Enhancing Adult Motivation to Learn

A Guide to
*Improving Instruction and
Increasing Learner Achievement*

Raymond J. Wlodkowski

Enhancing Adult
Motivation to Learn

Jossey-Bass Publishers · San Francisco

Substantial discounts on bulk quantities of Jossey-Bass books are available to corporations, professional associations, and other organizations. For details and discount information, contact the special sales department at Jossey-Bass Inc., Publishers. (415) 433-1740; Fax (800) 433-0499.

For sales outside the United States, please contact your local Simon & Schuster International Office.

Jossey-Bass Web address: http://www.josseybass.com

TCF Manufactured in the United States of America on Lyons Falls Turin Book. This paper is acid-free and 100 percent totally chlorine-free.

Library of Congress Cataloging-in-Publication Data

Wlodkowski, Raymond J.
  Enhancing adult motivation to learn

  (A joint publication in the Jossey-Bass higher
education series and the Jossey-Bass management series)
    Bibliography: p.
    Includes index.
    I. Motivation in adult education.   I. Title.
II. Series: Jossey-Bass higher education series.
III. Series: Jossey-Bass management series.
LC5219.W53 1985   374   84-43037
ISBN 1-55542-525-9 (paperback)
Figure 1 from *Motivation and Teaching: A Practical Guide* by
Raymond J. Wlodkowski. Copyright © 1978, 1984 by Raymond J.
Wlodkowski.
    Exhibit 4 is taken from *The Modern Practice of Adult Education*
(revised and updated), by Malcolm S. Knowles, New York, Cambridge,
The Adult Education Company, 1980, and is used by permission.

FIRST EDITION
HB Printing   10 9 8 7 6   Code 8522
PB Printing   10 9 8 7 6 5 4   Code 9325

A joint publication in
The Jossey-Bass Higher Education Series
and
The Jossey-Bass Management Series

Consulting Editor
Adult and Continuing Education

Alan B. Knox
University of Wisconsin at Madison

To my friend and teacher, Finley Hooper

Preface

Each year approximately 40 million adult Americans participate in educational activities. They go to college classes, in-service training sessions, business seminars, community workshops, and to church- and museum-sponsored lectures. In every one of these situations, someone must take the role of instructor—the individual responsible for helping the people present learn. Every instructor of adults seems to have two pressing concerns: How can I help these people learn effectively, and what is the best way to help them really *want* to learn what I have to offer? The latter is a motivational question, and its answer is the purpose as well as the advocacy of this book.

Enhancing Adult Motivation to Learn is designed to be a practical and immediately usable resource for educators, trainers, and staff developers whose primary task is instructing adults in business, industrial, and educational settings. It will also be useful to people who have occasional responsibility for teaching adults, such as ministers, community workers, medical personnel, coaches, and others in similar professions. The tenets of this book will help such individuals improve their effectiveness as instructors by allowing them to develop or increase the motivation to learn among the adults they teach.

Increasing learner motivation and helping adults *want* to learn are the topics that receive continual and major emphasis throughout this text. Currently, a number of books are available on teaching adults, but none of them is exclusively devoted to the use of motivation as a constant positive influence during learning activities. In the pages that follow, the reader will find out how to make the development of learner motivation an essential part of instructional planning, as well as which motivational factors are most useful and when to employ them. A large variety of specific strategies for increasing learner motivation are described in detail so that instructors can choose from among them, based on the subject being taught and the learning situation.

The education of adults is increasingly affected by technology and programmatic methods of instruction—approaches that tend to be dominated by behavioral psychology. There are many new and useful developments in motivational research, however, coming from the fields of linguistics, cognitive psychology, imagery, and systems theory, which can be of immense value in adult instruction. This book introduces this emerging information and shows how to use it in practical ways to the best advantage of adult learners.

Any instructor who has searched for a straightforward, realistic, and useful book on how to enhance adult motivation for learning will find this book helpful. Because this book's focus is motivation, there is little in it about learning theory, physical development, testing procedures, and philosophy of curriculum. However, the ample references provided will allow interested readers to pursue further study in most of these areas. My main concern is helping instructors enhance learner motivation during the process of instruction—when they are face-to-face with adult learners. I will discuss what needs to come before and after directly teaching or training adults, such as how homework, syllabus preparation, visual aids, and evaluation can be used to encourage learner motivation. Some promises to the reader:

1.   The least amount of jargon possible. It's obnoxious and confusing.
2.   No psychobabble. We're not going to "turn on to" anything, "go with the flow" anywhere, or understand the depth of "disassociative hysterical thinking."
3.   A little bit of humor. It lightens the sometimes heavy load of motivation.
4.   Many examples. They can clarify concepts and strategies and can tell us if we really understand what we're reading.
5.   A practical and consistent way to plan instruction that can enhance learners' motivation to master any subject. I've spent fifteen years learning how to do this and I want to share it.
6.   Motivational theories and methods positively supported by my personal experience. It may be written elsewhere, but if I write about it, I'll have at least tried it once as an instructor. If not, and it still sounds good, I'll warn you.

Overview of the Contents

This book is organized to provide the reader with the most important ideas and information I have found that can help to make effective instruction a motivationally consistent process, enabling optimal achievement and offering an inherently rewarding experience for *both* the adult learner and the instructor. Chapter One presents the theory and research supporting the idea that motivation is necessary for competent adult learning. It also elaborates a set of critical assumptions underlying my approach to motivation.

Chapter Two discusses the core characteristics—expertise, empathy, enthusiasm, and clarity—that are fundamentally necessary for a person to be a motivating instructor. Each characteristic is outlined according to performance criteria so that the reader can comprehend, evaluate, and learn those behaviors that are prerequisites to enhancing learner motivation.

Chapter Three takes an introductory look at the six major factors that motivate learning: attitudes, needs, stimulation, affect, competence, and reinforcement. These major motivation factors are then combined into the Time Continuum Model of Motivation, which is an organizational aid to motivation planning for instruction. This model offers the reader an immediate resource for making instruction consistently motivating.

Chapters Four through Eight provide the central content of this book. Each of these chapters is devoted to the comprehensive treatment of a specific major motivation factor: attitude is covered in Chapter Four, needs in Chapter Five, stimulation in Chapter Six, affect in Chapter Seven, and competence and reinforcement in Chapter Eight. These chapters pragmatically describe how each of these motivation factors has been found to be useful as a positive influence on adult learning. Specific strategies and detailed examples of the ways an instructor might incorporate these factors during instruction are also included. A total of sixty-eight motivational strategies are presented in these five chapters. Each strategy is discussed in terms of personal and situational influences and relevant adult characteristics. Wherever possible, the strategies are referenced to further readings that provide more information about theoretical elaboration and research.

Chapter Nine summarizes the previous chapters by means of a detailed outline of all the motivational strategies as well as their specific purposes. In addition, it explains two methods of motivation planning, the superimposed method and the source method. This chapter also includes four concrete illustrations of motivation planning and guidelines for instructor evaluation of learner motivation during the instructional process. Chapter Ten, the concluding chapter, discusses the concept of continuing motivation as it relates to adult learning. By carefully considering the growing body of knowledge from the field of intrinsic motivation, it presents useful suggestions for increasing the adult learner's capacity as a lifelong learner. These same suggestions are then considered as a means to enhance the intrinsic value of the process of instruction for the instructor.

Beyond all else, I have written this book to be a useful resource for anyone who wants learning to be a motivating experience for adults. To this end, I have described and discussed in detail the core characteristics that are fundamentally necessary for a person to be a motivating instructor: expertise, empathy, enthusiasm, and clarity. The six major motivation factors—attitudes, needs, stimulation, affect, competence, and reinforcement—that can positively influence adult motivation for learning are also fully analyzed. I have provided practical strategies for each major motivation factor, with clear examples of how to employ them during the instructional process. An organizational model, which allows an instructor to use motivation planning regularly to teach any subject or skill area, is offered along with numerous concrete illustrations of motivation planning. In addition to helping instructors enhance learners' motivation in face-to-face situations, it is hoped that the principles and techniques presented here will contribute to people's capacity for lifelong learning and the potential for intrinsically satisfying teaching.

Acknowledgments

I wrote this book while on leave from the University of Wisconsin at Milwaukee, and I am thus grateful to my department members and our university's administrators for relieving me of my duties to devote more time to scholarly activity. I am also indebted to Alan Knox for his initial support and continual guidance and availability throughout the preparation of this manuscript. Special thanks are due to Judith Kirkhorn, Donald Kirkpatrick, and Russell Robinson for their encouragement and insightful comments during the preparation of the first draft. I also want to express my gratitude to a corps of friends and colleagues, which includes David Prasse, Philip Smith, Anne Teeter, and Kenneth Wodtke, who were always available with cordial interest and helpful reactions when my writing as well as myself needed them.

It is commonplace to assign laurels to one's spouse for encouragement and support. In this instance, such a traditional response would be inadequate. My wife, Judith Jaynes, edited the entire first draft of the manuscript and, as a professional in her own field, clinical psychotherapy, provided innumerable insights regarding adult emotions and needs. I am most appreciative. Finally, I would like to thank Margaret Peterson for her masterful job of typing and organizing this manuscript.

Milwaukee, Wisconsin   Raymond J. Wlodkowski
February 1985

Contents

The Author

Raymond J. Wlodkowski is a writer and consultant in Boulder, Colorado. He received his B.S. degree (1965) in social science and his Ph.D. degree (1970) in educational and clinical psychology from Wayne State University in Detroit.

With a professional background as a university professor and licensed psychologist, Wlodkowski now serves as consultant to national and international organizations, including the Association for Supervision and Curriculum Development, AT&T Communications, and the East Asia Regional Council of Overseas Schools. He is coauthor of *Eager to Learn: Helping Children Become Motivated and Love Learning* (1990, with J. H. Jaynes) and author of *Motivation and Teaching: A Practical Guide* (1978), in addition to *Enhancing Adult Motivation to Learn* (1985), which received the 1986 Philip E. Frandson Award for Literature. His professional interests and publications are primarily in the areas of human development, instruction, and motivation.

In 1973, Wlodkowski received the University of Wisconsin,

Milwaukee, Award for Teaching Excellence. His most recent work includes the production of the video series *Motivational Thinking for Educators* (1989) and development of *Motivation to Learn,* winner of the Clarion Award as best training and development video program of 1991.

Enhancing Adult
Motivation to Learn

*A Guide to
Improving Instruction and
Increasing Learner Achievement*

1

How Motivation Affects Instruction

◆◆◆◆◆◆◆◆◆◆◆◆◆◆◆◆◆◆

There is more nonsense, superstition, and plain self-
deception about the subject of motivation than about
any other topic.   —*Thomas F. Gilbert*

Like the national economy, human motivation is a topic that
people know is important, continuously discuss, and would like to
predict. We want to know why people do what they do. But just as
tomorrow's inflationary trend seems beyond our influence and
understanding, so too do the causes of human behavior evade any
simple explanation or prescription. We have invented a word to
label this elusive topic, and we call it *motivation,* but even its
definition continues to baffle the most scholarly of minds. Most
scientists can agree that motivation is a concept that explains why
people behave as they do (Weiner, 1980a). After that very general
understanding, any more specific discussion of the meaning of
motivation becomes a cornucopia of differing assumptions and
terminology.

1

The biggest problem with motivation is we cannot see it and we cannot touch it. It is what is known in the psychological literature as a hypothetical construct, an invented definition that provides a possible concrete causal explanation of behavior (Baldwin, 1967). Therefore, we cannot directly measure motivation, and as long as this state of affairs lasts, there will be many different opinions about what it really is. Nonetheless, we do know that understanding why people behave as they do is vitally important to helping them learn, and psychology has made many inroads to the knowledge and skills that are useful for this purpose. Most psychologists concerned with learning and education use the word *motivation* to describe those processes that can (a) arouse and instigate behavior, (b) give direction or purpose to behavior, (c) continue to allow behavior to persist, and (d) lead to choosing or preferring a particular behavior. Thus, when we as instructors ask questions such as "What can I do to help my learners get started?" or "What can I do to help them put more effort into their learning?" or "What can I do to help them want to learn what I have to offer?" we are dealing with issues of motivation. Also, we continuously realize that the *motives* people bring with them to the learning situation strongly affect how and what they learn. This notion is quite accurate because a motive is any condition within a person that affects that person's readiness to initiate or continue an activity. For example, a person experiencing a need to understand how to be more physically fit has a good motive to read a book about physical fitness.

Although there have been some attempts to organize and to simplify the research knowledge regarding motivation to learn, instructors have received very few practical suggestions as to how to cohesively and consistently employ in their daily instruction the most useful elements of a large array of often conflicting information (Wlodkowski, 1981; Reigeluth, 1983). As a result, they have had to rely upon what has been traditionally used to enhance motivation for learning—intuition, common sense, and trial and error. Unfortunately, sometimes this approach leads to a rigid dependency on curriculum guides and an increased interest in a "bag of tricks" approach to instruction—the use of unrelated and often manipulative devices to spark learner interest in learning.

This is, indeed, troublesome for instructors. With no unifying motivation theory or model with which to organize and build motivational skills, they cannot easily change their practices, and what they learn about motivation from experience on the job as well as formal courses often remains fragmented and unconnected with instruction. There are a significant number of well-researched ideas and findings that can be applied to learning situations according to motivation principles. The following chapters will thoroughly discuss many of these motivational strategies and present a method to organize and apply them.

Why Motivation Is Important

We know motivation is important because, even without any specific agreement on the concept's definition, we know that if we match two people of the same exact ability and give them the same exact opportunity and conditions to achieve, the motivated person will surpass the unmotivated person in performance and outcome. We know this from personal experience and observation. We know this as we know a rock is hard and water is wet. We do not need reams of research findings to establish this reality for us. When research is consulted, our life experience regarding motivation is generally supported. To put it quite simply, when there is no motivation to learn, there is no learning (Walberg and Uguroglu, 1980). However, this extreme is not frequently the case, because motivation is not an either/or condition. It is often present to some degree, but when motivation to learn is very low, it is generally safe to assume that potential learning achievement will to some extent be diminished.

There is no major research study that thoroughly examines the exact relationship between adult motivation and learning. The best reviews and analyses of the relationship of motivation to learning are found in youth education. Here, there is substantial evidence that motivation is consistently positively related to educational achievement. Uguroglu and Walberg (1979) analyzed 232 correlations of motivation and academic learning reported in forty studies with a combined sample size of approximately 637,000 students in first through twelfth grades. They found 98 percent of the correlations between motivation and academic achievement were positive. They also noted that in their opinion the strength of the relation of motivation to learning is currently underestimated for historical, technical, and theoretical reasons (Walberg and Uguroglu, 1980). It appears reasonable to assume that if motivation bears such a significant relationship to learning for students as old as eighteen years of age, it probably has a similar relationship to adult learning. In support of this assumption, these researchers found that the relationship between motivation and learning increased along with the age of the students, with the highest correlations being found in the twelfth grade.

Motivation is not only important because it is a necessary causal factor of learning but because it mediates learning and is a consequence of learning as well. Historically, instructors have always known that when learners are motivated during the learning process, things go more smoothly, communication flows, anxiety decreases, and creativity and learning are more apparent. Instruction with motivated learners can actually be joyful and exciting, especially for the instructor. Learners who complete a learning experience and leave the situation feeling motivated about what they have learned seem more likely to have a future interest in what they have learned and more likely to use what they have learned. It is also logical to assume that the more that people have had motivating learning experiences, the more probable it is that they will become lifelong learners.

To be realistic, it is important to point out that although motivation is a necessary condition for learning, there are other factors such as ability and quality of instruction that are necessary as well for learning to occur. If people are given learning tasks that are beyond their ability, no matter how motivated they are, they will not be able to accomplish them. In fact, there is a point of diminishing returns for all of these mandatory factors, including motivation. For example, if learners are given an assignment that is difficult but for which they have the necessary capabilities, there is a point at which their abilities can carry them only so far before effort (motivation) is necessary to take them further, whether this be extra practice or increased study time. In terms of motivation, this could happen with ability or quality of instruction. Sports is a common example. There are many athletes who make tremendous strides in a particular sport because of exemplary effort but, finally, reach a level of competition where their coordination or speed is insufficient for further progress. Another case in point relative to quality of instruction might be a learner who wants to do well in math and has the ability and motivation but is limited by a complicated, obtuse textbook and an instructor who is unavailable for individual assistance. It is wise not to romanticize or expect too much of motivation. Such a view can limit our resourcefulness and increase our frustration.

It is difficult to scientifically understand exactly how motivation enhances learning and achievement. The nearest thing we have to a direct measure of it is effort (Keller, 1983). People work longer, harder, and with more vigor and intensity when they are motivated than when they are not motivated. Time spent actively involved in learning is definitely related to achievement (Levin and Long, 1981), so that explains some of it. Also, there is probably greater concentration and care in the process of learning while that time is being spent. Motivated learners are more cooperative. This would make them more psychologically open to the learning material and enhance information processing. It is much easier to understand what you want to understand. Finally, motivated learners get much more out of an instructor than unmotivated learners do. As instructors, we are much more willing to give our best effort when we know our learners are giving their best effort. It is important not to forget the reciprocity of this relationship and our responsibility to initiate it.

How Motivation Relates to Adult Learners

Adults are defined throughout this book according to the two criteria offered by Knowles (1980). First, a person is adult to the extent that that individual is performing social roles typically assigned by our culture to those it considers adults—the roles of worker, spouse, parent, responsible citizen, soldier, and the like. Second, a person is adult to the extent that that individual perceives herself or himself to be essentially responsible for her or his own life. Among the over twenty internationally recognized theories of motivation, there is not one that is exclusively devoted to an explanation of adult motivation (Madsen, 1974). There does exist a comprehensive theory of adult learning, andragogy, but its acceptance by most scholars in the field of adult education is questionable (Cross, 1981). However, there are generalizations of this theory that are widely regarded as accurate, the most important of which is that adults are highly pragmatic learners. Research consistently shows that vocational and practical education that leads to knowledge about how to do something is chosen by more adults than any other form of learning. Adults have a strong need to apply what they have learned and to be competent in that application (Knox, 1977). Knowles (1980), who developed the theory of andragogy, believes that the deepest human need is for self-esteem.

It can be generalized, therefore, that adults by definition, learning theory, and social research are responsible people who seek to build their self-esteem through pragmatic learning activities in which their competence is enhanced. From this perspective, there are motivation theories that are far more applicable to adult instruction than are others. These are the psychological theories that embrace competence as a central assumption, such as attribution theory, achievement motivation theory, personal causation theory, social learning theory, and cognitive evaluation theory. All of these support the idea that human beings strive for understanding and mastery, and tend to be motivated when they are effectively learning something they value. Among them, in my opinion, cognitive evaluation theory, as a single overview of human behavior, has probably the most natural relationship to the central assumptions of adult learning theory and research. The reasons why this harmonious relationship seems to exist will be discussed throughout this book.

If we accept that adults are responsible people who want to increase their competence in useful learning activities, what can we do as instructors to make this a reality during the process of instruction? That is what this entire book is about. To move more clearly in this direction, we can look at what motivation means from the adult perspective as well as the instructor's perspective. At this time, no one has scientifically investigated and explained each of these perspectives. However, it is important to understand what motivation means to both the adult learner and the adult instructor in order to build and utilize instructional strategies. Without some idea of what we want to happen, motivationally speaking, during the process of instruction, it is difficult to organize ourselves because we have no clear motivational purpose. And, if that purpose does not complement what the adult learners want to happen, motivationally speaking, we have a potential conflict. The following considerations can easily be theoretically supported and are based on my experience. At the bare-bones level, most instructors want adult learners who will responsibly begin, continue, and complete learning activities with a reasonable amount of effort and with successful achievement. That is really what most of us are looking for at the most basic level of our work. We want adults who will go through the entire learning process, put forth an honest effort, and be successful learners. If this were to continuously happen, we would not be concerned about motivation. The adult perspective on motivation is a bit more complicated but fundamentally parallels the instructor perspective. Adults want to be successful learners. This is a constant influence on them. If there is a problem with experiencing success or even expecting success, their motivation for learning will usually be detrimentally affected. There are myriad theories and research studies to support this notion (Spence, 1983).

After this assumption, it is important to see adult motivation as operating on integrated levels, the first of which is *success + volition*. It is critical that adults experience choice or willingness along with their success in the learning activity for their motivation to be sustained. This is the most critical and basic level of positive adult motivation for learning. There is almost no limit to the number of specific reasons why an adult might *want* to learn something, but unless an adult feels a sense of choice, motivation will probably become problematic (Knowles, 1980). At the very minimum, any instructor who is motivationally concerned can strive to make this instructional purpose for adult learners an actuality. The second level is *success + volition + value*. This means the adult learner does not necessarily find the learning activity pleasurable or exciting but does take it seriously, finds it meaningful and worthwhile, and tries to get the intended benefit from it (Brophy, 1983). Adults feel much better when they have successfully learned something they wanted to learn as well as something they value. This separates superficial learning from relevant learning and significantly adds to the self-esteem of the learner. The last level is *success + volition + value + enjoyment.* Simply put, the adult has experienced the learning as pleasurable. To help adults successfully learn what they value and want to learn in an enjoyable manner is the *sine qua non* of motivating learning and motivating instruction. I have never found an adult to be dissatisfied with it. It is the kind of instruction that receives awards and is long remembered and appreciated. This is not stated as an incentive for the reader but as the exposition of a reality. Instructors who can do this are truly masterful because they have made something difficult desirable. Every adult wants this learning experience, especially in the realms of life where competence is highly valued. And for instructors who want adult learners who successfully achieve with a reasonable amount of effort, it is the most challenging and rewarding route to follow.

Having generalized about the motivational perspective of adults toward the instructional process, there remain a number of research findings about their specific attitudes and characteristics that not only support, in some instances, the motivational perspective that has been offered but also are clearly informative for improving the overall quality of motivating instruction for adults. There have been a significant number of studies exploring *why* adults choose to participate in various kinds of learning activities (Cross, 1981). As mentioned earlier, most adults give practical, pragmatic reasons for learning. There is usually some problem to solve that may be as broad as how to successfully change careers or as narrow as learning how to earn extra money by refinishing furniture. Learning that will improve one's position in life is also a major motivation for participation. This varies with age, gender, occupation, and life stage. Young adults are primarily interested in education for upward career mobility. Older adults seek education for better job opportunities when this is possible, and those reaching career levels with few possibilities for career improvement are often interested in learning that will enhance the quality of life and leisure. In general, most adults have multiple reasons for learning, but the motives just cited tend to dominate their entry into group learning situations.

There is also a considerable amount of research regarding barriers to adult learning, reasons why they do not participate in learning activities. Among the various barriers studied, the one most pertinent to the content of this book is the *dispositional barrier*. Dispositional barriers are those related to attitudes and self-perceptions of people regarding themselves as learners. The two most commonly found barriers in this area relate to age and educational background. It is not uncommon for older adults to believe they are too old to begin new learning activities (Carp, Peterson, and Roelfs, 1974). Also, adults with poor educational backgrounds often lack interest in learning or confidence in their ability to learn.

It was once thought that aging was a realistic handicap to learning. If there is an age limit on learning performance, it is not likely to occur until around age seventy-five, when deterioration of bodily functions more significantly begins to set in (Kidd, 1973). That does not mean that aging does not affect the body until seventy-five, but that compensation for this gradual decline can be utilized to offset this deterioration. Eyeglasses, hearing aids, increased illumination, and increased time for learning are some of the ways to equalize learning opportunities for older adults. The time required for learning new things increases with age because, on the average, older learners perceive, think, and act more slowly than younger learners. However, there are substantial individual differences, and speed of response by itself should not prevent anyone from learning what that individual wants to learn (Cross, 1981). Knox (1977) concludes that when adults *can control the pace*, most of them in their forties and fifties have about the same ability to learn as they had in their twenties and thirties. Many people believe that because of the decline in vision, reading is a serious problem for older adults. However, in the absence of disease or serious impairment, the normal physical changes of the eyes can be accommodated through the use of eyeglasses and increased illumination (Cross, 1981). Hearing has also been well researched. There is a hearing loss as people become older and a translation problem as well. Rapid speech is more difficult for older adults to decipher.

But these changes can be treated and should not have much negative impact on learning capabilities until age sixty-five or older.

In terms of intelligence, it is safe to summarize that normal, healthy adults can be efficient and effective learners well into old age. There have been two types of intelligence that have been found to show different patterns in aging (Cattell, 1963). The first, fluid intelligence, is measured through such abilities as memory span, spatial perception, adaptation to new or novel situations, common word analogies, and abstract reasoning. It is less dependent on experience and education and appears to decline with age. People seem to perform best in their youth on tasks requiring quick insight, short-term memorization, and complex interactions. The second, crystallized intelligence, is measured through such abilities as vocabulary, general information, arithmetic reasoning, and reading comprehension. It is based on acculturation, including formal education and knowledge of the cultural and intellectual heritage of society. Crystallized intelligence increases or remains stable up to about age sixty. After this age, it is still capable of growth if the person is actively involved in intellectual pursuits. Fluid and crystallized intelligence are complementary. Research into both of these types of intelligence confirms the commonsense approach of many societies who revere the wisdom of the aged but rely on youth for quickness in learning new skills (Cross, 1981). As Knox (1977, p. 421) succinctly states, "During adulthood, as fluid intelligence decreases and as crystallized intelligence increases, general learning ability remains relatively stable, but the older person tends to increasingly compensate for the loss of fluid intelligence by greater reliance on crystallized intelligence, to substitute wisdom for brilliance."

Memory has received a good deal of attention by researchers in learning. Short-term memory seems to be more of a problem for older adults than long-term memory. When material is learned well and new information is integrated with previously learned material, memory appears to remain stable during most of adulthood (Moenster, 1972). Older adults seem to have their greatest problems memorizing meaningless material, complex material, and learning something that requires reassessment of old learning (Cross, 1981). It is believed that meaningless material is so poorly retained because older adults are poorly motivated to learn it and it is difficult for them to connect this material to previously retained learning. Memorization of complex material on a short-term basis seems to take them longer because they have to scan large stores of previous information to find proper associations and this interferes with recall. That is why distraction is so difficult for them. Generally, older learners will be more likely to have the most problems with initial learning and subsequent recall when learning activities are fast paced, complex, or unusual. Cross (1981, p. 164) has some very practical suggestions to help older adults with memorization: "First, the presentation of new information should be meaningful, and it should include aids to help the learner organize it and relate it to previously stored information. Second, it should be presented at a pace that permits mastery in order to strengthen the original registration. Third, presentation of one idea at a time and minimization of competing intellectual demands should aid original comprehension. Finally, frequent summarization should facilitate retention and recall."

In terms of personality, most people show consistency throughout life beginning with adolescence through later adulthood (Haan and Day, 1974). In a longitudinal study these researchers found style of cognitive engagement (verbal fluency, unconventional thought, wide-ranging interests, esthetic reaction, pride in objectivity, and intellectual level) to be among the most stable of all characteristics. Thus, people who are enthusiastically involved in cognitive activities during adolescence will probably stand out in a similar fashion during middle age. As people grow older, accuracy becomes more important to them and there is a greater dependence on previously learned solutions (Cross, 1981). Youthful learners are more likely to engage in problem solving with higher-risk behavior and trial-and-error solutions. There is increasing passivity in elderly learners, which means instructional processes will have to be flexible and nonthreatening to engage them and prevent withdrawal.

There are numerous other generalizations about adult development and characteristics that could be made relative to motivating instruction. However, these pertinent summarizations are distributed throughout the textual material that follows in order to more clearly accentuate their relationship to specific motivational strategies. In this manner, they become more sensible guidelines for the effective practice of instructional methods. For those more interested in adult development and learning as a specific topic, there are two excellent resources available: Knox's (1977) *Adult Development and Learning,* and Cross's (1981) *Adults as Learners.*

Critical Assumptions for Helping Adults Want to Learn

With a hypothetical construct as broad and complex as motivation, there is always room for controversy and argumentation. One of the things most likely to produce misunderstanding and reduce communication is for the receiver of a message to be unclear about the assumptions on which a message is based. This increases the tendency toward disagreement because of a lack of clarity rather than a lack of logic. The following assumptions are offered so that the reader can have a better understanding of why the numerous suggestions that this book offers for motivating instruction have been selected. These assumptions form a substantial part of the foundation and rationale for the theories and approaches that are advocated in this book.

The first assumption is that *people are always motivated.* They may not be motivated to learn, but they are motivated to do something. People are active in their relationships with their environment from earliest infancy onward (White, 1959). They constantly construct new meanings and interpretations from the events in their environment (Wittrock, 1974). This is important to realize because too often instructors dismiss particular learners as "not motivated." This implies a lifeless blob beyond assistance and increases the instructor's sense of helplessness. It is more accurate to say, "This learner is not motivated to learn with me." This implies there may be a difficulty with volition, the instructional process, or, perhaps, some personality disposition within the learner. It makes the issue more of a problem to solve than a hopeless case to dismiss or to withdraw from.

The second assumption is that *people are responsible for their own motivation.* We cannot directly motivate learners. We can make things stimulating and attractive. We can provide opportunity and incentives. We can certainly influence and affect learners, but we cannot totally control their motivation. What we do during instruction is mediated by the learners themselves (Wittrock, 1978). There is no direct line of control like a radio switch between instructor behavior and learner motivation. What we do with learners is perceived by them and filtered as well as modified by their values, beliefs, and judgments. These kinds of elements decide the final outcome of learner motivation. If this were not so, there could be no real responsibility on the part of adults for learning. They would be more like puppets than people. They could take no real pride in their choices and perseverance. Seeing learners as responsible allows us to develop mutual respect and interdependence with them. It also avoids total blame in either direction and helps to develop mutual problem solving when motivation is lagging. This assumption gives us the right to expect their cooperation as well as ours in making learning the reciprocal relationship it naturally is.

Thirdly, it is assumed that *if anything can be learned, it can be learned in a motivating manner.* There must be some degree of motivation to formally learn anything, even if that influence is limited to merely paying attention (Walberg and Uguroglu, 1980). Once we have someone's attention, there are a myriad of possible influences that can be used to sustain attention and interest. In a perverse way, national advertising is a testimony to the human ability to make anything attractive and appealing. If something is worth an instructional effort, one can assume that there is some degree of substance to the material. It must meet some kind of valid need or there would be no reason for making it the purpose of instruction. Finding that need, affirming it, and engagingly developing it through the instructional processes is, no doubt, a challenge but not an impossible one.

The fourth assumption is that *there is no one best way to instruct.* There are certainly better ways than others, but such variables as individual learner differences, type of learning task, learning environment, instruction style, and unconscious motives all work together in such complex ways that no scientific or psychological theory has yet discovered a way to make learner motivation consistently predictable through any particular method of instruction (Ames and Ames, 1984). We know much more today about motivation and learning than we did ten years ago. We continue to make progress. However, each step we take forward also tells us something about our limitations as well. For example, reinforcement theory, which seemed so scientific and mechanistic, must now deal with a cognitive reinterpretation of some of its most fundamental principles (Wittrock and Lumsdaine, 1977). The greatest implication of this awareness for instructional excellence is that instructors must still trust their personal judgment regarding what is best for them and their learners. The state of any method of instruction is not beyond improvement or revision. We do not have the scientific understanding to be rigid or dogmatic about the way we instruct. Close communication between the adult learner and the instructor is still needed, not to "debug" an instructional program but to continue the evolution of a very young and primitive science. One of the reasons adult educators have been so adamant about the right of adults to self-direct and participate in the development of the instructional processes that serve them is not only because of their respect for principles of adult development and behavior but because to shun adult learner input will narrow and limit the entire discipline.

Finally, it is assumed that *every instructional plan needs a motivational plan*. More often than not, the unstable variables that interfere with and complicate learning are human variables—the needs, emotions, impulses, attitudes, expectancies, irrationalities, beliefs, and values of people (Weiner, 1984; McLagan, 1978). Not surprisingly, these are motivational variables as well. Whatever the subject matter, it is usually rather stable and controllable. It has a logical structure and sequence. Finding an instructional design format for most subject matter is not an enormous problem (Reigeluth, 1983). There are many to choose from, but most do not adequately deal with the human variables just mentioned. However, motivational theories are vitally concerned with these variables and offer many methods and principles to deal with them. The challenge, then, is to integrate these methods and principles with instruction into a collective framework. Most instructors do this, but through intuition and spontaneous decision making. Their difficulties arise when motivation seems low or to be diminishing.

They have no formal plan for solving problems and often lack exact methods to revise, refine, or build upon. This often leaves them feeling helpless, hopeless, and prone to blame the learners themselves. When they turn to books on motivation, the vast array of competing and conflicting theories often leaves them only more confused. Another problem instructors face is how to maintain and develop further motivation in learners. Just as learning increases, most instructors would like to see motivation increase along with it. Again, without a motivation plan, it is difficult to build or strengthen this factor. There is no structure for consistent application. Probably one of the most helpful aspects of any plan is that it reminds us of what to do and when to do it. Without a plan, motivation too often becomes a trial-and-error affair lacking cohesion and continuity during instruction.

The unfortunate realization is that although the discipline of motivation has many constructive suggestions to offer the field of instruction, without some method of planning for them, they will probably tend to be weakly and inconsistently applied. This book is written as a means to solve this dilemma and to make motivating instruction a reality for both the adult learner and the adult instructor.

2

Characteristics and Skills
of a Motivating Instructor

> What all the great teachers appear to have in common
> is love of their subject, an obvious satisfaction in
> arousing this love in their students, and an ability to
> convince them that what they are being taught is
> deadly serious.
> —*Joseph Epstein*

Consider for a moment a motivating instructor who helped you as
an adult to genuinely want to learn what was presented; who was
able to influence you to go beyond another course finished, another
credit earned. See that person and remember, if you will, what
learning was like with that individual. Pleasant? Exciting? Scary?
Unpredictable? There are many possible reactions, but seldom the
ordinary. Most of us have had at least one such instructor. And every
one of us has the potential to be such an instructor to other adults.
The first step is to start with the basics.

Motivating instructors are not entirely magical. They are

unique. They do have their own personal style and strengths but observation, common sense, and research all point out that there are common elements that support the foundation of their instruction. These core characteristics can be learned, controlled, and planned for by anyone who instructs adults. I see them as the four cornerstones that provide the essential structural building points for any instructor. Upon them rests everything we have to offer adults. Without any one of them, there will be little continuing support for the many possibilities and complexities that can strain an instructional relationship with adults.

These four cornerstones are *expertise, empathy, enthusiasm,* and *clarity.* As instructors, our most advantageous approach to these building blocks is to see them as skills and not as abstractions or personality traits. They can be learned and they can be improved upon through practice and effort.

Instruction is a pragmatic art. We create and perform useful communication for the benefit of our learners. Every professional artist has a practice regimen. Fundamentals make up a considerable portion of it. As exercise is inherent to the lives of fine dancers and daily practice is a continual ritual for outstanding musicians, so are these few basic elements the ever-present foundation for motivating instruction. With steady use and attention to refinement, they can be developed and enriched. They are achievable.

Offering Expertise: The Power of Knowledge and Preparation

For many people, this cornerstone may have other names. Some people prefer to call it substance, knowledge, or competence (Hollander, 1976). No matter what the title, the practical definition of expertise for those of us who instruct adults boils down to three essential parts: (1) we know something beneficial for adults, (2) we know it well, and (3) we are prepared to convey it through an instructional process. Following these three criteria will allow our expertise to show itself and have the kind of positive effect that we and our learners both deserve.

1. We Know Something Beneficial for Adults.

Watch a group of unmotivated adults in any kind of learning activity—an in-service training session, a lecture, a business seminar.

(You've probably been a participant, at least a few times, in such a dreary experience yourself.) Their voices aren't shouting, but their minds and bodies are. "Don't waste my time." "Who are you kidding?" "Boy, I wish I could get out of here!" "I don't need this." It's almost palpable. As learners, adults are demanding, and rightfully so.

An instructor of adults is quite unlike a teacher of children or adolescents. This person is an adult among adults. The customary advantages of age, experience, and size cannot be counted on for extra leverage or added influence as they might be for an elementary school teacher. Many adults will have had experiences that far surpass the background of their particular instructor. As a group, they have out-traveled, out-parented, out-worked, and out-lived any of us as individual instructors. Collectively, they've had more lovers, changed more jobs, survived more accidents, moved more households, faced more debts, achieved more successes, and overcome more failures. It is highly unlikely that we can simply impress them with our title, whether it be trainer or professor.

Also, most adults come to learn for a definite reason. They are goal-oriented, pragmatic learners (Cross, 1981). They want their learning to help them solve problems, build new skills, advance in their jobs, make more friends—in general, to do, produce, or decide something that is of real value to them. The dominant question and request of adult learners for anyone who instructs them is "Can you really help me?"

The way to begin to answer this question is to know that we have something beneficial to offer our adult learners. This translates into an immediate question: What do we know that this group can understand, use, or apply that will help them? Once we have answered this question with *concrete examples* of the knowledge, skills, or awareness that we can offer this group, we will also have taken the first step in avoiding the classic mistake that many so-called experts make when instructing adults—thinking that knowing a lot about a subject is enough to teach it effectively. Colleges abound with knowledgeable professors who teach quite poorly. In many instances, this is simply because they have not considered what students might understand and be able to apply from what they profess. They have not taken the step to connect their knowledge to the daily needs and lives of their students. For this reason, there is no bridge for common understanding.

Clearly knowing that we have something of benefit to offer adults will not only increase our credibility with them, it will also be a boon to our own self-confidence. Anyone who instructs a particular group for a lengthy period of time eventually becomes quite naked. Our words and actions continuously strip away the camouflage of our announced degrees and experience to tell our learners whether what we know really makes a difference. Concretely understanding, before we begin to instruct, that we have something of value to share tells us that time is on our side and the effort it takes to competently do it is worth it.

2. We Know Our Subject Well.

There is no substitute for thoroughly knowing our topic. Nothing beats it. Whatever experience, reading, reviewing, or practice it takes, its payoff far outweighs its cost.

For instruction, knowing something well can be self-evaluated in an ascending order of questions. First, do we ourselves understand what we are going to teach? Can we explain it to ourselves in our own words? Secondly, can we give more than one good example of what we are teaching? A story, a joke, a fact, a piece of research, an analogy—there are many different types of examples. The main thing is to have more than one. This demonstrates the depth and breadth of our understanding as well as increases our ability to reach learners for whom a single example would not have enough explanatory power. Thirdly, if it's a skill we are teaching, can we personally demonstrate it? This is real credibility to the self and others. If not, or if this may be inappropriate, are there models, films, or videotapes that can do the job? Fourth, do we know the limits and consequences of what we are teaching? Say, for instance, we are explaining a managerial technique. Do we know what type of employees it may not work with or under what conditions it would be wise not to use it? What are its effects on production and morale? Does it entail any personal risk for the manager? Consideration of possible limits and future consequences reveals the sensibility of our expertise. Finally, do we know what we don't know? Where are the boundaries of our own knowledge and skill? How far are we from the cutting edge of our discipline? This awareness is a very intelligent modesty. Adults don't expect instructors to know everything, but they do want an honest understanding of what they are learning because they may apply so much of it. Instructors who know their own frontiers can better qualify and temper their instruction. This prevents learner disillusionment and misapplication, as well as points the direction to those areas of future needed learning for instructor and learner alike.

Knowing our subject matter well enhances our confidence, flexibility, and creativity as instructors. We may still have learners who are difficult to reach, but our fund of knowledge will not be what fails us. We can count on it. We can also be more open to questions and new directions that may come from our learners. Any time a person is really adept with a concept or a skill, that person can play with it. Spontaneity and improvisation are possible only for the competent. Consummate artists and scientists base their experiments on knowledge. As Zinker (1977, p. 22) writes, "The creative process begins with one's appreciation of what is there— the essence, the clarity and the impact of what is around us." What is taken as effortless, exhilarating instruction by the learner is often only the outcome of experience blended with many hours of study, and sometimes struggle, on the part of the instructor.

3. We Are Prepared to Convey Our Knowledge Through an Instructional Process.

Using an instructional process simply means conducting the necessary *immediate* planning and organization of materials for whatever it is we are going to offer as instruction on any given day. This is the intensive preparation just before the instructional moment. It is an awful truth. Valenti (1982, p. 19) said it well: "The most effective antidote to stage fright and other calamities of speech making is total, slavish, monkish preparation." Although much of instruction is not like speech making, his point is well taken and not far off the mark.

Brilliant and scholarly people who were at the zenith of their respective professions have been notorious for giving poor instructional performances. John Dewey, Abraham Maslow, and Albert Einstein are just a few whose eminence was more dull than sparkling at the lectern and in the classroom. Professor Einstein was known for burying his eyes in his notes with his words haltingly emerging through his monotone as well as his mustache. It is difficult to imagine, but some people actually conducted small talk while he lectured. Genius does not equal readiness to instruct.

No matter what the immediate planning, being well prepared for instruction culminates at two essential points. We have a relaxed familiarity with our materials and we can maintain eye contact with our learners. We can talk with them. We can look at them most of the time. This makes them living participants in moment-to-moment communication with us rather than a cardboard audience of faces. If we are tied to our notes, if we cannot put our manuals down, if we do not know what the next step is, our chances of being a motivating instructor are nil.

Vital instruction flows. There has to be a union of sorts between the instructor and the learners so that both parties feel part of a single process. Effective instructors set the stage for this fluid enterprise by knowing their material well enough to "read" learner cues, watching for signs of interest, insight, and even possible boredom. This allows the instructor to change qualities of voice, emphasis, and direction at will. Learners feel this type of instructor is talking with them rather than at them because the instructor's responsiveness to them is so apparent. They literally can see these reactions in the instructor's eyes and facial expressions. Questions and give-and-take between the instructor and the learners seem integrated into the stream of the lesson at hand. This can occur because of the instructor's excellent command of the subject matter. Like an expert navigator on a familiar ship in foreign waters, the instructor has the touch and feel of the material to sail a steady course.

The type of immediate preparation that allows for motivating instruction is whatever it takes for us to know that when the time for instruction comes, we will spend most of it looking at our learners and talking with them. For the experienced instructor, this may mean a few moments of quiet reflection; for the novice, this may mean hours of review, rehearsal, and organization. The range is wide. Notes, index cards, outlines, and even textual materials are appropriate to use as long as we can visually leave them to interact with our learners. If any section of our material seems insurmountable (occasionally this will happen to the best of instructors), we can make sure our learners can at least look with us. Visual aids, overhead projections, chalkboard outlines, and handouts are some possibilities. (It is important to note that this book is not oriented toward individualized forms of instruction such as computer-based training or distance education. In such instances, there is far less dependency on face-to-face involvement with the instructor and visual contact would certainly not be so strongly emphasized.)

Any significant achievement demands some degree of immediate readiness. Public speakers collect their thoughts. Hollywood actors reflect on their roles. Olympic athletes psych up. As motivating instructors, we can be no less prepared in our quest for involved learners. The time we spend mobilizing our knowledge and abilities just prior to instruction is probably the final step of our preparation. How we feel about it will carry over to how we feel when we meet our learners. It is our last chance for confidence.

Having Empathy: The Power of Understanding and Consideration

A woman in her mid-forties decides to take a communications course in her local college's extension program. She is an intelligent college graduate. For the last fifteen years she has committed herself to the role of homemaker. With her children older and more independent, she is considering graduate school or full-time professional employment. This course will be the first step. Her friends have encouraged her to take a basic communications class because it would be a reasonable but not too difficult introduction to current formal educational practices as well as a means to help her gain some useful skills for the job market. She is motivated.

The class meets once a week in the evening for two-and-a-half hours. At the first class session the instructor introduces himself, has the students introduce themselves to one another, and lists the requirements for the course—the reading of the course textbook and six assigned articles, a mid-semester and final exam, and a term paper. He mentions the fact that he is a tough marker and a real stickler for the use of appropriate English grammar in student papers. After a number of questions from the class regarding these requirements, he dismisses them early so that the students can get a head start on their required reading for the next week. Our student is a bit intimidated but determined. At the second class session, the instructor lectures on the history of communications theory and outlines a number of research studies that demonstrate the significant effect of different communication innovations. Our student is impressed by her instructor's knowledge but finds her interest waning. The third class session is a lecture on the topic of phenomenology and its philosophical implications.

Our student decides to drop the course and get a percentage of her tuition back before it's too late for any compensation. When her friends ask her why she didn't finish the course, she looks at them with a perplexed expression and replies, "It just didn't seem like something I needed right now. The course was about communication but it wasn't what I expected."

There are a number of different ways to look at this scenario. One might be to consider what the learner could have done to have helped herself in the course or to have avoided this particular course altogether. Perhaps she should have been more careful in selecting the class and found out more about both the instructor as well as the course content before she signed up for it. She also might have talked with the instructor and made her needs and expectations more clear to him. From another vantage point, it might seem that the instructor should have made his objectives clear from the beginning and taken some time to know his students and find out what their needs and expectations were. Wherever we place the responsibility, the same core issue remains: *Adult needs and expectations for what they are taught will powerfully influence how they motivationally respond to what they are taught.* In general, the more their needs and expectations are not met by what and how they learn, the lesser the chance that they will be motivated to learn.

As mentioned earlier, most adults come to learning activities for specific reasons. These reasons are based on what they think they need. These needs may be for social interaction, new skills, some type of certification, or simply relief from boredom. However, if the content or process of instruction does not in some way meet these needs, the learning will have very little meaning for adults. Involving adults in a learning process that does not seem to fulfill any of their personal goals eventually leads to an inevitable conclusion: "This is a waste of time."

Entire motivational theories are based on need gratification (Maslow, 1970), and any instructor of adults faces the challenge of looking at these learners and seeing their world and what they need from it as they see it. Adult learners learn in response to their own needs and perceptions, not those of their instructors. Empathy is the skill that allows instructors to meet this formidable requirement for motivating instruction.

The classical definition of empathy by one of its foremost proponents (Rogers, 1969, p. 111) is "when the teacher has the ability to understand the student's reactions from the inside, a sensitive awareness of the way the process of education and learning seem *to the student.*" Social psychologists and other writers have used words like *consideration* and *understanding* with similar intent. Researchers have found consideration to be a major dimension in effective leadership (Halpin, 1966). Vaill (1982) states unequivocally that leaders of high-performing systems (ranging from hospital emergency rooms to college marching bands) work on whatever the system *needs* at the moment. An instructional activity is a system: a group of interdependent people acting together to accomplish a predetermined purpose—learning. In this system the instructor is the leader and his or her awareness of the learners' needs for that learning will significantly influence their motivation to learn.

For those of us who instruct adults, the cornerstone of empathy is most readily useful when it is organized into the following three parts: (1) We have a realistic understanding of our learners' needs and expectations for what we are offering them to learn; (2) we have adapted our instruction to our learners' levels of experience and skill development; and (3) we continuously consider our learners' perspective. These three criteria will help us to know when we have reached a level of empathy that meets a standard capable of laying the foundation for motivating instruction.

1. We have a realistic understanding of our learners' needs and expectations for what we are offering them to learn.

It is no surprise that Grabowski (1976) in his substantial review of the research found that the competent adult educator understands and provides for the needs of adult learners. For the instructor, two important questions immediately arise relative to this information: How do I best find out what my learners' needs are? When do I know that I realistically understand what my learners' needs are?

For the first question, I have provided answers in Chapter Five. That chapter deals specifically with the array of methods that can assess and diagnose adult learner needs. The second question can be considered here. The way we know that we realistically understand our learners' needs is when we are personally confident that the objectives we have set for our course or module will include most of the goals and needs that our learners bring with them to the first meeting of our instructional program. That is to say, if we were to ask each learner at the initial session what they actually needed and expected to receive from the course, we could at the conclusion of those interviews hand out a previously prepared list of course objectives that would include most of their just-mentioned needs and expectations. I prefer to use the word *most* because *all* would be unreasonable, given the individual differences and complexities among a group of adults.

Another type of expectation that is crucial to instructor understanding is what the adult learner anticipates in the way of course requirements. Learners bring strongly felt expectations with them when it comes to what and how much an instructor asks them to do. In our learners' eyes, our fairness and our humanity will significantly depend on how our requirements measure up against their own personal expectations for this critical element. In reality, this is an issue of time. All course and training requirements take some time to do, whether it's reading, writing, practice, or problem solving. In most surveys, lack of time vies with cost for first place among obstacles to adult education (Cross, 1981). In fact, it is mentioned more often by people in their thirties and forties than by those younger or older. Sometimes instructors think that learners want fewer requirements because they want the easy way out. I think it is much more helpful to see requirements relative to the time they demand and to recognize that adult learners want to make sure they have enough time to fully demonstrate their real abilities. The issue is not "Give me a break." It's "Let's make sure I really have a chance to show you what I can do." Our understanding of the type of learners we have and the amount of time they can realistically afford is a necessary consideration to explore *before* we create our course and training requirements.

2. We have adapted our instruction to our learners' levels of experience and skill development.

Did you ever have the experience of being in a course or training program where you didn't have the skills or background necessary to do what you were asked to do? Were you ever in such a program and couldn't leave it? Maybe it was in the armed forces, in secondary school or, worse yet, in something you volunteered for. It's a special kind of misery, a mixture of fear, embarrassment, and infuriation. If there's no hope of learning, we usually try to get out of the situation. Our motivation is to escape, and if that's not possible, at best to endure and to avoid depression.

As instructors, we don't want to make people fail. In terms of empathy, *this means giving learners things to do that are within their reach.* If we give them assignments that are too easy or for which they've had too much experience, they will be bored and disinterested. It's a delicate balance. It is also one of the main principles of stimulation, as you will see in Chapter Six. The instructional goal is to match the learning process, whether it be materials, activities, assignments, or discussions, to the abilities and experience of our learners. It is the reason we do not want to assign books our learners cannot read or to expect them to be very interested in things they have already done.

If we are unfamiliar with our learners or if our subject matter is rapidly changing, we may want to use diagnostic or formative evaluation procedures to better understand their capabilities and experiences relative to our subject area. These can be interviews, paper-and-pencil tests, simulations, exercises, or whatever helps us to know what our learners can or cannot do relative to what we are offering them to learn. The purpose of these assessments is not to categorize learners but to help us create instructional procedures for better adult motivation and learning. Even among professional athletes, coaches begin training camps with exercises and tests that

are basically diagnostic. They know from years of hard-earned experience that you cannot take anyone from anywhere unless you start somewhere near where they are.

3. We continuously consider our learners' perspective.

This is really as much an attitude as it is a skill. It is strongly linked to what, in current jargon, is being called "high touch"— the need for the human element in an increasingly technological society (Naisbitt, 1982). More and more of education and training is being conducted with the use of machinery, computers, and electronic media. Performance objectives, task analysis, and instructional systems are just a part of an array of seemingly more efficient but also potentially more insensitive methods to deliver educational services. The need for human consideration on the part of the instructor is probably greater than it has ever been.

The more we mechanize and objectify the learning process, the more adult learners need to know we care about them as human beings. Hand in hand with this understanding is Saint-Exupéry's (1943, p. 70) marvelous maxim "What is essential is invisible to the eye." There are so many important things that go on during instruction between an instructor and a learner that no single human sense, no global standardized test, no amazing electronic equipment will ever pick up. In some ways, I wish this were not so. To some extent, it makes incomplete all the ideas and strategies found in this book. And yet, for anyone who has ever really been an instructor, we know this to be true. That is why considering our learners' perspective is as much an attitude as a skill. It is a constant desired awareness of what our learners are living and experiencing with us as they know and feel it. One could literally get a Ph.D. in communication skills, but if that person did not *want* to understand his* learners, he would not. To *want* to do this makes the necessary communication skills that much more effective. Of those skills,

---

*The traditional use of the pronoun *he* has not yet been superseded by a convenient, generally accepted pronoun that means either *he* or *she*. Therefore, I will continue to use *he* while acknowledging the inherent inequity of the traditional preference for the masculine pronoun.

listening is most important (Grabowski, 1976). It is the single most powerful transaction that occurs between ourselves and another person that tells that individual that we accept him as a human being. Do we understand? Do we interrupt? Do we look over that person's shoulder? Do we change the subject? Do we really know what that person is feeling? The way we listen tells learners more than anything else how much consideration we are really giving them. The choices we make as instructors based on this kind of empathic awareness will vary. There are no firm guidelines, but there is one clear message. We are in touch with our learners and they know it. The rest is up to both of us.

Empathy is not simply an altruistic notion. It doesn't just work because people want to be treated decently. It is part of something much larger for the motivating instructor. With expertise, empathy combines to make the instructor a powerful nurturant person in the eyes of the learner. Whenever an instructor can competently meet the needs of a learner, that instructor can be identified with by the learner. The learner then begins to take on some of the attitudes and behaviors of the instructor, to literally act in some ways like the instructor. Identification happens to some degree with almost any leader who significantly meets our needs, whether it be a parent, a political figure, or an instructor. This process is part of the reason we feel such a tremendous sorrow when such a person dies. A Gandhi, a former coach, any leader important to us can have this effect upon us. We have not just lost someone who meant something to us, we have lost a part of ourselves as well.

Identification allows each of us as motivating instructors to leave a legacy. And enthusiasm for our subject can be a noble inheritance.

Showing Enthusiasm: The Power of Commitment and Animation

An almost peerless example of enthusiasm is Leo Buscaglia, author, lecturer, and teacher. My introduction to him came about ten years ago when a student gave me an audiotape of Dr. Buscaglia's lecture at a local community college. All the student told me was that he thought I might find it interesting. Being very busy at the time, I decided to listen to it while I reviewed some correspondence. The tape was quite scratchy and the voice reproduction was very poor, but within minutes I had to put my notes down and just listen. The emotion and sincerity coming through that puny cassette recorder had drawn my attention like a powerful magnet. I could not turn away. Even though I might not agree with all of his message, I had to hear it completely, to the end. In person, Dr. Buscaglia is something to behold. Arms flying, suit coat tossed off to the side, sweat pouring down his face, eyes electric and then very soft, and a voice that covers at least two octaves, he epitomizes not only total commitment to what he is saying, but to every word he is saying.

Those of us a bit older might remember Julius Miller, another superlative model of enthusiastic instruction. This small, grey-haired man in shirt-sleeves was a physics professor who would now and then appear on the Steve Allen "Tonight Show." His routine, if you could call it that, was to demonstrate a basic principle of physics. Explaining atmospheric pressure, he would boil water in a can, seal it, and then spray the can with a hose. For the viewer, the attraction was not what happened to the can (a crumpling mess) but Dr. Miller's reaction to this phenomenon. Jumping up and down in excitement, he would shout, "Look at that!" There was no doubt that he thought what was happening was very important and that we should see it and understand it. He did more for my appreciation of physics than any high school or college teacher ever did. I remember him fondly.

The word *enthusiasm* originates from the Greek *enthousias-mos*, which means to be inspired or possessed by a god. Other dictionary meanings include strong excitement or feeling on behalf of a cause or subject. For instruction, I prefer a definition that includes the person's inner feelings as they are expressed in outward behavior. An enthusiastic instructor is a person who cares about and values his subject matter and teaches it in a manner that expresses those feelings with the intent to encourage similar feelings in the learner. Emotion, energy, and animation are outwardly visible in this person's instruction.

If we care about our instructional topic, there will be a natural inclination to display emotion and animation. If we do not care about our subject, it will be more difficult to produce feelings and gestures. We might be able to act out or invent such expressions for a particular occasion, but to maintain such zeal would be laborious and very stressful. Without a source of inspiration, it is difficult to be inspirational. The intent to encourage in the learner our value for our subject matter is important as well. This goal motivates us to have rapport with our students and to express our feelings in a way that engages our learners to share in our enthusiasm. Otherwise, we could become so involved in our own emotions that we could begin teaching for the benefit of ourselves rather than for the benefit of our learners. Arrogant instructors often suffer from this shortsightedness.

In educational research, enthusiasm enjoys a long history of being related to increased learner motivation as well as achievement (Rosenshine and Furst, 1971). According to Cruickshank and his associates (1980), all other things being equal, a teacher who presents materials with appropriate gestures, animation, and eye contact will have students who achieve better on tests than will the teacher who does not gesture, reads in a monotone, and generally behaves in an unenthusiastic manner. The eminent researcher Gage (1979) sees enthusiasm as a possible "generic" teaching behavior that is useful at all grade levels, in all subject areas, and for all types of students. From the direction of managerial studies, it has recently been reported that leaders of high-performing systems have *very strong feelings* about the attainment of the system's purposes. Vaill (1982) believes this characteristic appears 100 percent of the time in the actions of these leaders.

Enthuasistic instruction has such a powerful influence on the motivation of learners for a number of reasons. First and foremost is because instructors are sellers. We are advocates. We say, "Learn this, it's good for you." Some of us sell math or technical skills, others training programs or social skills. Our subject matter is our sales product. Whatever the content, the message is still the same—"Learn it. It's worth it." Whenever an individual is being sold something, especially an adult, a keen intuitive scanning of the salesperson takes place that summarizes itself in the question "What does this product do for you?" If we cannot show by our own presence, energy and conviction that this subject matter has made a positive difference for us, the learner is forewarned. If we appear bored, listless, and uninvolved with what we are asking the adult to learn, his response will be "If that's what knowing this does for you, by all means, keep it away from me." That is survival. It is also self-protection. No one wants to buy what has not done its own seller any good. It is an inherent learner wisdom that makes enthusiasm an absolute necessity for motivating instruction. For learners, *how* instructors say it will always take priority over *what* instructors say.

Enthusiastic instructors are potent models. That is why I have discussed expertise and empathy *before* the cornerstone of enthusiasm. When an instructor is seen by adults as competent and considerate, there is a tendency, through the identification process, for them to imitate the instructor's own behavior and attitudes toward the subject matter. If these two influential characteristics are missing, the spirited instructor could simply be dismissed as an enthusiastic jerk! Without substance or the ability to relate to learners, the zealous instructor appears foolish, more a person to be ridiculed than a person to be admired. Whereas when the expert empathic instructor displays such excitement about his subject matter, this person's enthusiasm can be seen by learners as the natural emotional outcome of justified commitment. Such an instructor can be a powerful, inspiring force for adult learners.

Enthusiasm by its very nature is energy, and energy attracts. It is not easy to disregard an animated person. Enthusiastic instructors are constantly producing stimulation by the way they act. Learners are more likely to pay attention and therefore understand what is said or demonstrated. This concentration increases comprehension, which spirals into a continual dynamic. Greater alertness produces better learning, which makes future stimulation more likely and rewarding. And on it goes. Thus a constant, self-perpetuating chain of events has been established. It is no wonder that learners "can't wait" for the next course session with an inspiring instructor.

One more quality that enthusiastic instructors effortlessly produce is believability. Because of their commitment to and involvement with their subject matter, they tend to use their own vital words and expressions. "Wow," "Who could imagine . . . ," and "That's incredible" may seem corny, but they are also undeniably authentic. In addition, such instructors are somewhat vulnerable to their own emotions. They would actually have a hard time hiding their feelings about what they teach. This kind of realism makes learners aware that enthusiastic instructors are speaking from their hearts as well as their minds. This accentuates their credibility and allows the learners to more easily embrace their instruction.

During instruction, the cornerstone of enthusiasm has basically two criteria: (1) We care about and value what we teach for ourselves as well as for our learners, and (2) this commitment is expressed in our instruction with appropriate degrees of emotion, animation, and energy. Attention to these two criteria will not only give some indication of our personal enthusiasm but will also have the added benefit of sustaining its force within our instruction.

1. We care about and value what we teach for ourselves as well as for our learners.

Our own personal interest in our subject matter is probably the surest indicator that we care about it. Do we devote time to understanding it better? Are we active members of groups or clubs that specialize in our discipline? Do we follow and learn from the best practitioners in our field? Do we read the magazines, journals, or newsletters of our subject area?

What is our area of specialty? Almost every artist, professional craftsman, or scholar has one, something unique they know or do better than most others in their field—a genuine source of pride. Whether it be the distinctive rhythm of a shoe shine man popping his rag or the esoteric experiments of a Nobel laureate, people who value their work usually try to develop a particular aspect of their skill or knowledge. It's our way of personalizing and showing appreciation for what we do. This specialty transcends each of us from an ordinary practitioner in the field into becoming a part of our subject matter by being a person who adds a singular contribution or style to the realm of our work. Enthusiastic instructors distinguish themselves and supplement their self-esteem by knowing they own such exceptional pursuits. Like some exotic faraway island, it gives us something special that only we have found to share with our learners.

Realizing the effects of what we teach helps us to care about our subject matter. Knowing which "firsts" our learners will have with us can be a powerful influence on our enthusiasm. The first time I ever read a Shakespearean sonnet was with a teacher. The first time I ever used a computer was at a workshop under the guidance of an instructor. The first time I ever learned how to prepare my own visual aids was with a trainer. The list is endless. What are the first-time experiences and skills that we bring to our own learners? That is why those adults are with us: to learn new things that help them to be more effective and knowledgeable. This is not something to be taken lightly or for granted. It is a needed contribution that every adult educator makes.

2. This commitment is expressed in our instruction with appropriate degrees of emotion, animation, and energy.

Displaying our commitment to our subject matter is the exhilarating quality that makes instruction enthusiastic. In some ways, we are like cheerleaders. We root for what we believe in.

Allowing ourselves to be emotional about what we teach is the key. Some examples: getting excited about new concepts, skills, materials, and future events related to our subject; showing wonder about discoveries and insights that emerge from our learners; and sincerely expressing feelings about the things we do with our learners—"I feel frustrated by these problems myself"; "I'm looking forward to beginning this new training with you"; "I'm happy to see the progress you're making."

A little bit of dramatization helps as well. Whatever the actor in us will allow is a good rule of thumb. This can be done by telling interesting stories about what we teach; role playing our subject matter (becoming historical figures, delivering quotes and speeches, simulating characters in problems, and so forth); and using the arts and media such as music, slide shows, and film excerpts to demonstrate and accentuate our subject matter.

Showing our interest in the world as it relates to what we teach is another very attractive way to display our enthusiasm. It not only vividly demonstrates our commitment, but it also broadens the importance of our subject matter. We can bring in articles and newspaper clippings of current events that relate to what we teach; take field trips; invite credible guest speakers who work in areas related to our subject matter; self-disclose about interesting personal experiences we have had as we learned about our field; and share any new learning that we might be carrying on at the moment. Some caution about these last two ideas is warranted. Going overboard with them could be interpreted as too self-centered, which would then be more harmful than helpful with adult learners.

Although emotional involvement, dramatization, and showing interest are ways to display our enthusiasm, how do we really know if our instruction expresses this quality? Collins (1976) has developed eight indicators of high teacher enthusiasm:

1. Rapid, uplifting, varied vocal delivery
2. Dancing, wide-open eyes
3. Frequent, demonstrative gestures
4. Varied, dramatic body movements
5. Varied, emotive facial expressions
6. Selection of varied words, especially adjectives
7. Ready, animated acceptance of ideas and feelings
8. Exuberant overall energy level

The Enthusiasm Rating Chart, Exhibit 1, can help you to determine just how enthusiastic you are. You can score your instructional behavior according to the eight categories as they are defined across the chart. Adding these eight scores will give you a composite score that can be identified according to the ranges of possible scores found at the bottom. An effective method would be to videotape a few of your instructional experiences and rate yourself. If you question your own objectivity, you might ask a respected colleague to observe and rate you or a videotape of your instruction. I personally favor the latter approach, especially if it is reciprocal, because I have found the discussion that results from these observations to be helpful and informative. Although Collins developed these categories of enthusiasm behaviors with preservice elementary teachers, they have also been used with vocational instructors (Allen, 1980) and should be useful for anyone who wishes to better understand or improve his enthusiasm for any instructional activity.

Sometimes as instructors we are faced with solving the problem of *loss of enthusiasm*. There are six potential destroyers of enthusiasm. A brief word about each may be beneficial to the novice as well as the more experienced instructor of adults.

• *Satiation.* You seem to be doing the same thing over and over again. The feeling is one of boredom. There is nothing fresh or new in your instruction. You feel you may be in a rut and B. B. King's anthem is far too clear to you—"the thrill is gone." One of the best antidotes for this condition is *change.* Change the content, process, environment, or population of your instructional situation. Ask yourself which aspect of your instruction would benefit from such an alteration and take the necessary steps. We know from systems theory that one significant change in a system can change everything. This principle may be positively applicable to your situation.

• *Stress.* You feel burned out, psychologically drained, and physically near exhaustion. Perhaps there is some depression as well. Instruction is taking too much out of you. If this is the case, make up your mind to control the stress and not let it control you. Stress does kill. There are myriad books and programs that offer realistic assistance. Contact your professional organization, local health department, or physician for appropriate references.

• *Lack of success.* You are just not getting the job done. You feel some degree of incompetence. Maybe your learners are not learning well enough, or they seem poorly motivated, or they are not applying what they learn. There may be even be discipline problems and personality conflicts between the learners and yourself. To a large extent, this book is devoted to resolving these issues. A realistic additional intervention would be to discuss the matter with a respected and trusted colleague. Literally, have yourself a consultation. Almost all professionals do when problems or questions come up in their work. Doctors, lawyers, therapists, and managers readily and wisely seek the counsel of fellow practitioners to resolve the many dilemmas that are common to anyone who provides a service to human beings.

• *Loss of purpose.* The ultimate values for which you instruct adults seem vague and distant, possibly even forgotten. You

Exhibit 1. Enthusiasm Rating Chart.

Categories	Low		High
	(1) (2) (3)	(4) Medium (5)	(6) High (7)
1. Vocal delivery	Monotone, minimum inflections, little variation in speech, poor articulation.	Pleasant variations of pitch, volume, and speed; good articulation.	Large and sudden changes from rapid, excited speech to a whisper; varies intonation and pitch.
2. Eyes	Looks dull or bored; seldom opens eyes wide or raises eyebrows; avoids eye contact; often maintains a blank stare.	Appears interested; occasionally lighting up, shining, opening wide.	Characterized as dancing, snapping, shining, lighting up frequently, opening wide, eyebrows raised; maintains eye contact while avoiding staring.
3. Gestures	Seldom moves arms out toward person or object; never uses sweeping movements; keeps arms at side or folded, rigid.	Often pointed, occasional sweeping motion using body, head, arms, hands, and face; maintains steady pace of gesturing.	Quick and demonstrative movements of body, head, arms, hands, and face.
4. Body movement	Seldom moves from one spot or from sitting to standing position; sometimes "paces" nervously.	Moves freely, slowly, and steadily.	Large body movements, swings around, walks rapidly, changes pace; unpredictable and energetic; natural body movements.

5. Facial expression	Appears deadpan, expressionless or frowns; little smiling; lips closed.	Agreeable; smiles frequently; looks pleased, happy, or sad if situation calls for it.	Appears *vibrant*, demonstrative; shows variety of emotions and many expressions; broad smile; quick, sudden changes in expression.
6. Word selection	Mostly nouns, few descriptors or adjectives; simple or trite expressions.	Some descriptors or adjectives or repetition of the same ones.	Highly descriptive, many adjectives, great variety.
7. Acceptance of ideas and feelings	Little indication of acceptance or encouragement; may ignore learners' feelings or ideas.	Accepts ideas and feelings; praises or clarifies; some variations in response, but frequently repeats same ones.	Quick to accept, praise, encourage, or clarify; many variations in response; vigorous nodding of head when agreeing.
8. Overall energy level	Lethargic; appears inactive, dull, or sluggish.	Appears energetic and demonstrative sometimes, but mostly maintains an even level.	Exuberant; high degree of energy and vitality; highly demonstrative.

Some cautions: Do not rely too strongly on the results of only one observation. Repeated observations will better allow you and your observer to evaluate level of enthusiasm. Try changing your low-enthusiasm performance to high by practicing to improve your lower-rated categories of behavior. In general, a score of 8–20, dull or unenthusiastic level; 21–42, moderate level of enthusiasm; 43–56, very high level of enthusiasm. Use this chart as a guide for more concrete understanding of your behavior but not as a precise instrument of measurement. For the latter purpose, consult the original research.

Sources: Adapted from Collins, 1976; Gephart, 1981, p. 4.

no longer feel the pride you once had in your craft. Instruction has become an ordinary, mundane task. You have survival but not self-esteem in your work. This is a common malady to almost anyone who does something frequently for long periods of time. It is often a form of taking one's occupation for granted. It happens in marriage as well as in many jobs. Some combination of distance, reflection, and the company of other enthusiastic practitioners can be helpful. Vacations, conferences, conventions, and retreats are some means to consider for self-renewal.

• *Living in the past.* The attack of the good-old-days bug. The learners aren't as good as they used to be. The instructional conditions have deteriorated. You see things as they once were. You see things as they are now. You feel depressed. You tell yourself things will not get better. You feel even more depressed. This can lead to cynicism. And if you associate with other cynics, feeding off one another's hopelessness can produce an endless cycle. Break this pattern by seeing things as you would like them to be. Tell yourself it can happen. Begin to take the necessary steps. Associate with others who are willing to work toward these goals with you.

• *Plateauing.* Your instruction may be effective but you no longer believe you can get better. You feel stagnant. Personal and professional growth on the job seem dead-ended. There is very little challenge to your work. You feel resigned rather than committed. If you cannot leave this situation, you may feel trapped. In both instances, whether you go or not, the beneficial alternative is the same—create another challenge for yourself. This means setting a desired concrete goal in your professional life for which the outcome is not certain. There will be some risk of failure but that is where the exhilaration comes from. It could be raising your instructional goals, trying a new training process, or developing a better evaluation scheme. Whatever it is, make it a moderate risk, meaning the odds for whatever you do are clearly in your favor. Then plan for it and act on it. The results will speak for themselves.

Demonstrating Clarity: The Power of Language and Organization

You are a trainee in a special program your employer has developed. You are attending the first training seminar that will help you gain the appropriate skills for your new work. It is the first hour of the session and things seem to be going smoothly. Materials have been passed out. The leader has introduced himself. He seems well qualified, experienced, and enthusiastic. In fact, he has just told you one of the most important prerequisites for success in your new job will be a positive attitude toward your fellow employees.

A trainee raises her hand and asks the following question: "I've often heard how important a positive attitude is. But what does that really mean? I think where I get confused is just understanding what an attitude is. Could you tell me what that word means?"

You had not considered it before but you now realize you are not too sure what an attitude is either. The instructor waits a moment and begins his answer. "Well, ah . . . an attitude is, um . . . sort of like a way of looking at something or maybe thinking about what you see, or feeling a certain way, so that you end up . . . no, let me say, act, uh . . . better yet . . . judge the situation and that makes you behave in a certain way. Like if you don't like someone, you won't talk to them. Or, . . . if you respect something, you'll take better care of it."

The instructor moves on. You are confused, and you notice by the expressions on their faces that most of your peers seem to be feeling the same way, too. Trainee motivation has seriously slipped in the seminar. You feel a bit worried that you will not be able to understand this instructor.

It happens to adult learners all too frequently. They have expert, well-intentioned, enthusiastic instructors who do not communicate clearly. In the example just cited, the instructor could have said, "An attitude is the combination of a perception with a judgment that results in an emotion that influences our behavior. For example, you see a neighbor at a party. You like this person. You feel happy to see him. You decide to walk over and say hello." At the very least, the instructor should have asked the trainee if more explanation or examples were needed. This would have allowed for further clarification and may have saved the day.

No matter how enthusiastic, expert, and empathic an instructor is, the fourth cornerstone of instructional clarity is still necessary for motivating instruction. People seldom learn what they cannot understand. Worse yet, it is frustrating to be in the presence of someone who seems to know and care about something but cannot convey what that something is.

Instructional clarity is teaching something in a manner that is easy for learners to understand and that is organized so that they can smoothly follow the intended lesson or program. But there is a catch—what may be easy for one person to understand may not be so for another. Therefore, there is a dynamic between what the instructor does and what the learner brings to the instructional situation. This interaction of instructor presentation with learner ability to comprehend is the reason why instructional clarity contains another necessary element. This is the process the instructor uses to give learners a way to understand what has been taught if it was not clear in the initial presentation. This process can take many forms. It may be a time set aside for questions on the lesson taught. Or it may be an opportunity for learners to practice and demonstrate what the instructor has taught under his direct supervision. Or it simply may be repeating things that are difficult to understand. The point is that every motivating instructor has a way to help learners clarify what has been offered through the instructional process.

There are many studies that reveal that instructional clarity is consistently and positively associated with learning (Gephart, Strother, and Duckett, 1981). There is also some evidence that teachers who are perceived to be clear behave in a similar manner regardless of geographic location. One can find them in Australia as well as in Tennessee. They are people who teach without sacrificing awareness of what is happening to the learner. They know their preferred methods of instruction, but they also reach out to discover what the learners need for better understanding.

Adult learners are especially baffled by a lack of instructional clarity because so often they bring with them a history of having been able to learn what they needed to know in order to survive and prosper. They are not first graders and their achievements testify to that. To know you have the ability but to feel unable to learn because the instructor's language or methods seem vague and confusing is extremely frustrating. Increasing this tension will also be the frequent reason for adults' participation in a formal learning experience—a real need for new learning to advance in their jobs.

It is difficult to prescribe what an instructor can do to guarantee instructional clarity. Significant research continues in this area and much evidence is still coming in. However, there are two helpful performance standards that current data tend to support: (1) Our instruction can be understood and followed by most of our learners; and (2) we provide for learners a way to comprehend what has been taught if it was not clear in the initial presentation. Following these two criteria as guidelines will help us establish and develop instructional clarity for our learners.

1. Our instruction can be understood and followed by most of our learners.

This guideline emphasizes our language and organization. We can begin by generally using words and descriptions that are familiar to our learners. We could be talking about something as simple as a smell or an odor, but unless we choose first to define them, we would be wise not to casually use the words *effluvium* or *redolence* to get across our meaning. When taking our learners into new areas of knowledge, we can use examples and analogies that are clear to them. To feel like Napoleon at Waterloo is much more comprehensible to most people than to feel like Alcibiades at Athens. There is, however, to all of this a critical mass. To use too much of our learner's language could be patronizing or inauthentic. We have to decide what is appropriate. The main goal is to avoid being vague and to describe as precisely as possible what is important for our learners to know. Our constant awareness of the expressions on their faces will give us a continual impression of how well they are comprehending our instruction.

Organization is the logical connection and orderly relationship between each part of our instructional presentation. Like a good map, can we be followed by our learners from one learning destination to the next? Are the most important concepts and skills properly emphasized and noted, just as larger cities might receive bolder designations on a topographical sheet? The best proof of how well our instruction is organized is our own ability to clearly

Exhibit 2. Instructional Clarity Checklist.

This is a checklist for learners to complete, but it can also be adapted to become a self-diagnostic instrument. In its present form, it can be given to learners for their feedback on your instruction. This will tell you from their point of view what you do well and what you need to do to improve the clarity of your instruction.

(After each statement, place a check mark under the category that most accurately applies to it.)

As our instructor you:

	Statement	All of the time	Most of the time	Some of the time	Never	Doesn't apply
0	1. Explain things simply.	—	—	—	—	—
0	2. Give explanations we understand.	—	—	—	—	—
0	3. Teach at a pace that is not too fast and not too slow.	—	—	—	—	—
0	4. Stay with a topic until we understand.	—	—	—	—	—
X	5. Try to find out when we don't understand and then repeat things.	—	—	—	—	—
0	6. Teach things step-by-step.	—	—	—	—	—
0	7. Describe the work to be done and how to do it.	—	—	—	—	—
X	8. Ask if we know what to do and how to do it.	—	—	—	—	—
X	9. Repeat things when we don't understand.	—	—	—	—	—
0	10. Explain something and then use an example to illustrate it.	—	—	—	—	—
X	11. Explain something and then stop so we can ask questions.	—	—	—	—	—
0	12. Prepare us for what we will be doing next.	—	—	—	—	—
0	13. Give specific details when teaching or training.	—	—	—	—	—
X	14. Repeat things that are hard to understand.	—	—	—	—	—
0	15. Use examples and explain them until we understand.	—	—	—	—	—
0	16. Explain something and then stop so we can think about it.	—	—	—	—	—
0	17. Show us how to do the work.	—	—	—	—	—
0	18. Explain the assignment and the materials we need to do it.	—	—	—	—	—
0	19. Stress difficult points.	—	—	—	—	—
0	20. Show examples of how to do course work and assignments.	—	—	—	—	—
X	21. Give us enough time for practice.	—	—	—	—	—
X	22. Answer our questions.	—	—	—	—	—
X	23. Ask questions to find out if we understand.	—	—	—	—	—
X	24. Go over difficult assignments until we understand how to do them.	—	—	—	—	—

Sources: Adapted from Kennedy and others, 1978; Gephart, Strother, and Duckett, 1981, p. 4.

outline our presentation for ourselves. If we can accurately follow it, the odds favor our learners' being able to do so as well.

2. We provide for learners a way to comprehend what has been taught if it was not clear in the initial presentation.

This guideline has many possibilities, depending on how and what we teach. The range spans reviewing difficult material to having announced office hours for learners who want personal help. The Instructional Clarity Checklist found in Exhibit 2 is a way of surveying these many options. It also provides us with a means to use learner feedback to diagnose how clearly we are being understood by them. Those statements that relate directly to guideline number 2 are preceded by an "X." Statements relating to guideline number 1 are preceded by an "O."

The Instructional Clarity Checklist offers us a concrete way to better understand how clear our instruction really is. By videotaping ourselves during instruction, we can use this checklist to evaluate the clarity of our instruction while we actually see and hear ourselves interact with learners.

We have had a chance to examine and discuss the four cornerstones of motivating instruction—expertise, empathy, enthusiasm, and clarity. They are four necessary, interdependent, and vital building blocks. They are a very strong foundation. They are not a complete structure. However, what follows in this book could not be considered without first acknowledging these core characteristics. Every motivational factor and strategy that follows is presented with the assumption that the instructor who uses them will do so in a context of instruction that is expert, empathic, enthusiastic, and clear. This will increase the probability that these strategies will be effective with adult learners.

3

What Motivates
Adults to Learn

Psychology cannot try to explain everything with a
single construct, such as association, instinct, or gestalt. A variety of constructs has to be used.

—Kurt Lewin

As a concept, motivation is a bit of a beast. A powerfully influential
and wide-ranging area of study in psychology, motivation at its core
deals with *why people behave as they do.* But in terms of mutual
understanding and tightly controlled boundaries of application,
motivation roams the field of psychology with almost reckless
abandon. There are over twenty internationally recognized theories
of motivation with many opposing points of view, differing exper-
imental approaches, and continuing disagreement over proper
terminology and problems of definition (Madsen, 1974).

This state of affairs is not simply the result of idiosyncratic
debate among scholarly egos but is more realistically due to the

44

complexity of human behavior and a lack of concrete measures of motivation. There are no ways to x-ray the thoughts of a species that is rational and irrational at the same time. In the fields of instruction and learning this has led to some difficult problems—whom to believe, which theories to apply, and how to make sense out of this wealth of confusing possibilities. In general, instructors and trainers can find very few guidelines that suggest how to cohesively and consistently apply the most useful and practical elements from this extensive array of motivational information (Wlodkowski, 1981).

Although the available knowledge does not fit into any single theory of motivation, there are a significant number of well-researched instructional strategies that can be applied to learning situations according to motivational principles. One way to presently resolve this dilemma is to utilize general motivation factors that can incorporate useful strategies from a variety of motivational theories. For example, most motivational theories have something to contribute to the understanding of how human attitudes are formed and operate. Anyone who instructs knows the importance of learner attitudes as they influence motivation for learning. By using the major factor of attitude, the instructor can consider strategies from numerous theories of motivation to more positively influence the learner in the learning task. With this approach, motivational strategies from classical conditioning, operant conditioning, gestalt psychology, consistency theory, rational-emotive theory, and social influence theory are all possible means to enhance learner motivation because each of these theories has a set of principles and related research that deal with attitude change.

There appear to be at least six major factors that are supported by numerous theories of psychology and their related research as having a substantial impact on learner motivation—attitude, need, stimulation, affect, competence, and reinforcement. The following sections of this chapter will consider how each of these motivational factors is a powerful influence on adult behavior and learning as well as how these major factors can be combined when designing motivational strategies for instruction.

How Attitudes Influence Behavior

In general, an *attitude* is a combination of concepts, information, and emotions that results in a predisposition to respond favorably or unfavorably toward particular people, groups, ideas, events, or objects (Johnson, 1980). For example, an accountant is required to take an in-service training course by her company. A colleague who has already taken the training tells her that the instructor is authoritarian and arrogant. The accountant finds herself a little anxious as she anticipates the new training. At her first training session, the instructor, in a matter-of-fact manner, discusses the course and its requirements. The accountant judges the instructor's neutral style to be cold and hostile. She now fears the instructor and resents the mandatory training. This accountant has combined information and emotions into a predisposition to respond unfavorably to a person and an event. If the accountant's colleague had told her the instructor was helpful and caring, it it less likely that the same outcome would have occurred.

Attitudes are powerful influences on human behavior and learning because they help people to make sense of their world and give cues as to what behavior will be most helpful in dealing with that world. If someone is going to be hostile toward us, it is in our best interest to be careful of that person. Attitudes help us to feel safe around things that are initially unknown to us. Attitudes also help us to anticipate and cope with recurrent events. They give us guidelines and allow us to make our reactions more automatic. This makes life simpler and frees us to cope with the more unique and stressful elements of daily living. In psychology this is called the "least effort" principle: Whenever possible, apply past solutions to present problems or, whenever possible, apply past reactions to present experiences. Not only does this help us to cope but this also helps us to be consistent in our behavior, which is a vital need for all human beings.

Attitudes are learned. They are acquired through processes such as experience, direct instruction, identification, and role behavior (teacher-student, parent-child, employer-employee, and so forth). Because they are learned, they can also be modified and changed. New experiences constantly affect our attitudes, making them shift, intensify, weaken, or reverse. They are in a dynamic process with people, the media, and life in general constantly impinging on them. Attitudes can be personally helpful as in the case of positive self-esteem, or they can be personally harmful as in the case of intense fear of failure. Attitudes are with us all the time and they constantly influence our behavior and learning.

New learning is usually risky business; the outcome is seldom a certainty. For adults, this risk may be even higher because the new learning may be required for a job, a promotion, or some important personal goal. Attitudes are very active in unpredictable situations because of the security they provide for the person. An instructor of adults can be quite assured that their attitudes will be an active influence on their motivation to learn from the moment the instruction begins. Adult learners will immediately make judgments about the instructor, the particular subject, the learning situation, and their personal expectancy for success. However, beyond knowing that learner attitudes are a constant influence, it is difficult to make broad, sweeping generalizations about the attitudes of adults with respect to learning in general. Kidd's cautionary statement (1973, p.117) is well worth noting: "As in so many areas, it seems that chronological age, compared with other factors, is of little utility in understanding or predicting attitudes."

There is evidence that adults of lower socioeconomic status more often hold negative beliefs and perceptions toward education than adults from the middle and upper ranges of socioeconomic status (Darkenwald and Larson, 1980). However, this generalization must be qualified by another generalization—a group of adults similar in age and socioeconomic status is far more heterogeneous than a group of children of similar age and socioeconomic status (Smith, 1982). As a person becomes older, the more time that person has to accumulate different life experiences. And since attitudes are learned and changed through experience, one can readily see the necessity for an open and flexible approach on the part of an instructor of adults.

How Needs Promote Desire

A *need* is a condition experienced by the individual as an internal force that leads the person to move in the direction of a goal. The achievement of the goal is capable of releasing or ending the feeling of the need and its related tension. Thirst (a need) leads to a search for water (a goal). When enough water has been drunk, the need or tension of thirst is ended. Needs exist in the tissues and memory of human beings (Deci, 1980). They can be physiological, such as hunger, or learned, such as the need for achievement.

All people live with an unending sense of need. Which need a person is currently experiencing will depend on the individual's history of learning, the current situation, and the last need that was fulfilled. Some needs seem more dominant and continuous (for rest and safety), while others are less predictable (for understanding and orderliness). No single theorist in psychology has created a list of needs that are acceptable to most other psychologists. Yet no psychologist would deny the powerful influence of needs on human behavior. People actually can feel *driven* to acquire food, money, or knowledge, which are just a few of the many compelling needs that seem to motivate human beings.

Most often, needs act like strong internal feelings that push a person toward a general goal. The more strongly the person feels the need, the greater the chances the person will feel an accompanying pressure to attain the related goal. This tension or pressure can translate into a *desire* when the individual becomes aware of this feeling and *wants* to achieve a *particular* goal. A person feels hunger and a need for food (general goal). He desires to cook himself a gourmet meal (particular goal). Another person feels a bit lonely and needs some social company (general goal). He desires to call his best friend (particular goal). Desire usually leads to satisfaction and enjoyment. It is what people *want* to do. When adults need and desire what they are learning, they will tend to be highly motivated. Instructors can influence motivation based on need by being sensitive to apparent needs and by formulating how and what they present to adult learners in a manner that gratifies those needs. For example, "Those of you who are taking this training to improve your relationship with your employees will learn three management techniques that will help you to do exactly that."

Probably the most widely known approach to the concept of need is the one developed by Maslow (1970). This holistic and dynamic theory assumes that need gratification is the most important principle underlying human development. Maslow organized a hierarchy of needs arranged in order of prepotency. Table 1 shows the hierarchy of needs, common conditions of deficiency and fulfillment, and an everyday example of such fulfillment.

Prepotency means that when needs are satisfied at one level, the next higher order of needs becomes predominant in influencing behavior. Physiological needs are the lowest in the hierarchy while self-actualization needs are the highest. Unless a lower need is at least partially fulfilled, it is difficult for the next higher need to be influential on the person's behavior. Thus, a very lonely person (love and belongingness needs) would have difficulty concerning himself about becoming highly competent (esteem needs) at a particular job. However, it must be stated that there is very little empirical support for prepotency at every level of Maslow's hierarchy (Whaba and Bridwell, 1976).

There is considerable research support for the physiological and safety needs being active on a prepotent basis. People do need to feel physically well and personally safe before they can commit themselves to learning. After these two needs are satisfied, people appear to respond to the rest of the needs in the hierarchy on almost a totally situational basis. Maslow's hierarchy (especially the higher needs) is probably most useful as a comprehensive list of needs that helps instructors to categorize motivational strategies and instructional objectives after they become empathically aware of the needs that have brought the adults to the learning situation.

There is evidence that supports the understanding that adults who are less educated and in the socioeconomically lower classes will be more interested in learning and education that is aimed at their survival needs (physiological and safety), while the more well-educated middle and upper classes will be more open to learning and education that is aimed at personal development, achievement, and self-actualization (Cross, 1979). Nevertheless, in the beginning of any learning situation, instructors of adults are more effective when they recognize the needs that have brought the adults to the learning situation, and they can intensify the adults' desire for learning by applying motivational strategies that enhance what the learners *want* to acquire through their participation.

Table 1. Maslow's Need Hierarchy and Conditions of Deficiency and Fulfillment.

Need Hierarchy	Conditions of Deficiency	Conditions of Fulfillment	Illustration
Physiological[a] (lower-level)	Hunger, thirst Sexual frustration Tension Fatigue Illness	Physical well-being Pleasure from senses Relaxation Comfort Healthy state of being	Feeling satisfied after a good meal
Safety[a] (lower-level)	Insecurity Fear	Security Calmness	Being secure in a full-time job
Love and belongingness (higher need)	Loneliness Self-consciousness Isolation	Sense of friendship Free expression of emotions Sense of unity with others	Experiencing total acceptance in a love relationship
Esteem (higher need)	Incompetence Inferiority	Competence Confidence	Receiving an award for outstanding performance on a project
Self-Actualization (higher need)	Absence of meaning in life Uncreative	Work that embodies personal values Creative living	Realizing a personal potential as in writing a valued book

[a]Evidence for prepotency exists.

How Stimulation Maintains Attention

What is stimulation? Is it excitement, entertainment, or provocation? Sometimes it is. But frequently it is not. *Stimulation* is any change in our perception or experience with our environment that makes us active. We see something more colorful and are attracted to it. We hear something new and listen more carefully to the sound. We touch something unexpectedly and retract our hand from it. Someone shows us something for the first time and we think about it for a while. A surprise jolts our emotions. All of these are stimulating experiences. They can be interesting, frustrating, invigorating, or irritating. Whatever their quality, they will get our attention and tend to keep us actively involved.

Human beings seek stimulation. There is considerable evidence that sensory stimulation is important to the development and maintenance of normal motivated behavior (Petri, 1981). Prolonged periods of inadequate stimulation can lead to problems ranging from retarded physical growth to excessive fear and hallucinations. Sensory-deprived people will work very hard to maintain stimulation. From the Count of Monte Cristo to prisoner-of-war diaries, there are numerous literary and historical references that document the tragic consequences of lack of normal stimulation.

Petri reports that a considerable amount of research in neurophysiology suggests that an actual need for stimulation exists. It appears that stimulation increases the activity of the brain and keeps human beings aroused and alert to deal with their environments. Small or moderate changes in arousal are reinforcing to us and cause us to direct our attention toward these various forms of stimulation. As long as these changes such as novelty, uncertainty, and complexity continue, we continue to pay attention to them. Once these changes stop, we tend to become bored and explore in other directions to maintain our alertness.

Stimulation directly helps to sustain adult learning behavior. If a person does not pay attention to instruction, very little learning will take place. The instructional process and its related materials make up the main body of most learning activities. Adults can have a desire to learn something as well as a positive attitude toward it, but if they do not find the process of learning stimulating, their attention will diminish. People do not *want* to become bored but they *become* bored. Self-discipline and will power can only take concentration so far. A continually repetitive and uninteresting stimulus can wear down the best intentions of most people. Once boredom sets in, *fatigue* and *distraction* are not far behind. Being adults, we are more vulnerable to these two oppressors of learning because, unlike children for whom school may be their first priority, adults have other serious responsibilities and learning may be one more demand added on to an already stressful life-style.

To be a stimulating instructor of adults is a great challenge and a real necessity. I believe it is the area of instruction where the least amount of practical knowledge exists. However, this text accepts this gauntlet; Chapter Six will provide a formidable array of strategies to maintain stimulation during the instructional process.

How Affect Motivates Behavior

The major motivation factor of affect pertains to the emotional experience—the feelings, concerns, and passions—of the individual learner or group while learning. No learning takes place in an emotional vacuum. Learners feel something while learning, and those emotions can motivate their behavior in a number of different directions.

Some psychologists have proposed that emotions are the "chief movers" of behavior (Tomkins, 1970), and most psychologists accept the idea that thinking and feeling interact to mutually influence one another as well as to lead to changes in behavior. Weiner (1980b), widely known as a cognitive psychologist, has recently offered evidence that a feeling in and of itself can motivate behavior. The following example is offered to represent his understanding.

A college student asks another college student for her notes to a particular class. She tells her she has been in an accident and was forced to miss class because of it. She is wearing bandages and an arm splint. The student feels compassion for her and lends her the notes. In this scenario the student has a cognitive understanding that leads to a feeling (compassion) that causes her to lend her notes.

It is important to emphasize that it is *the degree of her feeling* that mostly caused her behavior. If she had felt less sorry for the injured student, she may not have given her the notes. Although the perception and feeling are related, it is the intensity of her feelings at that moment that had the strongest influence on her immediate behavior. People constantly make judgments and interpretations about the causes of their own behavior and the behavior of others that lead to emotional feelings. But it is the intensity of those emotions that seems to play the largest part in influencing imme-diate future behavior. If people wait a period of time after a certain perception, their emotions will often change or lessen, leading to a different behavior from the one that might have actually occurred if they had acted immediately after the perception had taken place. Someone says something that angers us and we immediately want to argue with the person. After some time passes, our anger may diminish and we choose not to debate with the individual. This is probably why conventional wisdom encourages us to postpone important decisions while we are feeling any emotion very strongly—the emotion itself can trigger behavior that may not be in our best interest.

Every learning environment is constantly influenced by the normal emotional reactions of its participants. Also, because adult learning so often deals with success and failure in achievement and accomplishment activities, the personal feelings of these learners are continually rampant as they react to their progress or lack of it. The emotional state of an adult at a particular instance of learning is a significant influence. Ask any group of adult learners about how they *feel* about what they are doing and you will receive an indicator regarding their future involvement, perseverance, completion, or return to the learning activity.

It is also important for instructors to keep in mind that emotions not only influence behavior but may affect thinking as well. For example, a learner notices he has forgotten an important assignment and feels a degree of fear. To reduce this anxiety, he may think of acceptable reasons to tell his instructor about why he forgot the assignment.

This constant dynamic of thinking, feeling, and behaving is what puts vitality and humanity into the learning situation. Instructor and learner emotions give meaning and relevancy to learning. Affect can be an intrinsic motivator. When emotions are positive while learning, they sustain involvement and deepen interest in the subject matter or activity. If reading fine literature fills a learner with wonder and joy, that learner will very likely want to read more of the same literature. Harmony between emotions and thinking, so that they can influence motivation to learn as a supportive integrated force, is in the best interest of effective instruction.

How Competence Builds Confidence

According to White (1959), human beings *inherently* desire to gain competence over their environment. Competence theory assumes that people naturally strive for effective interactions with their world. By virtue of being a human being, a person is intrinsically motivated to master the environment and finds successful mastery of tasks to be gratifying. We are genetically programmed to explore, perceive, think about, manipulate, and change our surroundings to promote an effective interaction with our environment. "The behavior that leads to the building up of effective grasping, handling and letting go of objects, to take one example, is not random behavior produced by a general overflow of energy. It is directed, selective, and persistent, and it is continued not because it serves primary drives, which indeed it cannot serve until it is almost perfected, but because it satisfies an intrinsic need to deal with the environment" (White, 1959, pp. 317-318).

Researchers have demonstrated that infants as young as eight weeks old can learn particular responses to manipulate their environment. In one such study, infants were placed in a crib with a mobile above their head (Watson and Ramey, 1972). By turning their head to the right, an electrical apparatus in their pillow was activated and caused the mobile to move. Not only did these children learn to "move" the mobile but they displayed more positive emotions (smiling, cooing) than infants for whom the mobile movement was controlled by the experimenter.

The history of the human race is a continuous, colorful catalogue of bold scientists and daring adventurers who have relentlessly reached out to master their environment. We are apparently active and reasoning creatures who want to shape the course of our development. In general, competence is the concept or major motivation factor that describes our innate desire to take the initiative and effectively act upon our environment rather than remaining passive and allowing the environment to control and determine our behavior.

A number of different psychological theories embrace competence as a central assumption. Attribution theory, achievement motivation theory, personal causation theory, cognitive evaluation theory, and social learning theory support the idea that human beings strive for understanding and mastery (Weiner, 1980a). Their combined research is an outstanding documentation that adults tend to be motivated when effectively learning something they value.

Because awareness of competence is such a powerful influence on human behavior, adults who are learning and can feel an actual sense of progress and real accomplishment are usually well motivated to continue their efforts in a similar direction. In addition, since there is considerable evidence that adults enter educational programs with a strong need to apply what they have learned, there will be a continual attentiveness on their part toward how effectively they are learning (Knox, 1977). They know their families, jobs, and communities will be the arenas in which they test this new learning and under those conditions, there is little margin for error or incompetence.

In general learning situations, a sense of competence occurs when there is an awareness of personal mastery: the realization by the person that a specified degree of knowledge or level of performance has been attained that is acceptable by personal and/or social standards. This usually comes toward the end of the learning process when the person has had a chance to apply or practice what is being learned. When the person knows (usually through feedback) how well he can do what he is learning and can make internal statements, such as "I really understand this" or "I am doing this proficiently," feelings of competence will occur.

Once the person knows with some degree of certainty that he is able or adept at what he has learned, he will feel self-confident.

This comes from the person's realization that he has intentionally mastered whatever has been learned through his own ability and effort. This self-confidence emanates from such internal statements as "I can do it" or "I will be able to do it again."

The relationship between competence and self-confidence is mutually advantageous. Competence allows confidence to develop, which leads to emotional support for effort to master new skills and knowledge. Competent achievement of this new learning further buttresses confidence, which can now again support and motivate more extensive learning. This can result in a spiralling dynamic where competence and confidence grow in continued support of one another. To personally feel assured that one's own ability and effort can eventually lead to new learning and achievement is a powerful and lasting motivational resource. It is also the mark of a true expert or champion in any field. Instructors can help learners to achieve this by emphasizing and establishing conditions for competent learning. It is a wonderful gift.

How Reinforcement Enhances Learning

One of the most fundamental laws of psychology is the principle of reinforcement. *Reinforcement* is any event that maintains or increases the probability of the response it follows (Vargas, 1977). In countless studies with animals and humans, in laboratories, classrooms, and clinical settings, psychologists have found that behaviors can be made more or less likely through the judicious application of positive and negative reinforcement. The effective use of reinforcing events, such as the results of one's work, praise, social approval, and attention, have been established as important variables to be considered in the design of educational environments (Glaser and Cooley, 1973).

Reinforcement is designed and employed in this text in essentially the theoretical framework of Skinner (1968). This means that it is used in an "operant" or "instrumental" sense where learner behavior is emitted (mainly occurring spontaneously) and is instrumental in bringing about reinforcement. Talking, writing, and reading are operants that can be instrumental in bringing about instructor reinforcement. A learner writes a paragraph using correct grammar and is complimented by her instructor for the specific use of this grammar. The learner, having been reinforced, will be more likely to use this type of grammar in future paragraph writing. According to *operant conditioning,* if no one reinforced a person's writing, that person would not learn how to write. This approach is very much in the Darwinian tradition. "Operant learning is a process much like Darwinian selection is for species. In a given environment those acts which are in some way effective survive and those which are ineffective die out. Over a period of time, patterns of behavior, like species, evolve from the kinds of individual operants that survive" (Vargas, 1977, p. 35).

In this type of reinforcement theory, positive reinforcement plays a major role (Karoly, 1980). *Positive reinforcement* happens when a behavior is followed by a presentation of a desired stimulus that increases the behavior's rate of occurrence (Alberto and Troutman, 1982). A *positive reinforcer* describes the consequent event itself. Positive reinforcers can be *tangible,* such as money and prizes, or they can be *social,* such as approval and affection. People do seem to study with greater effort and learn more effectively when their specific learning behaviors are positively reinforced by their instructors (Wlodkowski, 1982). Good grades, high test scores, academic awards, and instructor attention have been educational incentives for many years. It is difficult to believe any academic setting could positively survive without them. Although recent studies have indicated that *how* these reinforcers are applied must be carefully qualified (and these qualifications and cautions will be fully considered in Chapter Eight), research in adult learning and work continues to support their effective use (Korman, Greenhaus, and Badin, 1977; Pittman, Boggiano, and Ruble, 1983).

A *negative reinforcer* is an aversive stimulus or event that can be removed or reduced in intensity. *Negative reinforcement* is the contingent removal or reduction of an aversive stimulus following a behavior that increases the future rate and/or probability of the behavior's occurrence. An example of negative reinforcement would be an instructor telling a learner that a certain boring drill can be terminated when a specific level of achievement has been reached. Penalties, disapproval, and threat often act as negative reinforcers. However, because negative reinforcement is an aversive approach to learning with many of the potential drawbacks of punishment, I evaluate this procedure as potentially too dangerous and do not advocate its use or application (Karoly, 1980). In general, adults in this culture do not respond well when they know or feel their learning is coerced. Consequently, their motivation for learning under such conditions tends to diminish over time. For these reasons, negative reinforcement will not be further considered in the following sections of this book. Therefore, the major motivation factor of reinforcement, as it continues to be discussed, is synonymous with positive reinforcement.

Organizing the Major Factors of Motivation for Maximum Usefulness

We have seen how important and yet how confusing motivation as a general concept can be. One way for instructors to make sense out of the array of theories that make up motivational psychology is to consider major motivational factors that are broad enough and scientifically supported so that they can serve as categories to arrange instructional strategies based on these many theories. To this end, six major factors of motivation have been offered: attitude, need, stimulation, affect, competence, and reinforcement. Each of these major factors has a wealth of multiple theories as well as related research that supports its powerful influence on learner motivation. The question now is "How do we arrange and use these major factors for instructional planning?"

This also seems like an appropriate time to say a few words about motivation planning in general. I am convinced that one of the logical reasons why ineffective and unmotivated learning so frequently occurs is because of the lack of motivation planning on the part of many instructors. Ask yourself or any other instructors how often and consistently do they do motivation planning for what they teach. When it comes to motivation, even the best of us tend to use common sense, intuition, and trial and error as our means for instructional planning. This is not willful negligence. This is the best that we can do when such a confusing and conflicting array of motivational theories exists. Until this book, no general programmatic design for comprehensive motivation planning has been presented in the literature on instruction for adults.

Lesson planning and instructional design have existed, but not with continuous attention to and detail for motivated learning *throughout* the instructional sequence. Attention to stimulation has usually been woefully lacking. One can plan an effective learning sequence, but that does not mean the learners will be motivated while learning. This is the problem with instructional objectives. In their orthodox use, there is hardly any attention to affect or stimulation. I contend that for an adult to *learn and want to learn* (motivated learning), motivation planning is necessary. Otherwise, a person may, at best, learn but also dislike what has been learned or the learning process itself.

Motivation planning can be integrated with instructional planning or it can be used in addition to instructional planning. This will help to avoid two other pitfalls common to instruction, the first of which is *instructor ignorance when instruction seems unmotivating*. If a person does not have a motivational plan, what does that person do when instruction seems boring or lifeless? What is the logical approach? With no plan, the instructor is back to trial and error and intuition. Sometimes this is successful, but it is more frequently inefficient and prone to consequent feelings of impotence and exasperation. The second problem emerges when the instructor, having no motivation plan to analyze for possible solution to motivational difficulties that arise during instruction, places the entire responsibility for this state of affairs upon the learners. Blaming the learners for being unresponsive to instruction that is actually poorly designed or implemented in terms of its motivational influence is a common reaction among many instructors. It is difficult for us to be openly self-critical. Defense mechanisms like rationalization and projection act to protect our egos. With no motivation plan to fall back upon, we are that much more likely to be influenced by such defense mechanisms and to see our learners as responsible for the difficulties we are having. Motivation planning helps to keep our attention on how we instruct and what we can do about that instruction when it is not as vital as we would like it to be. This diminishes our tendency to blame, which is a common reaction to problems that seem unsolvable.

Instruction is systemic in nature. It is a network of interactions between an instructor and learners that leads to learning.

Therefore, motivation planning has to be systemic as well. No single major factor, such as need, exists without somehow being related to the other factors, such as stimulation and competence. Learning activities are arranged in patterns or sequences that lead to the attainment of learning objectives. For example, learners listen to a lecture, which is followed by a discussion, which is followed by some problem solving based on the previous lecture and discussion. The learning objective is that the learner will correctly solve a certain kind of problem, and three learning activities were sequenced to reach this objective.

Every learning sequence, whether it lasts twenty minutes or twenty hours, can be divided according to a time continuum. There is always a beginning, a middle, and an end. There are effective things that can be done during each of these phases to enhance learner motivation. Each phase has a maximum potential for the employment of motivational strategies that can optimally influence the learner's motivation. Each phase also relates to the others in forming a dynamic whole that, when proper motivational strategies are applied according to their particular phase, enhances the overall learning experience and catalyzes the learner's positive return to the learning situation. The various learning activities that make up the sequence can be analyzed in terms of when they occur and which motivational strategies they can incorporate in order to maximize their motivational influence throughout the sequence. The Time Continuum Model of Motivation organizes motivational strategies according to this rationale (Wlodkowski, 1981) (see Figure 1).

In the Time Continuum Model of Motivation there are three critical periods in any learning sequence or process during which particular motivational strategies will have maximum impact on the learner's motivation.

1. *Beginning*. When the learner enters and starts the learning process.
2. *During*. When the learner is involved in the body or main content of the learning process.
3. *Ending*. When the learner is finishing or completing the learning process.

Figure 1. The Time Continuum Model of Motivation.

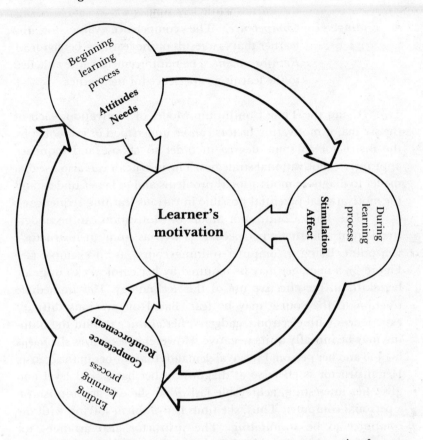

For each of these critical periods, there are two major factors of motivation that serve as categories for strategies that can be applied with maximum impact during those periods of time.

- *Beginning:* *Attitudes.* The learner's attitudes toward the general learning environment, instructor, subject matter, and self.

  Needs. The basic needs within the learner at the time of learning.
- *During:* *Stimulation.* The stimulation processes affecting the learner via the learning experience.

Affect. The affective or emotional experience of the learner while learning.

- *Ending:*   *Competence.* The competence value for the learner that is a result of the learning behavior.

Reinforcement. The reinforcement value attached to the learning experience for the learner.

Using the Time Continuum Model of Motivation, each of the six major motivation factors can be understood or evaluated by the instructor to some degree in order to choose and sequence appropriate motivational strategies. The instructor can also use this model to diagnose motivational problems and to better understand the motivational potential possible in various learning sequences.

The Time Continuum Model of Motivation can be understood from a learner's perspective as well as from an instructor's viewpoint. Using a computer training course as an example (see Figure 2), a manager may be required by her employer to upgrade her skills in the effective use of this technology. Her immediate reaction to the course may be fear. Based on previous difficult experiences with electronic gadgetry, her *attitude* toward the training may be initially quite negative. However, she realizes she *needs* her job and her personal survival demands that she begin the course. Her instructor is effective at diagnosing her basic skill level and gives her interesting, achievable tasks that she can accomplish on a personal computer. Thus, she finds her problem solving with the computer to be *stimulating.* The instructor also arranges for periodic "break-out" sessions during the course where the trainees can share their questions and reactions to their learning. These are *affectively* satisfying to the manager and she finds the group's morale to be very emotionally supportive. As her skills and independent work with the computer increase, she finds herself feeling *competent* and confident with this technology. Toward the end of the training her instructor *reinforces* her progress by giving her free time to use the computer to set up programs for application in her home office. At the end of the course she is a bit amazed to realize how motivated she is to use the computer on a regular basis in her work setting. This example serves to illustrate how the six major motivation factors interact on a dynamic basis to influence learner

Figure 2. Positive Motivational Dynamic of a Manager in a Computer Course.

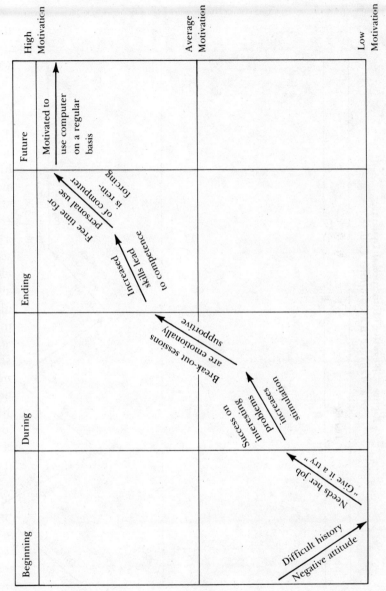

Figure 3. Negative Motivational Dynamic of a Manager in a Computer Course.

	Beginning	During	Ending	Future
High Motivation				
Average Motivation				
Low Motivation				

Difficult history
Negative attitude

Needs her job
"Give it a try"

Unsolvable problems decrease stimulation

Break-out sessions add some emotional support

Few skills, sense of incompetence

Lack of progress means little reinforcement

Low motivation to use computer on a regular basis

motivation along a time continuum. This is a very positive example. But it can be just as easily understood that if the trainer had given her difficult problems she could not solve, so that she was not stimulated and did not develop the consequent competence, her motivation could have suffered accordingly (see Figure 3).

The earlier discussions of the six major motivation factors in this chapter as well as the Time Continuum Model of Motivation and these above examples all stress the generalization that *each of the major motivation factors exerts maximum influence at a particular time in a learning sequence.* Deci's cognitive evaluation theory (Wlodkowski, 1981) is highly supportive of this interpretation. Through memory, physiology, and situational perception, needs and attitudes influence the learner at the *beginning* of the learning sequence. These two factors seem to have the greatest motivational impact on the learner whenever that person starts a new learning process. "Do I need it?" and "What do I think of it?" are internal questions that immediately come to the minds of adults when they begin a learning task. These result in the formulation of *motives* that are the goals that the learner wants to achieve through the learning experience. These needs and attitudes combine to interact with the stimulation and the affective processes that occur *during* the main body of the learning experience itself to further influence learner motivation. Every learning sequence has a series of main activities (reading, problem solving, lectures, discussions, drills, and so forth) to increase learning. Unless these activities are stimulating and/or affectively positive, there will be little motivational influence to sustain learner attention and involvement. Beginning attitudes and needs can carry the learner only so far. The process of learning itself should be stimulating and affectively positive to maintain the learner's effort to continue learning. At the *ending* of the learning sequence, the competence value and the reinforcement gained interact with the previous four major motivation factors to influence the learner's motivation at that moment, and for the future as well, resulting in new attitudes and needs. Through appropriate ending activities, the learner applies new skills or becomes aware of new knowledge, thereby feeling competent and having a learning product to be reinforced. If the learner cannot experience the consequent skills or new knowledge attained through the achievement of the learning objective, there will be no feelings of competence and, worse yet, what is there for the instructor to reinforce? Such an ending results in superficial learning with little transfer and feelings of frustration on the part of the learner.

Applying the Time Continuum Model of Motivation

Although the Time Continuum Model of Motivation shows motivational influence in three separate phases because time is linear in its progression, the overall influence of the major motivation factors is probably more dynamic and constant. Also, the six major motivation factors are probably not equal in their motivational influence upon the learner. Each is quite powerful. Therefore, the most productive route is for the instructor to plan motivational strategies for each factor so that a continuous and interactive motivational dynamic is organized for maximum effective instruction. This is a "leave no stone unturned" approach to motivation. *What is most critical is that each time phase* (beginning, during, and ending) *within the learning sequence includes significant positive motivational influence on the learner*. If any of these periods is motivationally vacant, learners will have difficulty sustaining their motivation for learning. This is analogous to nutrition for daily living. Most people eat three meals a day to sustain their energy. These meals usually correspond to beginning, during, and ending phases of their daily routine. Without such timely nutrition, their entire sequence of living habits can be disrupted. The six major motivation factors are selective sources for positive motivational influence, just as the major food groupings are selective sources for vitamins and protein. Thus, there are six basic questions to be considered by an instructor in the planning of any learning sequence or experience:

1. What can I do to establish a positive learner attitude for this learning sequence? (emphasis on beginning activities)
2. How do I best meet the needs of my learners through this learning sequence? (emphasis on beginning activities)

3. What about this learning sequence will continuously stimulate my learners? (emphasis on main activities)
4. How is the affective experience and emotional climate for this learning sequence positive for learners? (emphasis on main activities)
5. How does this learning sequence increase or affirm learner feelings of competence? (emphasis on ending activities)
6. What is the reinforcement that this learning sequence provides for my learners? (emphasis on ending activities)

If each of these questions is adequately answered by the instructor (and integrated into the learning sequence with appropriate activities), learners will have an excellent chance of being motivated to learn throughout the learning sequence.

The primary value of the Time Continuum Model of Motivation is that it is an organizational aid. It can be applied to groups or to individuals. By continuously attending to its six related questions, the instructor can, in any learning situation, design motivational strategies for learners throughout the learning sequence. Each of these questions pinpoints a major motivational factor and can be used by the instructor as a guide to the selection of motivational strategies from a wide array of motivational theories. These strategies can then be translated by the instructor into learning activities or instructor behaviors that are integrated into the learning sequence. Table 2 illustrates the six basic questions as they might be used by an adult basic education instructor to select one motivational strategy for each of the six major motivation factors for an instructional objective in arithmetic.

As Table 2 shows, there are six sequenced motivational strategies that are based on six different motivational theories. Each has also been translated into an actual learning activity or instructor behavior. The Time Continuum Model of Motivation allows for as many strategies to be used as the instructor believes are needed. The instructor's knowledge of motivation, subject matter, instructional situation, and time constraints will determine the quality and quantity of the motivational strategies employed. With this model, an instructor who knows only a few principles of motivation, as well as an instructor who knows many, can at least have a means

Table 2. Six Questions Based on the Time Continuum Model of Motivation as Applied by an Adult Basic Education Instructor.

Instructional Objective: After two weeks, learners will add and subtract mixed fractions at a 90 percent achievement level.

Question	When Used	Motivational Strategy	Motivational Theory	Learning Activity or Instructor Behavior
1. What can I do to establish a positive learner attitude for the learning sequence?	1. Beginning of learning sequence	1. Positively confront the possible erroneous beliefs, expectations, and assumptions that may underlie a negative learner attitude.	1. Rational-Emotive Theory (Ellis)	1. Ask learners how many have heard that fractions are really difficult to do and discuss with them their feelings and expectations.
2. How do I best meet the needs of my learners through this learning sequence?	2. Beginning of learning sequence	2. Reduce or remove components of the learning environment that lead to failure or fear.	2. Safety Needs, Self-Actualization Theory (Maslow)	2. Organize a tutorial assistance plan by which learners who are having difficulty can receive immediate help from the instructor or a fellow learner.
3. What about this learning sequence will continuously stimulate my learners?	3. During main phase of learning sequence	3. Whenever possible, make learner reaction and involvement essential parts of the learning process, that is, problem solving, games, role playing, simulation, and so forth.	3. Equilibration (Piaget)	3. Use games and creative problems to challenge and invite daily learner participation.

4. How is the affective experience and emotional climate for this learning sequence positive for learners?	4. During main phase of learning sequence	4. Use a cooperative goal structure to maximize learner involvement and sharing.	4. Cooperative Theory (Deutsch)	4. Have teams of learners solve fraction problems with one member of the team responsible for diagnosing the problem, another responsible for finding the common denominator, another for working it through, and another for checking the answer; alternate roles.
5. How does this learning sequence increase or affirm learner feelings of competence?	5. Ending of learning sequence	5. Provide consistent feedback regarding mastery of learning.	5. Cognitive Evaluation Theory (Deci and Porac)	5. Use answer sheets and diagnostic and formative tests to give feedback and assistance to learners.
6. What is the reinforcement that this learning sequence provides for my learners?	6. Ending of learning sequence	6. When learning has natural consequences, allow them to be congruently evident.	6. Operant Conditioning (Skinner)	6. Construct a "class test" where each learner creates a mixed-fraction word problem for the other learners to solve. Each learner is responsible for checking and, if necessary, helping the other learners to solve the problem.

beyond trial and error for cohesively applying them to the instructional setting. The model also fits the actual process of instruction as it is conducted in learning environments, with sequenced activities and particular objectives having a holistic patterned framework that includes a time orientation, subjective viewpoint, and a logical method to combine strategies of motivational theories that are often set apart by their conflicting assumptions. Four case examples of effective motivation plans based on the Time Continuum Model of Motivation that are of greater depth and magnitude are presented in Chapter Nine.

How much to use any major motivational factor is a vital question. This will remain unique and vary according to the instructor, learners, and learning situation. Some of us, by virtue of values, experience, and talent, may emphasize those major motivation factors that best suit our beliefs, abilities, and situation. An analogy for this is to see learner motivation and instruction as a musical arrangement. Each major motivation factor represents a series of notes that may be played relative to our talent and taste. How often and in what pattern we (instructors) select these notes (motivational strategies) will result in a certain melody (learner motivation) that we may care to play again or alter, depending on its results (learning). There are many different melodies as well as types of music. To me, this is the art of instruction. Just as perfect art does not exist, neither does perfect instruction. But technology and science advance art as well as instruction, and we are wise to pay attention to those motivational strategies that are well supported by theory and research.

Each of the next five chapters centers on a major factor of motivation and its specific motivational strategies with their related learning activities and instructor behaviors. These strategies are not perfect solutions, but they are realistic methods that have a logical probability of enhancing learner motivation. Your understanding of these strategies and how to use them can significantly increase the creativity, skill, and impact of your motivation planning. The following strategies will stress what the instructor can do to enhance adult motivation for learning. This does not mean that adult learners bear no responsibility for their own motivation or that they are completely dependent on the instructor for feeling motivated while learning. The purpose of this entire book is to support, strengthen, or increase whatever amount of motivation adults possess when they are learning, to make the instructor an active, valuable resource and vital partner in their realization of a motivating learning experience.

4

Helping Adults Develop Positive Attitudes Toward Learning

~~~~~~~~~~~~~~~~~~~~~~~~~~~~~~~

Exhortation is used more and accomplishes less than almost any behavior-changing tool known to man.
—Robert F. Mager

People spend a great deal of their time trying to influence other people's attitudes. This is especially the case if we have some responsibility for the work or effort of another individual. We talk, show evidence, list logical reasons, and, in some instances, actually give testimony to the positive results of this desired attitude in our own lives. We are trying to be persuasive. Intuitively, we know it is best for people to like what they must do. Instructors want learners to feel positively toward learning and the effort it takes to accomplish it. However, exhorting, arguing, explaining, and cajoling are usually very inefficient means to help someone develop a positive attitude toward learning. All of these methods have a glaring weakness—they are simply words, "talk," if you will, that have nowhere near the impact of the consequences, conditions, and people involved in the learning task itself. When successful, it is the *process* of learning that will tell the story for the learner. When unsuccessful, these methods become a form of linguistic static, badgering, or nagging that undermines and prevents the development of a positive attitude within the adult learner.

In general, it is probably best not to try to talk adults into learning. There are far more powerful things we can do in the presentation of ourselves and our subject matter as well as in our treatment of adults to help them build positive attitudes toward their learning and themselves as learners. This chapter will examine a number of strategies that enable adults to learn, grow, and flourish as they involve themselves in our instruction. These strategies can help us to work in such a way with adults that they genuinely want to learn with us, are motivated to use what they have learned, and, most important, are eager to learn more.

Four Important Attitudinal Directions

A useful functional definition of an *attitude* is that it is a combination of a perception with a judgment that often results in an emotion that influences behavior (Ellis, 1962). The attitudes that adults have that will directly influence their learning usually take one or more of the following directions: (1) toward the instructor, (2) toward the subject and learning situation, (3) toward themselves as learners, and (4) toward their expectancy for success in the learning activity. See Table 3.

The examples in Table 3 illustrate the influence that attitudes can have on behavior and performance in learning tasks. Whenever we instruct, we want to establish a learning environment in which these four important attitudinal directions are positive and unified for the learner. We want adults *to like and respect us and our subject matter, and to feel confident as learners who realistically believe they can succeed in the learning task at hand.*

If any one of these four attitudinal directions becomes seriously negative for the adult, motivation for learning can be impaired. A person could respect the instructor, feel confident as a learner, and objectively expect to do well but still intensely dislike

Table 3. Attitudinal Directions.

Perception +	Judgment →	Emotion →	Behavior
I see my instructor.	He seems helpful.	I feel appreciative.	I will cooperate.
The instructor announces the beginning of a new unit on family relations (subject matter).	Learning more about being an effective parent is helpful to me.	I feel interested.	I will pay close attention.
It is my turn to present my project to the seminar (self as learner).	I am knowledgeable and well prepared for this.	I feel confident.	I will do a good job and give a smooth and articulate presentation.
The instructor is giving a surprise quiz (expectancy for success).	I have not studied this material and will probably flunk this quiz.	I feel very anxious.	I can't think straight and won't be able to answer the questions.

the subject area. This sometimes happens with required courses or training where competent instructors find able adults disinterested and apathetic. In a similar vein, an adult might like the instructor and the subject, be confident as a learner, but realize he doesn't have the time or proper materials to prepare and be successful in the learning task. It is quite likely that this person would have his overall motivation to learn significantly reduced. Trying hard for this person would probably only increase his sense of frustration. This is often the case when someone has to compete against someone else whose preparation and material advantages seem far superior to his own.

In most instances, adults experience their attitudes immediately, without premeditation or serious reflection. They hear or see something and the attitude begins to run its course. The instructor introduces the topic and the learner's attitude toward that topic emerges. The instructor assigns homework and the learner's attitude toward the assignment is quickly felt. "Wait and see" makes a great deal of sense, but that is not how attitudes work. This self-advice against possible erroneous attitudes is a direct appeal for caution because we understand how instantly attitudes influence us. "Wait and maybe I can change this attitude" is probably a more accurate self-admonition. Once a person has had an experience, the attitude will occur, like it or not. It may only be a vague feeling, but it is still an influence on behavior. That is why an instructor has to be aware of what can be done to positively influence learner attitudes at the beginning of any learning experience. They will be there from the very start. Having them *work for* our learners and ourselves gives the best chance for motivated learning to occur. Although some of the following strategies can be implemented throughout the learning experience, their exemplification will stress usage at the beginning of learning and training activities.

Creating a Positive Attitude Toward the Instructor

In a literal sense, the instructor or trainer is often the medium through which the learning activity takes place. We introduce, guide, evaluate, give feedback, and continuously respond to our learners. If we do not actually teach, we at least do "touch" almost everything the learner will come into contact with while learning with us. This ranges from handing out bibliographies to setting up technical equipment. Learning is associated either directly or indirectly with us. We want that association to be positive. It is more difficult for someone to accept what they are offered when the person who is giving it to them is someone they do not like or respect. A learner's negative attitude toward an instructor makes that instructor a *barrier* between the material to be learned and the learner. Instead of feeling consonant and at ease because a respected instructor is offering an attractive lesson, the learner may feel dissonant and psychologically tense because a disliked instructor is offering an attractive lesson. The same principle occurs in everyday behavior. We feel uneasy purchasing a car from a salesman we don't like or accepting a gift from someone we disrespect. In most instances, it seems better for us not to buy the car or not to accept the gift because then our actions are consistent with how we feel toward the person. For learning, this means adults will be more open, accepting, and responsive to materials and tasks they receive from an instructor they like and respect. They will be quite the opposite with an instructor they don't like or respect. Optimal motivation for learning will probably decrease.

As discussed in Chapter Two, the core characteristics of expertise and empathy will be of significant influence in establishing a positive attitude toward the instructor on the part of the adult learner. Probably one of the main pitfalls to avoid in working with adult learners is any semblance of behavior on the part of the instructor that might appear as arrogant or patronizing. Because adults have had such a wide range of experiences and are involved in a multiplicity of responsible roles, they are logically repelled by an instructor with a blatantly superior demeanor. We may know more about our subject matter, but it is doubtful that we know more about life. As workers, parents, and citizens with decades of handling the risks and responsibilities of those roles, adult learners bring a richness to the learning environment that makes some degree of humility on the part of the instructor a realistically wise choice.

The following strategies are ways to demonstrate our empathy and expertise to the best advantage for both our learners and ourselves.

Strategy 1: Share something of value with your adult learners.

The next time you go to hear a professional speaker, whether it be at a banquet or a conference, check to see how much time elapses before that person tells a joke or a humorous anecdote. It will probably be less than three minutes and it will happen about four out of every five times. Professional speakers know the value of *sharing humor*. It does far more than break the tension between speaker and audience. It says if you can laugh with me, you can listen to me. You can identify with me. You can see I am a human being and that I have emotions too. All sharing has this potential— to break down images and to allow the learner to experience our common humanity without self-consciousness. Humor is a very efficient means to this end. It also tells the learner that there are at least times when we do not take ourselves too seriously, that we have some perspective on life, and that the way we teach will allow for the vitality of laughter within the learning process itself.

Another type of effective sharing is to relate a *mutually credible intense experience.* This may be some trouble we've had on the job, a difficult learning experience, a crisis within our family, an unexpected surprise, an accident—something that tells the learners that we have mutual concerns and a shared reality. This form of sharing should relate to the topic at hand or it can seem forced. I sometimes tell about problems I have had with unmotivated learners. I know most of my audience has had similar problems and this gives me a chance to share what I have learned from these dilemmas. This type of sharing has also taught me how much of this process is a two-way street. Seeing the concerned faces in the audience increases my identification with them as well.

Sharing *your involvement with the subject matter*—whether it be problems, discoveries, research, or new learning—is a way to show your enthusiasm as well as your humanity. Adults are interested in seeing how their investment in the subject matter will pay off for them. When we share our involvement with the topic at hand, we model this potential for them and reveal something about our real selves as well.

Another powerful form of sharing on an ongoing basis is giving adult learners *our individual attention.* At moments like this, we are committing one of our most valuable assets as instructors to our learners—our time. Being available to learners before, during, and after class directly tells them we care about them. Also, being in one-to-one contact with someone allows for a situation that is more personal and spontaneous.

In general, sharing *something about our real selves,* when done tactfully and appropriately, gives adult learners a chance to see us beyond the image of an instructor. Most people are a bit surprised when they see their instructors in common settings like supermarkets, shopping centers, and theaters. Part of this is due to novelty, but part of this is also due to how dramatically set apart most learning environments seem from the real world. By wisely self-disclosing our reactions to common experiences like television shows, sporting events, travel, and maybe even a little trouble we've had with life along the way, we give adult learners a chance to positively identify with us and become more receptive to our instruction (Jourard, 1964).

Strategy 2: Concretely indicate your cooperative intentions to help adults learn.

Almost everyone who has something to learn from somebody is vulnerable to a nagging fear—what if I really try and I can't learn it? This is often true for adults because so much of what they must learn will directly influence their job performance or family relations. For instructors to let them know at the outset that there is a concrete means of assistance available will help them to reduce this fear as well as to save face. This may mean announcing our availability during office hours, arranging tutorial assistance by appointment, or creating a device whereby learners who are having difficulty can use special materials or aids. Essentially, the message is "As instructor and learner, we are partners in solving your learning problems. I want to help you and it's okay to seek help." This tells the learners that their vulnerability will be safeguarded and that they will have a nonevaluative and interested response to their requests for assistance (Johnson, 1980). This is immediate evidence that we do care about the people who learn with us.

Strategy 3: To the degree authentically possible, reflect the language, perspective, and attitudes of your adult learners.

In psychotherapy this is called *pacing* and it is considered the essence of what is needed to establish rapport with other people (Charny, 1966). It is the instructor matching the verbal and nonverbal behavior of his adult learners—literally reflecting their speech, mannerisms, and perceptions.

Friends pace each other naturally. They "understand" each other, usually have something in common, and speak a similar language. Strangers striking up a relationship follow a similar pattern. They cast about for some common interest like the weather, sports, or current news. When they hit a similar chord, they share perspectives that may lead to some common viewpoint that further intensifies the relationship. Feeling "connected" with someone usually means finding mutual interests, values, and outlooks in another person. Friends who have not seen each other for a long time often talk about the "old days" to renew their sense of rapport with similar past experiences. People are sometimes accused of "talking shop" at parties, but this professional rapport is usually the actual foundation for their relationship. It could be difficult for them to have a genuine conversation without referring to the work place.

One of the easiest things we can do to make ourselves understood and accepted by our adult learners is to fluently use their language and their perspective. People understand other people by their own definitions and their own attitudes. Not only do people have a difficult time understanding someone who speaks differently than they do but they have a more difficult time trusting this person as well. This is a universal historical fact. Assuming the language and perspective of our adult learners makes us more clearly understandable, more trustworthy, and more effective as models. This is why listening is so important. Until we really understand someone, it is difficult to accurately use their language. This is not "talking down or up" to anybody. This is a sensitive awareness of the predicates, figures of speech, common interests, and similar values that our adult learners have with us. It is using our awareness of these factors to construct a language and perspective that is used with integrity to effectively and clearly communicate. If a person uses the expression *bottom line* to mean personal limit and displays a very analytical approach to a political question, we are wise to use both a similar expression and approach if we want ourselves well understood regarding the same political question. The goal is not to be a chameleon but to select wisely from among the expressions and perspectives we hold in common with our adult learners to enhance our rapport with them.

Strategy 4: When issuing mandatory assignments or training requirements, give your rationale for these stipulations.

Adults hate busywork. Many of them have had teachers who were simply authoritarian and handed out assignments without rhyme or reason. Because requirements demand time, energy, and responsibility, even the most motivated adult learner will feel cautious when the assignments are handed out. (Notice how quiet it gets!)

By stating the rationale for these stipulations, our adult learners will know that we have carefully considered the matter, that we realize the obligations, benefits, and results of these requirements, and most important, that we respect them enough to share this information. It is also no mean advantage to the instructor that revealing this rationale ensures the assignments against misinterpretation of motive or purpose.

As in most matters of communication, difficult news is best received when it is direct and concise. For example, "At the end of this unit, I will ask each of you to role play a conflict resolution problem in a small group setting. Each of you will be asked to solve a management problem by applying the five steps of the conflict resolution process. This will give me the opportunity to give each of you guided practice and feedback so that you can refine your skills and have a chance to test the method under simulated conditions."

Another example—"In addition to the reading of your textbook, I've assigned three outside articles and put them on reserve at the local library. I realize this may be somewhat of an inconvenience for you. However, each of these articles contains a case study that is far more realistic, comprehensive, and relevant than any of those found in your text. These case studies will provide much better examples of the principles you are studying and give you a chance to explore the benefits of these theories in situations much closer to your own real life experiences."

With even the clearest rationale, assignments are assignments, and usually no one applauds after they are given. Respect the silence for what it usually means—the serious concern of any adult learner who accepts a new responsibility.

Strategy 5: Allow for introductions.

Introduce yourself. This is definitely for the first meeting of the group and seems quite obvious, but it is amazing how many instructors fail to extend this common courtesy. Say a few things about who you are, where you're from, why you're conducting the course and, by all means, welcome the group.

This really shouldn't take more than a couple of minutes. It is also a good idea to give the learners a chance to introduce themselves as well. This emphasizes their importance and our interest in them as people. It also does a great deal to help everyone learn each other's names and to significantly reduce the emotional tension so often present at the beginning of most courses, seminars, and training sessions. Scores of articles (Johnson and Johnson, 1982) have been written describing different exercises for helping people to get acquainted in new social situations. I have no particular advocacy in regard to such devices, except to say that they can be immensely helpful when used briefly and in healthy respect for the learning tasks at hand.

Building a Positive Attitude Toward the Subject and Learning Situation

Read the following words out loud:

English	Grammar	History	Computers
Math	Reading	Biology	Music
Spelling	Composition	Algebra	Chemistry

Which word evoked the strongest emotional reaction in you? Was it a positive or a negative feeling? Most of the above subject areas are common to the educational experience of adults. They have taken such courses and they usually have distinct attitudes toward them. Any new learning that involves elements from these former subjects will cause immediate attitudinal reactions on the part of adults. That is why questions like these are so often asked by adults at the beginning of new courses and training sessions: How much reading will I have to do? What kind of math does this training require? What will I have to write? Adults have strong opinions about both their abilities and their feelings toward such requirements.

For children, much of their learning seems like an accumulation of specific topics. They take arithmetic, reading, and spelling in the fourth grade and then they take more arithmetic, reading, and spelling in the fifth grade. Not only do adults have to integrate such skills in their new learning but they also carry attitudes toward them that are often decades old and very entrenched (Smith, 1982). New learning often causes mixed reactions in adults. They might want to learn about computers but honestly have real fears if any math is involved in the training.

To some extent, new learning goes against the grain of the personal autonomy and security of adults. Independent thinking and self-responsibility for philosophical beliefs are characteristic of mature adults (Kidd, 1973). They have usually found a way to successfully cope with life and have formulated a set of strongly held convictions. New learning often asks them to become temporarily dependent, to open their minds to new ideas, to rethink certain beliefs, and to try different ways of doing things. This is somewhat threatening to them, and their attitudes can easily lock in to support their resistance.

It has also been documented that adults may react with apprehension to specific areas of content, such as math and foreign languages (Smith, 1982). For some, speaking in front of the group is a real ordeal. Others find specific learning techniques, such as role playing and videotaping of themselves, to be quite anxiety producing.

Whatever we can do as instructors to minimize adult negative attitudes and to foster the development of their positive attitudes toward our subjects and instructional processes will improve their motivation for learning. With the constant present force of the core characteristic of enthusiasm, the following strategies are a means to this end.

Strategy 6: Eliminate or minimize any negative conditions that surround the subject.

Mager (1968) has written that people learn to avoid the things that they are hit with. It is a common fact of learning that when a person is presented with an item or subject and is at the same time in the presence of negative (unpleasant) conditions, that item or subject becomes a stimulus for avoidance behavior. Things or subjects that frighten adults are often associated with antagonists and situations that make them uncomfortable, tense, and scared.

Therefore, it is best not to associate your subject with any of the following conditions that tend to support negative learner attitudes and repel adult interest:

- *Pain*. Acute physical and psychological discomfort, such as continuous failure (learner effort makes no difference), poorly fitting equipment, or uncomfortable room temperature.
- *Fear and anxiety*. Distress and tension resulting from anticipation of the unpleasant or dangerous, such as threat of failure or punishment, public exposure of ignorance, or unpredictability of potential negative consequences.
- *Frustration*. An emotional reaction to the blockage or defeat of purposeful behavior, such as when information is presented too fast or too slowly, or the learner receives unannounced tests or inadequate feedback on performance.
- *Humiliation*. An emotional reaction to being shamed, debased, or degraded, such as when a person receives sarcasm, insult, or public comparison of inadequate learning.
- *Boredom*. A cognitive and emotional reaction to a situation in which stimuli impinging on the learners are weak, repetitive, or infrequent, such as learning situations lacking variety, covering material already known, or containing excessively predictable discussion respondents (the same people talk over and over again).

This list is quite dismal. However, just as a slate must be swept clean before new clear and lucid writing may appear, learning environments have to have these negative conditions removed before positive conditions can effectively occur. Otherwise, the best efforts of motivating instructors can be contaminated and diffused by the mere presence of such oppressive elements.

Strategy 7: Ensure successful learning.

It is difficult for anyone to dislike a subject in which they are successful. Conversely, it is rare to find anyone who really likes a subject in which they are unsuccessful. Competent learning in a subject is probably one of the surest ways to sustain a positive attitude toward that subject. According to Bloom (1981), most learners (perhaps over 90 percent) can master what is generally taught. The important qualification is that some learners take a great deal more time to learn something than others do. In general, his preliminary studies indicate that slow learners may take six times as much time to learn the same material as faster learners do. With effective instruction and efficient use of learner time, he believes this ratio can be cut down to three to one.

Some adults may be discouraged when they realize how much extra time and effort they will need to expend to master what we are teaching. However, we can positively influence their attitudes as well as those of our faster learners when we guarantee the following three conditions: (1) quality instruction that will help them to learn if they try to learn, (2) concrete evidence that their effort makes a difference, and (3) continual feedback regarding the progress of their learning.

In addition, it helps us as instructors to realize that few adults know for certain how much time and effort it will take to master a particular subject. When the three conditions just cited are present from the very beginning of a course, learners have a much better chance to experience success. Here are Bloom's guidelines for establishing these conditions:

1. In addition to your main instructional techniques (lecturing, discussion, textbook, and so forth), have a number of alternative instructional processes available to meet the needs of individual learners. Some alternatives:

- *Group study procedures* available to learners as they need them. Small groups of learners (two or three) could meet regularly to go over points of difficulty in the learning process. If this is done, avoid competitive forms of evaluation so everyone feels able to gain from cooperating with one another.
- *Other suggested textbooks* that may offer a clearer or better-exemplified discussion of material the learner is having difficulty grasping in the adopted textbook.
- *Workshops, programmed instruction units, and computer-assisted instruction* may provide the drill and specific tasks that regular instruction cannot. Some learners need small steps and

frequent reinforcement to overcome particular learning difficulties.

- *Audiovisual methods* can sometimes provide the illustrations and vivid explanations not found in regular learning procedures.
- *Tutorial help* is often a last resort, but it is certainly a legitimate and helpful one for many learners.

2. Set clear (understandable to the learner) standards of mastery and excellence. When adults know the criteria by which their learning will be evaluated, they know better what to do in order to do well in a particular subject.

3. Avoid interlearner competition. When adults do not have to fear each other's progress to protect their self-esteem, an extra and valuable corps of instructional assistants is available in the learning environment for other participants.

4. Break down courses or training into smaller units of learning. Such a learning unit may correspond to a chapter in a book, a well-defined content portion of a training seminar, or a particular time unit. Segmenting instruction into smaller increments allows progress to be more easily understood by the learner, just as gauging a minute on a clock is easier to do than gauging an hour. Every time we can help our learners say that they have concretely learned something, we have helped them feel a sense of progress. This also helps them to maintain their concentration.

5. Frequently use *formative evaluation*. These are exams and tests, whether they be written, oral, or performance, that are used in a diagnostic-progress sense. This means they are *nongraded,* assess learner progress, indicate points of learner difficulty in learning, and are tailored to the particular unit of learning. For those learners who have mastered the unit, formative evaluation will give them positive feedback and reinforce them as well as their learning. They can honestly say, "With that instructor, I really know how well I'm doing." For those learners who lack mastery of a unit, formative evaluation will point out the particular ideas, skills, and processes they still need to work on. Bloom has found that learners respond best when they are referred to particular instructional materials or processes intended to help them correct

their difficulties. They can at least say, "I know where I am and I know what I have to do to help myself."

Ensuring successful learning is a powerful strategy. Bloom's own words (1981, p. 173), testify to this: "Perhaps the clearest evidence of affective change is the interest the student develops for the subject he has masterd. He begins to 'like' the subject and to desire more of it. To do well in a subject opens up further avenues for exploration of the subject. Conversely, to do poorly in a subject closes an area for further study. The student desires some feeling of control over his environment, and mastery of a subject gives him some feeling of control over a part of his environment. Interest in a subject is both a cause of mastery of the subject as well as a result of mastery. Motivation for further learning is one of the more important consequences of mastery."

Strategy 8: Make the first experience with the subject as positive as possible.

This strategy is based on the idea that "first impressions are important." According to Scott (1969, p. 67), "Organization inhibits reorganization." Therefore, the first time learners experience anything that is new or occurs in a novel or different setting, they are forming an impression that can have a lasting impact. This could be the first day of a training session, or the beginning of a new unit of learning, or the introduction of a new piece of equipment. These are *critical periods* in determining the ways learners will respond to and feel about what they are experiencing. All of these are examples of an initial contact where the learners have not totally organized their beliefs and attitudes toward the subject. Therefore, they are more flexible, fluid, and open to change regarding their impressions of the event. However, their first impression, once formed, will strongly influence how they accept and receive future experiences with the subject. This essentially comes from their need for survival and predictability. Those who have a positive first experience will feel more safe and willing to learn the subject at a later date. Those who have a negative experience will tend to want to avoid the subject for reasons of self-protection. Anything we can do as instructors to make that first lesson or initial contact as *safe, successful,* and *interesting* as possible will increase learner motivation for future involvement with the particular subject. In this respect, an office manager introducing a new word processing system to his staff might on the first day of training use guided practice to show them how to successfully employ an editor program that automatically corrects all grammatical and spelling errors in business correspondence. Likewise, a foreign language instructor might on the first day of class have each person fluently learn some of the most essential expressions for visiting and traveling in the related foreign culture.

Strategy 9: Positively confront the possible erroneous beliefs, expectations, and assumptions that may underlie a negative learner attitude.

Some learners have mistaken beliefs that support their negative attitudes. For example, "If I have to do any math in this course, I won't do well in it"; "Communications training has never helped anyone I know"; or "If I make a mistake, I'll really look bad." Assumptions of this sort lead to fear of and resistance toward a subject (Ellis and Greiger, 1977). People maintain their negative attitudes by repeating such beliefs to themselves. If an instructor thinks such beliefs are operating within an individual or a group, an appropriate discussion along the following guidelines might help to significantly reduce the negative attitude:

1. Tactfully find out what the learner might be telling himself that leads to the negative attitude. ("You seem somewhat discouraged. Could you tell me what might be happening or what you might be thinking that's leading to such feelings?")

2. If the learner appears to have a self-defeating belief, point out how negative feelings would naturally follow from such a belief. ("If you believe making a mistake will really make you look foolish in front of your peers, you probably feel fearful and anxious about even trying some of the group exercises.")

3. Indicate other assumptions that might be more helpful to the learner. ("You might try telling yourself that this is guided practice, where everyone including your instructor expects some mistakes, and that the purpose of the exercises is to refine skills, not to demonstrate them at a level of perfection.")

4. Encourage the learner to develop beliefs based on present reality that promote his well-being. ("When you start to feel discouraged or negative, check out what you are telling yourself and see if it really helps you. Consider if there might be some other beliefs or expectancies that would do you more good. You might want to discuss this with me so I can give you feedback and other possible ways of looking at the situation that might be more helpful.")

Strategy 10: Associate the learner with other learners who are enthusiastic about the subject.

In the best of group learning situations, there are sometimes a few members who retain a negative attitude toward the subject. While the majority of learners may be beaming and responsive, we can easily identify those individuals who seem dismal and distant. Sometimes they remain isolated, but frequently they can band together and become a clique that detracts from the motivational momentum of the entire group. A possible way to respond to such learners is to create opportunities for them to work with the more enthusiastic members of the group. Keep the ratio at two to one (two positive to one negative). If you have enthusiastic learners who are informal leaders (highly influential group members that do not have official status), make certain they are your first choices for membership in these small working groups.

Enthusiasm is contagious. If the reluctant learner has the opportunity to work with, be tutored by, or cooperatively pursue a project or goal with learners who are interested in and optimistic about the subject, he will have peers to model and will experience some group pressure to feel likewise. This person will not be able to easily deny the value of the subject, and the resulting dissonance may lead to positive attitude change.

Developing Positive Self-Concepts for Learning

Goethe (Ungar, 1963) believed that the greatest evil that can befall a person would be that he should come to think ill of himself.

Some learners may not have a negative attitude toward their instructor or the subject, but they may have a negative attitude toward themselves. This is often called "poor self-concept." If this is true, it will probably negatively affect their motivation to learn. Combs (1965) and Rogers (1969) have written that the maintenance and the enhancement of the perceived self are the motives behind all behavior. Numerous researchers have found that self-concept is positively related to academic achievement—the higher the self-concept, the better the odds that the person will do well on academic tasks and vice versa (Wlodkowski, 1982).

It is difficult to say which comes first, a positive self-concept or higher academic achievement. In all likelihood, it is an interactive process that works both ways. It is also important to note that one's general self-concept is made up of more specific self-concepts including the physical, social, and emotional as well as the academic (Shavelson, Hubner, and Stanton, 1976). One might feel quite physically adept but very inadequate in school situations. This kind of breakdown exists within the academic self-concept as well. A learner might feel quite superior in English and very inferior in math. People can modify their self-concepts for specific areas of learning. No matter what a learner's self-concept is, we have a chance within our special instructional or training session to positively affect that person's self-estimation. Like an oasis in the desert, our particular learning environment can nourish and replenish even a poor self-concept that has been weakened by other harsher and more barren learning situations.

There are some cautions. The older the learners, the stronger the relationship between self-concept and achievement (Woolfolk and McCune-Nicolich, 1984). When an older person's learning self-concept is negative, it will not be easy to alter. The adult has a firmer and more fully formed self-concept than does the child (Brundage and MacKeracher, 1980). It is not uncommon for adults to harbor doubts about their personal learning ability. Often their capacities tend to be underestimated and underused (Knox, 1977). Their own family members may reinforce their self-doubts by questioning their abilities or need for certain learning. Later adulthood and old age are periods when many learners are especially prone to this source of anxiety. For adults to undertake a return to school or an in-depth learning project is a move into unknown territory.

Regardless of the state of the adult's self-concept upon entering our learning situation, we can provide the experiences from which each adult can derive a positive sense of self-esteem as a learner. Before we move to the particular strategies that are available to us, it is important to again emphasize the strategy of *ensuring successful learning*. This strategy powerfully affects both attitude toward the subject as well as attitude toward the self as learner. In fact, it is the prerequisite for all the strategies that follow. The fundamental basis for acquiring a positive self-concept for learning is the reflection of self as an achiever. Bloom (1981, p. 173) states this clearly: "Each person searches for positive recognition of his worth and he comes to view himself as adequate in those areas where he received assurance of his competence or success. For a student to view himself in a positive way, he must be given many opportunities to be rewarded. Mastery and its public recognition provide the necessary reassurance and reinforcement to help the student view himself as adequate." Although Bloom's research has been largely directed at younger students, a significant proportion of it has dealt with college-age students. Also, from the perspective of adult personality theory, his generalizations regarding mastery and success are strongly supported (Knowles, 1980).

Strategy 11: Encourage the learner.

This strategy can be used on a group or individual basis. Encouragement is any behavior on our part by which we show the learner: (1) that we respect the learner as a person, no matter what he learns; (2) that we trust and believe in the learner's effort to learn; and (3) that the learner *can* learn. For an adult to realize that he is respected by the instructor only because of learning performance is dehumanizing. Such a criterion for instructor acceptance denies the adult's other worthy qualities and makes the person into a "thing" that learns without feelings or dignity. The primary foundation for encouragement is our caring and acceptance of the learner. This forms the context for the ways we choose to show confidence and personal regard for the learner's effort and achievement. These include the following:

1. *Give recognition for real effort.* Any time a person attempts to learn something, that individual is taking a risk. Learning is a courageous act. No one learns 100 percent of the time. Some risk is usually involved. We can help by acknowledging the learner's effort and by making perseverance a valued personal trait. Any comment that says "I like the way you try" can help the learner see effort as something to value in the process of learning. Also, for insecure learners to honestly know that their effort is respected by the instructor until adequate achievement occurs does a great deal to reduce their performance anxiety and its debilitating effects.

2. *Minimize mistakes while the learner is struggling.* Sometimes learning is like a battle. The critical edge between advancement and withdrawal or between hope and despair is fragile at best. Emphasis on a learner's mistakes at such a critical moment is accentuated by the emotions at hand and is a sure way to encourage self-defeat.

3. *Emphasize learning from mistakes.* Help the learner to see a mistake as a way to improve future learning. When we actually help learners learn from a mistake, we are directly showing them that thinking and trying are in their best interest and that we have confidence that they will learn.

4. *For each learning task, demonstrate a confident and realistic expectancy that the learner will learn.* Essentially this translates into the message "You can do it," but without implying that the task is easy or simple. Whenever we tell a person that something is easy, we have placed that person in a "lose-lose" dilemma. If the person successfully does the task, there is no feeling of pride because the task was easy in the first place. If the person fails, there is a feeling of shame because the task was implied to be simple.

5. *Show faith in the adult's capacity as a learner.* This is a functional attitude toward the learner that translates into "Sometimes it may be difficult, but I believe you can learn and I will work with you toward that goal." Whenever we give up on a learner, we also give up on ourselves as instructors. Realistically, some of our learners actually may prefer this. It makes it easier for them to stop

trying. By showing consistent trust in the learner's capacity to achieve, we maintain our responsibility as instructors and we emphasize the learner's responsibility for continued effort.

6. *Work with the learner at the beginning of difficult tasks.* It's amazing what can be lifted and moved with just a little help. Sometimes a learner might have a momentary confusion or not know what to do next. Our proximity and minimal assistance can be just enough for the learner to find the right direction, continue involvement, and gain the initial confidence to proceed with learning.

7. *Reinforce the "process" of learning.* This means acknowledging all parts of the learning endeavor—the information seeking, the studying, the practicing, the cooperating, and so forth. If we wait for the final product—the test results, project, or whatever the final goal is—it may be too late. Some learners may have given up by this time. It also means the learner must wait until the end of learning to feel good about learning. Even waiting for some minimal progress to acknowledge can sometimes be a mistake. Learning is not a linear progression. There are often wide spaces, deep holes, dead ends, and regressions in learning. Real encouragement says the task of learning is itself important and emphasizes the intrinsic value in the entire process of learning.

Strategy 12: Promote the learner's personal control of the context of learning.

It is very important for learners to be successful and to feel encouraged, but for people to build confidence as learners, they must realize that it is their own behavior that is most responsible for their learning. This means that they must feel a sense of personal causation in the process of learning—that they mainly *control* how, what, and when they learn (deCharms, 1968). At first this may seem obvious. Of course, if a person pays attention, studies, and practices, that person will feel responsible for any successful achievement. However, when we remember that instructors usually establish requirements, issue assignments, give tests, generally set the standards for achievement, often control the learning environment, and sometimes pressure learner involvement, it is not too difficult to understand that a learner may come to believe that it is the instructor who is most responsible for his achievement. If this is the case, it is probably not good for the self-concept of the learner. Even when successful, this person may feel very dependent as a learner, less resourceful, and consequently bound to the demands and directions of the instructor for future learning. In this way, a person can become a puppet or a pawn in the game of learning without any real development of self-esteem as a learner.

Because adults are inclined toward autonomy in so many aspects of their daily lives, the following methods to increase their sense of personal causation while learning should effectively complement this characteristic of their development.

1. *When appropriate, allow the learner to plan and set goals for learning.* A person who plans for something has a functional experience that validates that the individual is the originator and guide of that process.

2. To the extent possible, *allow the learner to make choices about what, how, and when the learner is to learn something.* Choice is the essence of responsibility. It permits the learner to see that he is in charge of the learning experience. He can choose topics, assignments, when to be evaluated, how to be evaluated, and so forth. The possible list is infinite to the creative instructor.

3. *When appropriate, allow the learner to use self-evaluation procedures.* When a learner knows how to understand both the mistakes and the successes of his own learning, the person receives a concrete sense of participation in the learning act. Sometimes mistakes seem more instructor created than learner committed. Self-evaluation procedures reduce this misperception and give the learner a sense of control from the beginning to the end of the learning experience. When you can actually tell yourself whether you've really learned something, you feel more responsible for that learning.

4. *Help the learner to be aware of personal strengths and abilities in learning tasks.* For example, "You have a number of assignments to choose from, but it seems to me you have a real talent for explaining things well and could probably give a very interesting oral presentation. What do you think?" A learner who

knows and takes advantage of personal assets while learning feels a real sense of power and confidence.

5. *Let the learner record or log personal progress while learning.* This concretely allows the learner to feel personal growth and learning are taking place.

6. *When appropriate, let the learner participate in analyzing potential blocks to progress in learning.* For example, "What do you think the difficulty might be?" or "In your estimation, where do you think the confusion begins?" By participating in solving his own learning problem, the learner feels more commitment to its resolution and concretely is more aware of his role in the learning process. An added plus for instructors—it is not infrequent that adult learners know better than we do where problems in learning are occurring.

7. *When advisable, ask the learner for a commitment to the learning task.* This accentuates the learner's personal choice. It prevents denial or withdrawal from personal responsibility for learning. When we ask a learner "Are you sure you're going to do it?" or "Can I feel certain that you're going to try?" and we receive a sincere affirmative answer, we are helping to amplify the learner's sense of self-determination. However, we are not to use this technique without careful forethought or use it unwisely, or it will lack impact and emotional substance, becoming a mere manipulation and insult to the learner.

8. *Make feedback promptly available.* While learning, prompt feedback leads to stronger feelings of personal control and responsibility. This is one of the main reasons why computer-assisted instruction can be motivationally fantastic. The computer has the mechanical ability to give immediate feedback. The learner has a moment-to-moment awareness of progress in learning. This constant back-and-forth "dialogue" between computer and person gives the learner a strong sense of control in the learning process. In so many ways, the computer tells the learner it will not respond until the learner responds first. The learner's personal control is undeniable. On the other hand, the longer it takes for a person to know if a response has had an effect, the more difficult it can become to know whether that response had any effect at all. Imagine having a conversation with someone who waited at least five

minutes to answer any question you asked. It is likely that you would wonder if you were actually being heard. Anything an instructor can do to ensure the best possible pace of accurate feedback will concretely help to emphasize learner responsibility. See Chapter Eight for a more comprehensive discussion of the appropriate use of feedback.

It is not self-defeating for a learner to see an instructor as a source of knowledge and as a guide for learning. At its most basic level, learning is usually the result of a cooperative act between a learner and an instructor. The purpose of these methods is to emphasize that the *majority* of responsibility for learning is under the control of the learner. For a learner to feel that "I can do it" when it comes to future learning, that person has to first be clearly aware that "I did it" from previous experiences in learning.

Strategy 13: Help learners to attribute their success to their ability and their effort.

While the last strategy dealt with the *context* of learning, this strategy focuses on the *outcome* of learning. That outcome is *success,* and the term is used here in its broadest sense. It could be passing a test, receiving an excellent grade, completing a fine project, satisfactorily demonstrating a new skill, correctly answering a problem—any achievement that turns out well in the eyes of the learner.

Adults try to be logical. *If they have a success, they will often reflect upon a reason or a cause for that success.* Some cognitive psychologists call these inferred causes *attributions* and have created a theory and body of research to demonstrate their significant effects on human behavior (Weiner, 1980a). For instructors, the important understanding is this: *When people have had a learning success, it will probably best enhance their self-concept and their motivation to believe that the major causes for that success are due to their ability and their effort.* One might suppose that if a learner had a good deal of personal control over the learning context and was successful, at least the attribution for effort would be automatic. Certainly this possibility would be more probable, but some learners find attributions like luck, help from others, ease of task, and fear just as plausible. There is no way to guarantee what a person will think. Because of this, whatever we can do to directly help learners to see ability and effort as the causes of their learning success is important. A helpful attribution is to a learner's awareness of personal control of the context of learning like a period is to the end of a declarative sentence. It establishes closure and clarity of meaning. ("I know I am responsible for my learning success." is quite different from "I know I am responsible for my learning success?")

There are multiple reasons why the attribution of ability and effort are so beneficial to the learner. Both of these are *owned* by the learner (internal locus of control). It is the person's ability and the person's effort that made the learning success possible. Therefore, the person can feel genuine pride. Ability also has a stable quality to it (it lasts) and the person can feel more confident when similar learning tasks arise. Effort is unstable (sometimes it's difficult to persevere), but it is probably the aspect of a learner's behavior over which he has the most control and influence. Knowing effort makes a difference reduces the learner's feelings of helplessness and increases his tendency to persevere.

Here are some ways to help learners realize these attributions.

1. *Provide learners with learning tasks suitable to their ability.* "Just within reach" is a good rule of thumb. These will challenge their ability and demand effort for success.

2. *Stress the importance of effort for success on learning tasks prior to their initiation.* This should be a reminder and not a threat. For example, "Given the challenge of this task, it's going to take some real work." This alerts the learners to their responsibility and increases the chances for an attribution to effort upon successful achievement.

3. *Provide verbal and written messages that accurately accentuate learner perceptions of ability and effort for success.* Here are a few examples: "Great to see your hard work pay off." "Your skills made a real difference." "That's a talented performance." "Your knowledge is apparent in your writing." "I know a lot of perseverance went into this project." The important thing about such statements is that they can be distributed all the time. We are literally a fount of attributions for our learners.

Strategy 14: When learning tasks are suitable to their ability, help learners to understand that effort and persistence can overcome their failures.

The term *failure* is used here in its broadest sense—mistakes, errors, lack of completion, poor test results, low grades, unskilled performance, any lack of achievement that turns out poorly in the eyes of the learner. If a learner experiences an unsuccessful learning outcome, there is very little the individual can do to improve unless that learner believes further personal effort has an impact on future learning tasks. To paraphrase Seligman (1975), intelligence, no matter how high, cannot manifest itself if the person believes that his own actions will have no effect. If a person believes failure is due to lack of ability, then more effort will seem to make little difference because ability is so difficult to change. The result will be discouragement. Bad luck, too difficult a task, and poor materials are all attributions that indicate personal effort makes only a small impact on influencing performance outcomes. Sometimes these attributions on the part of the learner are correct, but sometimes they are rationalizations that ease the learner's guilt and frustration. If we honestly have good reasons to believe that greater effort will improve learners' performance, it is wise for them to know this as well. It emphasizes their power and responsibility in the learning task and can give them real hope for future performance when similar tasks will be undertaken. Our tact in revealing this to the learner is an immeasurable asset. For example, "I realize you might be feeling quite badly about how this assignment turned out, but my honest estimation of your performance is that with continued effort you can definitely improve. Here are the units that seem to need further review. . . ."

Establishing Expectancy for Success

It is possible that a learner could initially like a subject, feel positively toward the instructor, have a good academic self-concept, and still not expect to succeed. The person might just decide he does not have enough time to study for the training or the course. For adults, time is a critical issue because of their many other roles and

responsibilities. The investment of time in a learning activity may
be as important a decision as the investment of money or effort
(Kidd, 1973). Sometimes learners do not understand what is necessary to do well in a course and this confusion leads to discouragement. Sometimes the materials and training are so new and different
to the learners that many of them actually have difficulty seeing
themselves as potential performers in the necessary learning tasks.

There are many different reasons why adult learners might
not expect to succeed. When this is the case, it is probably in their
best interest for them not to get enthusiastic. If they do, they will
experience greater pain and disappointment if they fail. In fact, to
try at something people do not believe they can do is usually not
very intelligent behavior and is often a waste of time. When
expectancy for success is low, learners tend to protect their psychological well-being by remaining withdrawn or negative. Instructors
often interpret this as apathy or resistance, but for the learners it is
really self-protection. Demonstrating clearly that the learning task
is concretely possible to achieve is a significant positive influence
on the learner's attitude toward learning.

Strategy 15: Make the learning goal as clear as possible.

When learners understand exactly what they are to learn,
confusion cannot detract from their expectancy to succeed. This
may mean distributing instructional objectives (Gronlund, 1978)
(for example, "Each technician will take a blood sample and obtain
the blood type, hemoglobin content, and Rh factor, using standard
laboratory procedures"); handing out a list of learning outcomes;
or writing the purpose of a particular unit of study on the
chalkboard. Basically we can say it, write it, or show it—whatever
it takes to clearly let the learners know what they are expected to
learn.

Strategy 16: Make the criteria of evaluation as clear as possible.

In the view of most learners, how they are evaluated will play
a crucial role in determining how they objectively expect to do in
any course or training session. Evaluation procedures will impinge

upon their feedback, feelings of the reinforcement, sense of progress, and self-concept as learners. The criteria of evaluation have to be clear to them from the beginning of learning if they are to know which elements of their performance and production are essential. When the criteria are clear, they have a "road map" to success and can self-evaluate their learning as they proceed. This should enhance their motivation because they can anticipate the results of their learning efforts and regulate their behavior (studying, writing, or practicing) with more certainty and efficiency.

There are so many different things to learn and so many different ways to evaluate that no short, comprehensive list is possible. Instructional objectives contain their own evaluation criteria and they may be a helpful method. In general, the idea is to verbalize or demonstrate the ways we as instructors will use to assess the different degrees of excellence or mastery in learning and to put these into print for our learners to see and understand. This usually means defining terms, standards, and calibrations of measurement so that learners can comprehend how these are applied, scored, and integrated as measures of learning.

The more we can be *public* about our evaluation criteria, the more learners can self-evaluate and self-direct their learning. In addition to explanations and demonstrations of our evaluation criteria, we can also distribute concrete learning products that have already been evaluated by these criteria. Past tests, papers, projects, and media can give learners realistic examples of how these criteria have been applied. A varying display (from poor to excellent performance) of these concrete models of applied evaluation criteria can dramatically help learners to understand what is expected of them.

Strategy 17: Use models similar to the learners to demonstrate expected learning.

Because learning is often so new as well as abstract to many adults, they honestly wonder if they can do it. Any time we can provide examples of people such as the learners themselves successfully performing the expected learning activity, we have taken a significant step toward enhancing learner expectancy for success.

This strategy is based on the research of Bandura (1982, pp. 126–127), who has written about the reasons for its effectiveness. "Seeing similar others perform successfully can raise efficacy expectations in observers who then judge that they too possess the capabilities to master comparable activities. . . . Vicariously derived information alters perceived self-efficacy through ways other than social comparison. . . . Modeling displays convey information about the nature and predictability of environmental events. Competent models also teach observers effective strategies for dealing with challenging or threatening situations."

   With film and video technology, we have wonderful ways to organize and demonstrate what we want our learners to achieve. Past students and trainees are another source for live modeling sessions. Whether it be a skill, technique, or discussion, if it can be learned and demonstrated, with today's technology, we have a way to bring it to our learners and to concretely raise their expectations for success.

Strategy 18: Announce the expected amount of time needed for study and practice for successful learning.

   As mentioned previously, time is precious to adults. It is often very difficult for adult learners to estimate the amount of time a given course, assignment, or practice regimen might take. Some will overestimate. Some will underestimate. Others will procrastinate as busy people often do. When any learning activity requires a significant amount of time, it is best for learners to know this. Such awareness will help them to plan more effectively, to realize their responsibility, and to avoid procrastination.

Strategy 19: Use goal-setting methods.

   This is an effective individualized approach to increasing a learner's expectancy for success. The advantage of this method is that it brings the future into the present and allows the learner to become aware of what is necessary to do in order to have a successful learning experience. Not only does it prevent the learner from making an unrealistic expectation, but it also gives the learner a chance to specifically evaluate and plan for those obstacles that prevent achievement. With the goal-setting model, the learner knows that he is in command and can calculate what to do to avoid wasting time or experiencing self-defeat. Thus, before even beginning the learning task, the learner knows that expended effort will be worthwhile and he has an actual sense that there is a good probability for success.

There are many different methods of goal setting. The one that follows is an eclectic adaptation from various models in the literature. If the learning experience is to be initiated, the following criteria are to be met as well as planned with the learner:

1. *Achievability*
   - Is there enough time to reach the goal? If not, can more time be found, or should the goal be divided into smaller goals?
   - Can the learner do it with the skills and knowledge at hand? If not, is there any assistance available, and how dependable is that assistance?

2. *Believability*. What is the level of the learner's self-confidence for the goal? Does the learner at least think he has a reasonable chance of doing it?

3. *Measurability*. How will the learner specifically be able to gauge progress or achievement? This can be something as simple as problems completed, pages read, or exercises finished. The main thing is that a way of measuring is decided upon so that feedback is a tangible reality for self-evaluation.

4. *Desirability*. Is the goal something the learner *wants* to do? The learner may *have* to do it or *should* do it, but is it wanted as well? If it isn't, then the satisfaction level and sense of personal responsibility for the learner will be less. Goal setting can be used for "must" situations, but this is best handled if we are open about it and admit to the learner the reality of the situation to avoid any sense of manipulation.

5. *Focus*. Some plan by which the goal is daily placed in the learner's awareness is important to avoid forgetting or procrastination. Repression, denial, and the attractiveness of other realities are powerful barriers to progress. Effective reminders, such as outlines,

chalkboard messages, or daily logs, help to reduce these obstacles and aid us to refrain from unnecessary dependencies and nagging.

6. *Motivation.* Is the process of reaching the learning goal somehow stimulating, competence-building, reinforcing, affectively positive, or need-gratifying? This is necessary to maintain perseverance because initial motivation may wear thin.

7. *Commitment.* Is the goal so valued that the learner can make a formal or informal gesture to pledge effort and responsibility? This can be anything from a statement such as "I'm really going to try" to a handshake to a contract. This affirms the learner's self-awareness of accountability and allows for the development of self-esteem.

If these criteria are not met, the learning goal is probably in need of alteration or abandonment. If the criteria have been met, there is an excellent probability that the goal can be achieved. At least three more things can then be done.

8. *Identify resources within and outside of the learner.* The learner benefits from knowing his talents. Accentuating the learner's ability to write, speak, organize, and so forth will indicate what can be utilized with confidence. Identifying resources outside the learner, such as tutors, libraries, or materials, helps the learner to more easily reach out and use such assistance for learning.

9. *Preplan to consider and remove potential obstacles to learning.* The question for the learner is "What do you think might interfere with the achievement of your goal?" This may include anything from other obligations to lack of a quiet place to study. Planning ahead for the reduction of these inhibitors will decrease their obstructive power and give the learner added leverage to contend with them.

10. *Arrange a goal review schedule.* A small amount of time to check progress will give us and the learner a chance to evaluate and regain momentum. Minor distractions and interferences can be more easily eliminated. Time sequencing and refinement of planning will help to encourage the learner. If progress has deteriorated, reexamine the criteria. A question such as "What did you do instead?" may help to uncover hidden distractors or competing goals.

Strategy 20: Use contracting methods.

Sometimes it is useful to base a learning project on more precise planning, especially when increased competence is necessary. Requirements in business, industry, education, and government often bring adults into learning situations where further training is mandatory. In such circumstances, a learning contract (which is really a short form of goal setting) may be used as an agreement between the learner and the instructor that specifies the exact ways to achieve and demonstrate the necessary learning goal. Because contracts detail what is to be done and how it is to be accomplished, there is far less chance of the possible ambiguity that often leads to learner anxiety, fear of failure, and other negative emotions in job-related training.

Such a contract contains:

1. What the learner will learn (learning goal or objective).
2. How the learner can demonstrate learning of the specified information, skills, or concepts (performance task or exam).
3. The degree of proficiency expected of the learner (evaluation criteria or evidence of accomplishment).
4. The choice of resource and activity alternatives for learning.
5. The target dates for completion.

The example in Exhibit 3 illustrates a possible contract for the active listening component in a communication skills program.

This chapter has discussed numerous ways to build more positive attitudes toward learning. Which strategies to select will be based on your sensitive awareness of yourself, your learners, and the entire learning situation. When all four of the important attitudinal directions are positive—toward yourself, your subject, the learner's self-concept, and expectancy for success—you will have a powerful motivational force to support any instructional endeavor. Also, since attitudes operate at the *beginning* of any human contact, execute strategies for them *early* in your instructional process.

Exhibit 3. Sample Learning Contract.

Learner: Ed Jaynes

Learning Unit: Active Listening

Learning Objectives	Learning Resources and Activities	Target Date for Completion	Performance Task	Evidence of Accomplishment
1. To describe the characteristics of effective attending behavior.	1A. Read two articles by A. Mehrabian and E. T. Hall. 1B. Complete assigned practice sheet (3 pages).	1. End of Week 1	1. Mastery exam of picture-dialogues.	1. Can describe 2 characteristics of effective attending behavior in 90% of the picture-dialogues.
2. To differentiate between the intellectual and the emotional content of messages (active listening).	2A. Read chapters 3 and 4 of the book, *Leader Effectiveness Training*. 2B. Listen and respond to the audio practice tapes.	2. End of Week 2	2. Mastery exam of written oral messages.	2. Can correctly identify the intellectual and the emotional content in 90% of the written oral messages.
3. To apply active listening skills to actual communication situations.	3A. View videotapes of active listening scenarios. 3B. One hour of role playing active listening situations with fellow trainees.	3. End of Week 3	3. Participate in active listening exercise under instructor's supervision.	3. Can contribute appropriate active listening responses to 80% of the communicated messages.

5

Recognizing
and Responding to
Needs of Adult Learners

> In what areas do most people appear to find life's
> meaning? We have only one pragmatic guide: mean-
> ing must reside in the things for which people strive,
> the goals which they set for themselves, their wants,
> needs, desires and wishes.
> —*Edward C. Lindeman*

As Chapter Three has indicated, needs motivate adults, especially
at the beginning of any learning sequence. One way to view
successful instruction is as a process that meets the fundamental
needs of learners. When adults do not want to learn what we have
to offer, it is quite probable that they either experience needs that
interfere with the learning process or that our instruction neglects,
satiates, or threatens their current need state. Take, for instance, an
adult college student who refuses to initiate a composition assignment that is achievable, stimulating, and offers practice in the

course's required writing skills. The student may not want to do the assignment because: (1) he is worried about failing a test in another subject and wants to prepare for it (safety need); (2) he is concerned about a family problem and has to have time to deal with it (belongingness need); or (3) he is simply feeling ill and wants to rest (physical need). Undoubtedly, there are many other possibilities. The critical realization for instructors is that adults usually take the logical and the shortest route to goals that are based on their most pressing felt needs. When they do not want to start to learn or when they want to stop continuing to learn, a basic question for us is "What fundamental need is now influencing them?" Answers to this question will help us to know what to do to help adults want to learn.

Researchers in psychology and adult education are critical of the concept of need because of its many different definitions, variety of uses, and value-laden qualities (Monette, 1977). Nonetheless, total clarification of the term is not currently possible, and the concept of need still provides important understanding of adult motivation. Therefore, in the following sections of this chapter, the way in which the term *need* is being used will be specified in order to promote accuracy and appropriate application.

Deciding Which Adult Needs Are Most Important in the Learning Situation

The first meeting of an instructor and a group of adult learners is, indeed, a critical period. Both the instructor and the learners will be making many influential decisions at this time. As learners, we have all had this experience. Our minds race with computerlike efficiency as we judge the instructor, situation, subject, and our peers. Questions tumble out with rapid-fire frequency. Can I pass this course? How much work does it involve? Will I learn anything I need? How intelligent is this instructor? What are the requirements? Do I understand the requirements? What kind of people are in here? How do I fit in? And so on.

Adult learners make at least two sets of crucial decisions whenever they start a new group learning experience. The first set of decisions are those judgments that lead the person to take or enroll in a specific course of study or training. The second set of decisions are those considerations that occur at the beginning of the course or training and influence future performance in that learning experience. Tough (1979) has found that there are twenty-six possible steps of judgment that these combined decision sets can include. No one learner will perform all of these steps, but each learner will perform some of them. Tough's eighteenth step (1979, p. 68) is offered below as an example of the kind of judgments that many adults might be making in those first few hours of a new learning experience.

> The person becomes more precise or accurate in his estimates of the various costs of the learning project. These costs can include (a) time for planning, arranging, and learning; (b) money; (c) the sacrifice of other things that would be possible if that time or money had not been spent at the learning project; (d) space for equipment or books; (e) frustration, difficulty, effort, the need to perform boring or unpleasant learning activities, or other negative feelings; (f) unpleasant physical consequences (such as aching muscles after practicing tennis . . .); (g) negative reactions in other persons, including their feeling that the learning project is strange or peculiar; and (h) the need to accept help from others, or to put himself in the hands of some person or group.

The above example clearly emphasizes safety needs. The basic needs of adults will play a crucial role in determining motivation for learning at the beginning of an instructional process. As instructors, we often cannot singularly influence adults to take a course with us. People may be in our classes or training sessions for many reasons such as job requirements, personal needs, and professional goals over which we have little or no control. However, once the learners are with us and that initial meeting takes place, our influence can be quite strong. A *needs assessment* is an instrument for strategies that can help us enhance learners' motivation by directly responding to their needs at the beginning of the learning process.

Conducting a Needs Assessment

Needs assessment refers to any systematic process for collecting and analyzing information about the educational needs of individuals, groups, or organizations (Moore, 1980). The needs assessment approaches in adult education literature tend to be large and complex (Pennington, 1980). They are often used for programmatic decision making by administrators and educators in business, industry, education, and other large institutions. As referred to in the following strategies, needs assessment is a modest and informal process used by an instructor and his learning group.

Strategy 21: Use needs assessment techniques to discover and emphasize the felt needs of learners in the learning process.

Felt needs are in the conscious awareness of the learner and they are needs that the learner wants or desires to gratify (Monette, 1977). For example, a felt need of an adult in a woodworking class might be "to make something for his home." Or a felt need for a parent in a family relations course might be "to learn how to effectively discipline his children." Felt needs are usually stated as goals, desires, or interests. Most of them can be fitted into Maslow's (1970) hierarchy of needs, but they will usually be stated by the learner as specific expectations or desires for course content and outcomes.

Felt needs *are not* to be considered as adequate measures of the real needs of adult learners. Learners are limited by their experience and perceptions that may not include awareness of all the possibilities, applications, and ramifications of what they are studying. However, since adults do have awareness of the practical needs that have brought them to the learning situation, they are reasonable to expect some gratification of these needs. Their motivation to learn will be enhanced when they find an instructor who respects these needs and creates a learning process by which these needs can be met. To deny the felt needs of adult learners would be to insult their intelligence and self-determination. Furthermore, instructors can usually incorporate their expertise regarding the real needs of their learners along with the learners' expression of their felt needs. Needs assessment is an excellent device to assist this productive coalition.

The simplest and most direct method is to ask the learners, through *interviews, group discussion,* or *questionnaires,* some semblance of the question "What do you most want to get out of this learning experience?" Once this information is gathered, we can evaluate it and integrate these learner-felt needs with those that our expertise and research support as relevant to the learners in our course of instruction. We can then report this information back to our learners and show how course objectives and content reflect this understanding. *In fact, I believe if this method or any of the following needs assessment techniques are conducted, the instructor is obligated to share his findings with the learners who have cooperated.* Adults do not want to be treated as guinea pigs, and their effort and cooperation are to be respected through the sharing and utilization of the information gathered.

While the above direct methods are efficient, they sometimes may be too superficial (Knowles, 1980). Another needs assessment technique that is more probing is to *make a listing of the critical topics, objectives, and/or processes of the course* and to have the learners individually or collaboratively rank order them in terms of perceived importance to themselves. In this manner the instructor has more control over what is offered, and yet the learners can use their felt needs to emphasize their priorities in the learning content and processes. As an example of the application of this technique for needs assessment, here is a list of twenty possible topics for a graduate-level adolescent development course:

Obesity	Runaways	Depression	Moral development
Aggression	Sexuality	Insecurity	Emotional development
Chemical abuse	Peer relations	Identification	Family relations
Alienation	High school dropouts	Generation gap	Motivation
Rebellion	Delinquency	Cognitive development	Discipline techniques

As the instructor for this course, I was initially perplexed about how to teach it. For myself, there were too many topics with too little class time for in-depth coverage. The graduate students in this course were from many different backgrounds (education, social work, psychology, nursing, corrections, therapy, and parenting), with many very practical needs. To solve this dilemma, I offered the students the opportunity at the first class meeting to randomly break off into small groups and through a consensus decision-making process to rank order the ten of these possible topics they wanted to have presented during course time. Collecting this data and using a point system, I further ranked the groups' priorities and came up with the ten most wanted topics. These were indicated to the students the following week along with their order of presentation and assigned readings. It was a success—the students felt their needs were being met and I found a way to give in-depth coverage to desired topics during class time. Student course evaluations have consistently and emphatically encouraged continued use of this needs assessment technique.

Sometimes in more general adult education courses, such as language arts or the social sciences, it is helpful for the instructor to know what are the felt needs of learners as reflected through their common interests. This knowledge can aid the instructor in using more relevant examples, selecting stimulating topics for discussion, or assigning independent study activities. A *series of sentence completion items* that are organized to increase instructor awareness of the learning group's interests, concerns, and desires can be used for this purpose. An example of such a group of sentence completion items is as follows:

1. When I read the newspaper, I like to read about . . .
2. My favorite TV programs are . . .
3. Something I want to do more often is . . .
4. The question I want this course to answer is . . .
5. I want this course to help me . . .
6. An important goal for me is . . .
7. Sometimes I'm concerned about . . .
8. From this course, I want to know more about . . .

9.   When I get free time, I like to spend it . . .
10.   If I could get the chance, I would like to try . . .

Sentence completion items like these could be distributed to learners for written completion. The instructor would indicate that the purpose for this activity is to gather information to better understand ways to make the course content more relevant, stimulating, and useful. The instructor should also inform the learners that each individual's answers will be kept private and that no academic judgments would be based on any individual's responses. It may be interesting to do a frequency count on items such as questions 1, 2, and 5, and to report this data back to the group. Such sentence completion activities are not scientific tools but are really alternative creative ways to gain more insight about learner-felt needs. No sentence completion item is to ever be considered as an absolute. If any learners would object or refuse to complete certain items, their rights are to be respected.

All of these needs assessment activities are examples of ways to better comprehend learner-felt needs. When adults know from the very beginning of a course that their instructor has actively sought to understand their desires and will, to a significant extent, respect their wants through the basic content of their learning, their motivation to learn is enhanced. For them, one of their most fundamental questions has been positively answered—"This course will not waste my time."

Strategy 22: Use needs assessment techniques to discover and emphasize the normative needs of learners in the learning process.

A need may be defined as *normative* when it constitutes a deficiency or gap between a desirable standard and the standard that actually exists (Monette, 1977). The individual learner or group that falls short of the desirable standard is said to be in need. Viewed from the learners' perspective, when a normative need is the discrepancy between what those individuals want themselves to be and what they are, adult education literature commonly refers to it as an *educational need* (Knowles, 1980). In this manner, it represents the distance between an aspiration and a reality.

Normative needs can be quite narrow, such as the need of a person to type sixty words per minute, or quite broad, such as the need of a person to understand psychology. Normative needs are not absolute. They are based on standards that reflect the values and perceptions of those who set them. Experts often disagree among themselves over standards—Who is the best batter in baseball? What is an effective secretary? What makes a worker excellent? Also, there may be disagreement between the institution and the individual over the criteria for required competencies. Unions and business fight this battle every day and we have only to look toward public education to see the heated debate over minimal competency testing. For the purposes of this book, the issue of required competency as it relates to normative need is much more focused, between instructor and learner.

There are two general categories of normative needs assessment that have a good chance of enhancing learner motivation. The *first* is a normative needs assessment where the required levels of competency are established by the instructor and can be explained by the instructor to the learner with a convincing rationale and/or supportive evidence that is acceptable to the learner. If the learner does not trust or accept the required competencies on such a needs assessment, the results of his performance may cause him to feel resentful or, at best, merely resigned to learn whatever is required to make up the indicated discrepancies. For example, a typist who can type fifty-five words per minute may see a required competency of seventy words per minute as unreasonable. He may learn to type faster but begrudge every minute of the learning experience.

When learners do accept the required competencies in the normative needs assessment, they are pleased to have concrete evidence that clarifies their aspirations and identifies their needs. When the instructor indicates that his instruction will be based on this awareness and aimed at reducing the found discrepancies, the learners know the learning experience will be worthwhile. Motivation to learn has been enhanced right from the start of the course or training. The question "Why are we here?" has been answered. Learners now can see their learning as designed to personally help them.

There are many methods of normative needs assessment: interview, questionnaire, tests, group problem analysis, records and reports study, job analysis, or performance review. A comprehensive discussion of each of these would be too long for a book of this size. Two excellent references with more thorough treatments are *The Modern Practice of Adult Education: From Pedagogy to Andragogy* (Knowles, 1980) and *New Directions for Continuing Education: Assessing Educational Needs of Adults* (Pennington, 1980). What follows are a few examples of normative needs assessment that model the purposes and content that such devices can include.

Probably one of the most commonly used types of normative needs assessment is the diagnostic test. Reading, composition, foreign language, and mathematics are subject areas where such tests are often used. Pretests are usually given before designing instructional activities for the learner. The advantage of the diagnostic test is that it is capable of identifying specific areas of deficiency and aids the instructor in tailoring the most helpful learning interventions. Also posttests can show learner progress and concretely reinforce gained competencies.

Another type of normative needs assessment can be problem-solving activities where learners are given situations to analyze and to apply their skills and knowledge. These can be "live" problems such as simulation exercises, role playing, critical incidents, or business games. By comparing the various solutions tried and their effects, the learners gain some insight into their understanding and the level of skills they possess to deal with such problems.

Sometimes the learners themselves can be involved in the feedback and evaluation of their fellow learners during a normative needs assessment. This is often possible on performance tasks and has the positive effects of helping one another to learn as well as allowing for the validity of peer perceptions. Because there are a larger number and variety of learners than the instructor himself, their feedback has a more convincing tone and authority. This is a common technique in public speaking classes where each partici-pant early in the course makes a short speech and has it rated by other participants on scales related to vocabulary, gesturing, pro-nunciation, pacing, and so forth. The composite rating of the participants can then be transposed onto a profile sheet such as is illustrated in Exhibit 4, giving the learner a quick understanding of the areas of skill needing most improvement. Similar profiles can be drawn up from learner ratings in real or simulated situations for such other skills as instruction, interviewing, discussion leading, conflict resolution, counseling, and any of the wide variety of skills involved in artistic and physical activities. The Enthusiasm Rating Chart in Chapter Two is another example of a normative needs assessment suitable to this type of application.

The instructor's *normative needs assessment* process involves four steps: (1) the development of a model of required competencies; (2) the assessment of the learner's present level of performance by the instructor or cooperating learners in each of these competencies;

Exhibit 4. Profile of Ratings of Public Speaking Skills.

Name of Student: ___Richard Walden___ Date: ___Dec. 16, 1983___

Skill Components	Mean Ratings
	Low 1 2 3 4 5 6 7 8 9 10 High
Vocabulary	X
Clarity of expression	X
Pacing, pausing, emphasis	X
Voice projection	X
Gesturing	X
Logical development	X
Adequacy of supportive facts	X
Adequacy of illustrations	X
Appropriateness of humor	X
Quality of opening	X
Quality of closing	X
Rapport with audience	X
Conveying of sincerity	X
Pronunciation	X
Enunciation	X

Source: Knowles, 1980, p. 231. Used by permission.

(3) the assessment of the discrepancies between the required competencies and the learner's present performance, and (4) the presentation of this information to the learner. All of these steps require tact,
empathy, and effective communication on the part of the instructor.

The *second* general category of normative needs assessment,
the *self-diagnostic normative needs assessment,* allows the learners
to diagnose their own needs. Thus, once the model of required
competencies has been developed, the instructor allows the learners
to (1) assess their present level of performance in each of these
competencies, (2) assess the discrepancies between the required
competencies and their present level of performance, and (3) report
this information to him. Exhibit 5 is an example of this type of
assessment for a workshop on self-directed learning.

As Exhibit 5 indicates, self-diagnostic normative needs assessments are not very scientific or extremely precise measures of
learner needs. They are, however, realistic and sensitive ways to help
adults make better judgments about what they need from a course
of study or training experience. They can significantly help learners
to concretely realize how a learning experience will benefit them.
Such assessments are being more widely used in adult education,
nursing, and business for just these reasons. Because the learners
have greater personal control in determining and understanding
what their learning needs are, their motivation and involvement for
the resulting learning experience should be enhanced. Most adults
want to help themselves. When they have personally authored and
created their own illumination of what they need to do, it is a
message difficult to resist.

Using Adult Basic Needs to Create Strategies
for Motivated Learning

This section deals with needs in the broad general sense of
universal human biological and psychological requirements as
discussed in Chapter Three. Maslow's hierarchy will be used as a
categorical structure to explain and organize the motivational
strategies that follow. The *felt* and *normative* needs that are
identified through needs assessment techniques can also fit into
these categories. Therefore, instructors may want to use the infor-

Exhibit 5. Possible Model of a Self-Diagnostic Normative Needs Assessment for Self-Directed Learning.

Name: _____

Three Recent Self-Directed
Learning Projects:

_____

_____

_____

Instructions: The statements below reflect some of the necessary competencies for successful self-directed learning. Consider three self-directed learning projects that you have recently conducted. List these and spend a few moments reflecting upon them. Then complete the form in the following manner: (1) place a **P** in the column that most accurately reflects your *present* level of performance for each competency; (2) place an **R** in the column that most accurately reflects the *required* level of performance you need to achieve for each competency to be a successful self-directed learner. You will then have an understanding of the gaps between where you are now and where you need to be in order to be a more successful self-directed learner.

	Never	Seldom	Some-times	Often	Always
1. I *choose* learning projects that *I* want to accomplish.					
2. I *plan how* to achieve the learning projects that are chosen.					
3. I *complete* the learning projects that are chosen.					
4. I *evaluate the results* of my learning.					
5. I *practice* those skills that are necessary to my learning until I am satisfied with them.					
6. I *have patience* to reach the learning goals that take time to achieve.					
7. I *check my own progress* in learning.					
8. I *have personal standards* by which I judge the quality of my learning.					
9. I *creatively use my environment* to solve problems when I am learning.					
10. I *take moderate risks* when learning to stretch my abilities and talents.					
11. I *choose challenging learning projects.*					

mation gathered about such needs through these techniques in conjunction with the following strategies to further enhance adult motivation to learn.

There is considerable evidence that adults constantly involve themselves in both self-directed and institutionally guided learning activities based on their perceived needs. Tough's (1979) reported research, *The Adult's Learning Projects,* shows that almost all adults undertake at least one or two major learning activities a year, with the average number being about eight. These highly deliberate efforts to gain certain knowledge or skill (or to change in some specific way) are usually initiated for purely practical reasons. People average 700 hours a year at these learning projects, with only about 10 percent of the projects being associated with educational institutions. It appears that most people become ready to learn something when they experience a need to learn it in order to cope more satisfyingly with real-life tasks or problems. Knowles' (1978) theory of andragogy assumes that adults are ready to learn those things that they "need" to learn because of the developmental phases they are approaching in their roles as workers, spouses, parents, leaders, leisure time users, and the like. As instructors, we can use Maslow's hierarchy to better understand these needs and to create motivational strategies that incorporate these needs in a manner that positively influences learning.

Two types of strategies will be outlined for each of Maslow's categories. One type of strategy deals with how the *content* of the subject matter presented relates to a specific need. The second type deals with the *process* of learning itself and how the presentation and approach to learning by the instructor can enhance motivation with respect to a basic need.

Physiological Needs. Unless the basic physiological needs are met, learning is a difficult task because most of the learner's energy is devoted to coping with the pain and tension the learner is feeling. These basic needs are usually for food, water, air, rest, activity, sex, stimulation, and satisfactory temperature. This is why properly timed breaks, sufficient ventilation, and adequate bathroom facilities can make or break any well-planned learning activity. Hungry or tired learners are not usually very cooperative or attentive learners. No special strategy is necessary here. Humane consideration of the learner will usually suffice to establish a learning environment that respects these needs. The only exception is probably the need for stimulation, which will be fundamentally addressed in Chapter Six.

One of the first cues to unmet physiological needs among learners is restlessness. When adults become restless and that behavior continues, it is time for the instructor to do something about it. The appropriate instructor response can be an empathic diagnosis of the learning situation: Have the learners been sitting too long? Are they getting hungry? Is the room too stuffy? Or if the physiological need of the learners is not obvious, an open-ended question to them may be helpful. For example, "I notice some restlessness is starting to develop and I'm wondering what the cause might be?" This question could be to an individual or to the group, and issued privately or publicly, as the situation may warrant. Such a question also allows for learner participation in resolving the problem of restlessness. The important thing is that restlessness be recognized and acknowledged, especially when it is obvious to the adults themselves. Prolonged restlessness is one of those "silent but deadly" motivational issues that may not be publicly addressed but that can erode the learner's confidence in the sensitivity and empathy of the instructor. Because physiological needs deal so much with the basic conditions of learning, there is only one motivational strategy in this category.

Strategy 23: When relevant, select content, examples, and projects that relate to the physiological needs of the learners.

When an instructor can relate a subject to how we sleep, or the air we breathe, or the energy we need, we are likely to be interested. Personal survival is a profoundly compelling topic. People like to learn how to stay healthy and fit. Since the physiological needs directly address how people stay alive, their inclusion as topics, examples, and goals of learning for any subject area will usually encourage greater learner interest.

Whether we like it or not, most adults perk up and show increased interest in topics that deal with sex or violence. This need not be a tacky ploy by a desperate instructor for more learner involvement. Even Mother Goose and Walt Disney could not avoid these themes because they are fundamental forces in nature and human existence. By finding imaginative and appropriate ways to deal with these topics, instructors show respect for their daily influence in the lives of adults and add to the credibility of their subject matter.

Safety Needs. These needs deal with the basic security of the individual. They are arrived at through a sense of stability and freedom from fear and anxiety. They are partly made up of the needs for structure, order, and reasonable limits. Safety needs bring learners to the learning environment as well as operate in the learning environment itself.

Tough (1979) found that most adults in most learning projects are motivated by some fairly immediate problem, task, or decision that demands certain knowledge or skill. Many of these problems and tasks relate directly to safety needs such as upgrading new skills to keep one's job, solving personal problems that threaten one's family, learning home repair to save money, and adapting to new environments and cultures. Knowles' discussion (1980, pp. 27-28) of the adult need to prevent personal and professional obsolescence is a stark but realistic testimony to the power of safety needs. "This need arises from the fact that most adults alive today were educated in their youth according to the doctrine that learning is primarily a function of youth and that the purpose of education is to supply individuals in their youth with all the knowledge and skills they will require to live adequately for the rest of their lives. But the rapidly accelerating pace of change in our society has proved this doctrine to be no longer valid. Facts learned in youth have become insufficient and in many instances actually untrue; and skills learned in youth have become outmoded by new technologies. Consequently, adult years become years of creeping obsolescence in work, in play, in understanding of self, and in understanding of the world."

Learner preference for a predictable and orderly learning environment is another example of the influence of safety needs. Although someone might imagine that because of the potency of safety needs, adults could be intimidated or threatened into learning, this would be, indeed, a mistake. In this culture, one of the most critical psychological criteria for adulthood is when people see and conduct themselves as self-directed. Unless the adult is in some specific role with an authoritarian hierarchy, such as a soldier or a police officer, direct commands for performance are usually deeply resented. Adult development is a progression toward self-determination and personal responsibility for choices and decisions. Since adults want to control their own lives, instructor coercion makes for a hostile and counterproductive learning situation. Showing adults that we as instructors can help them to meet their safety needs is a cooperative relationship they can appreciate and accept.

Strategy 24: When relevant, select content, examples, and projects that relate to the safety needs of the learners.

With adults, finding ways to improve job performance, financial savings, family relations, and personal efficiency are just a few of the many topics that naturally appeal to their desire for greater security. The main thing is for instructors to find those areas of concern specific to the learners' safety needs and to show how they can be better dealt with as an integral part of what is being taught whether it be math or mysticism. In general, our empathic understanding of what worries our learners can be a guide to potential topics or projects that can enlist learner involvement. Any time we offer learning experiences that help adults overcome and neutralize their fears, we are teaching something they will certainly value.

Strategy 25: Use imagery techniques to help learners clearly remember specific problems or tasks that are relevant to the knowledge or skill being taught.

When safety needs are a significant reason for what is being learned, the more clearly the person can visualize the problem or task for which the learning will be used, the more likely there will be enhanced motivation to learn. This process helps adults to more concretely experience the problem or task and to actually anticipate the benefits of their learning in an immediate and realistic manner.

For example, when conducting a course in parenting skills, it is reasonable to expect that those adults who have a particular problem in mind, to which the skills can be applied, will be more motivated to learn than those parents who cannot imagine where to employ these skills. I often ask trainees to "see" an actual problem for which they can use a particular motivational strategy before I teach the strategy. This request consistently increases participant motivation to learn.

There are numerous books and a reputable journal in the field of imagery (Sheikh, 1983). At its most basic level, helping learners to visualize a memory involves *relaxation* and *focusing*. The first step is to help the learners to relax. The best posture for relaxation is either seated or lying down with feet uncrossed, hands loosely at the sides, and the back straight. If you do not know a relaxation technique, the following deep breathing exercise can be used (Bry, 1979, p. 36).

Close your eyes. Get yourself comfortable.

Pay careful attention to your breathing. Recognize how slow and deep breathing will help to induce relaxation. Exhale. Then take a deep breath in through your nose and blow it out through your mouth. Breath from your abdomen, deeply and slowly. Allow your abdomen to rise and fall as you breathe.

With each inhalation and exhalation, count your breaths. Count *one* on the inhalation and *two* on the exhalation. Focus only on the breath and your counting.

If a thought comes into your mind which causes you to lose track of your counting, just return to the count.

If a thought comes into your mind, look at it as though it were someone else's. Neither grab hold of it nor chop it down. Neither stop it or pursue it. Simply watch it come into view and disappear. Then continue your counting.

Count your breaths until you feel deeply re-

laxed. Breathe in and out slowly, counting each
breath, until you feel quiet, relaxed, and still alert.

The state you want to create in the learners is one of receptive
stillness or relaxed attention. Once you see the learners are relaxed,
ask them to see a blank movie screen or a white sheet of cloth and
to see as clearly as possible on this surface a moving picture of the
problem they want to solve or the task they want to accomplish. Ask
them to see the persons involved in the setting in which the task or
problem takes place, to hear their words, and to see their actions.
Give them about thirty seconds to a minute for this activity. Then
take some time to discuss what they saw, heard, and felt. Use this
information to show how the forthcoming learning experience will
relate to their needs.

Although this strategy has been introduced with safety needs,
it is also quite helpful for clarifying learner problems and tasks
related to any need. Furthermore, it is a possible device to use as a
means to anticipate and react to the potential outcomes and effects
of newly acquired skills, particularly in the areas of communication, problem solving, and human relations. For example, management techniques, sales strategies, and conflict negotiations are just
a few of the many possible areas where imagery might be a useful
means to further understanding and enhanced learner motivation.

*Strategy 26: Reduce or remove components of the learning
environment that lead to failure or fear.*

Most of the applied suggestions pertinent to this strategy
have been included in the motivational strategies related to the
sections in the previous chapter dealing with attitudes toward the
instructor and subject. However, there are two more instructor
behaviors that require emphasis and best fit into this strategy.

1. *Remove or eliminate any aspects of age, cultural, sexual,
or social discrimination.* In this respect, from the beginning of a
course or training session, we are sensitive to our learners, our
materials, and, most especially, ourselves. To check ourselves, we
need to ask such questions as: Do we accept and respect *all* learners
in our courses? Do we have fair standards and expectancies for *all*

learners? Do our instructional processes, language, and materials reflect these standards?

As instructors, we can model attitudes and behaviors that enhance the relations of our learners. By showing acceptance and fairness to all groups of adults, we reduce mistrust and fear, making the learning situation a safe and cohesive environment for motivated learning. A reference that gives greater scope to these guidelines is *Multicultural Nonsexist Education* (Colangelo, Foxley, and Dustin, 1979).

2. *If any discipline is necessary, be sure it is fair, learner accepted, well understood, and consistently applied.* Many adult instructional situations do have penalties that may be applied such as those for absenteeism, tardiness, or incomplete projects. If these appear necessary, they should be explained and discussed with the learners from the outset of the learning experience. When such rules can be formulated with the learners themselves, it is best to do so. Their participation in deciding the sanctions will make them more respectful and accepting of the created rules. After the limits have been decided upon, consistency of application is mandatory. When adults have assurance that rules are applied by the instructor in a predictable and fair manner, adults know they are equally respected and can relax about the boundaries of their safety.

Strategy 27: Create a learning environment that is organized and orderly.

One of the surest ways to make a person insecure is to make that person dependent on someone and then to have that someone treat the person in a totally inconsistent manner. Adults, no matter how self-directed, are dependent to some extent on their instructor for information, feedback, and guidance. They need a sense of routine and orderliness in their learning situations. This reduces stress and provides the energy to make learning possible and the risks for achievement more attractive. Think tanks and Nobel laureate laboratories are relaxed and orderly environments.

What is advocated here is that each course or training session should have a regular procedure by which materials are received and shared, by which learners know how to cooperate, by which information is processed and evaluated, and by which basic order is maintained. This does not mean that learning should not be imaginative, exciting, or sometimes even unpredictable. The routines and organization provide the foundation from which the learner can mentally, emotionally, and physically leap into the process of learning, just as the floor provides the foundation for every dancer's step and graceful motion.

Strategy 28: Introduce the unfamiliar through the familiar.

New learning can be quite scary for adults. They often have to relinquish long-held beliefs and comfortable skills. First time learning experiences demand a "temporary surrender of security" (Sheehy, 1976). People who anticipate totally new experiences often ask "like" questions: "What does it taste like?" "Who does he act like?" "What does it feel like?" This helps the person to assimilate the potential new experience with the known past and to feel more secure about attempting it. The same is true for building initiative in adults for novel learning experiences. So if you are starting a completely new topic for learners, connect it to one with which they have some familiarity. If you are beginning to train adults in a brand new skill, compare it to a skill already learned by them. If you are trying a more complex lesson for the first time, show how it relates to a more simple one. This usually makes adults feel safer, more confident, and, therefore, more willing to risk learning.

Love and Belongingness Needs. These needs make up the adult's innate desire for affectionate relationships and for a place in the group with an accepted identity. For learners this means that they want to feel respected and a part of the learning group, giving and receiving genuine affection among their fellow learners and instructors. This also means adults come to courses and training with a desire to learn things that will make them more able and successful in their families, social relationships, and communities.

The need for affection and belonging is probably stronger today among adults than in previous years. Naisbitt (1982) accounts for this with his high tech/high touch analysis: Whenever new technology (computers, electronic media, and so forth) is introduced into society, there must be a counterbalancing human response. He sees the self-help and personal growth movements as a human attempt to compensate for the ever-accelerating technological presence within our culture. The more technology we introduce into our society, the more people will aggregate and want to be with other people, whether it be in a movie theater, in a shopping mall, or in a classroom. Cross's (1981, p. 94) recent review of the research in adult education gives support to the notion that social motives for learning seem to be increasing. "Despite the difficulties in interpretation, there seems to be only one consistent trend in the reasons people have given for taking courses over the past decade: a steady increase in the proportion taking courses for personal or recreational reasons—a category that includes education for participation in community activities, for personal and family interests, and for social and recreational interests."

Maslow would have contended that love and belongingness needs have always been dominant forces within the psyche of most adult learners. The fact that Benjamin Spock's book on baby and child care (19 million copies sold) and Dale Carnegie's *How to Win Friends and Influence People* are two of the most popular books ever published is another indication of how powerful these needs are for most adults. It seems safe to declare that an instructor of adults can positively influence the motivation of his learners by incorporating these needs in selected motivational strategies.

Most motivational strategies related to belongingness needs are found in Chapter Seven because affect, a major motivational factor, is fundamentally influenced by social relationships. This positioning also emphasizes the constant use of belongingness needs *during* the learning sequence. Present discussion will deal with those motivational strategies that incorporate belongingness needs and are seen to be influential at the *beginning* of the learning sequence.

Strategy 29: When relevant, select content, examples, and projects that relate to the love and belongingness needs of the learners.

If any of the topics or applications of your subject matter or training can be related to the learners' family, community, or social relationships, indicate this in your introduction of the material to be learned. Show learners how they will be able to use what they learn in their personal lives.

Realize the power of identification. When learners see and hear things they feel a part of or a bond with, they are much more likely to pay attention and become involved. This means using familiar characters, locales, and topics as subjects of study and understanding. People like to know more about their neighborhoods, their cities, their popular heroes, and their work settings. Better understanding of a *town like theirs* or a *family like theirs* makes adults more interested in learning about them. Even using figurative names that reflect the ethnicity of your learning group can make a positive difference. Mr. Hernandez is preferable to Mr. Smith, as an example, in a community of Hispanic learners, as long as such exemplification is not trite or so rare as to be insulting by its inclusion.

Most adults have some romantic bent within them. Topics such as friendship, kinship, romance, loyalty, commitment, passion, and quests are vitally appealing to adults. The goal is to find a way to legitimately and realistically make them a part of the focus or content of our instruction. When we can, we are wise to do so.

Strategy 30: Create components in the learning environment that tell learners they are accepted and respected participating members of the group.

1. *Learn and use the names of the adults in your courses or training sessions as quickly as possible.* People like very much to be addressed by their names. It tells them they are acknowledged as unique individuals. It is also equally important for adults to learn each other's names in a learning group. This makes them more comfortable, approachable, and increases the likelihood of better communication and social contact within the group. Name tags and mixer games can be used for this purpose. These exercises are found in most human relations and communication sourcebooks. A mnemonic device for this purpose that is quite efficient is to go around the group and to have each person say their name and something that is unique about themselves; for example, Bob the chef, Yvonne from Australia, Cheryl who skydives, and so forth.

Then have volunteers identify as many people as possible until the entire group is acknowledged. Learning sessions can begin with these types of brief exercises until it is apparent that most people know each other's names.

2. *Use seating arrangements where people can see and hear each other.* Circles and U-shaped or V-shaped clusters are best. The message is symbolically and functionally in the structure of the room: Everyone is to be seen and heard because everyone is valued and respected.

3. *If your course or training is of long duration, arrange to interview each learner personally.* This will help you to better understand each learner's goals, needs, personal life styles, family situations, hobbies, and interests. This is a radical activity. It is time-consuming and seldom done, but consider the benefits:

- Each learner will have a face-to-face contact with you in which that person can relate beyond the instructional task.
- Each learner will know that you know him better as a person and will also have a sense of you as an individual.
- This interview will affirm your caring and involvement with each learner.
- You will probably give each learner an experience that the person has had with few instructors. This is often enough to stimulate a sense of reciprocal commitment.

It is important to remember that the interview should be reasonably short and light, a dialogue between two friendly adults. Another option is to construct a personal data questionnaire for the learning group and to report interesting averages and information back to the learners. For example, "Our mean age is thirty-two; 67 percent of us are parents, 15 percent are left-handed," and so forth. This gives the group a sense of identity and promotes cohesion.

4. *When necessary, designate course and training responsibilities so that each learner becomes a functioning member of the group.* Rotate roles of leadership, tasks of assistance, committee work, and privileges to give everyone a chance. This is a dynamic system where every adult has a participating role. In this manner, the learning group is analogous to a family in which every member

has rights, responsibilities, and privileges. Unless such tasks are shared, people become more easily isolated and can eventually feel alienated. Such a distribution of responsibilities and roles provides for the giving and receiving elements necessary for a healthy group.

Esteem Needs. Esteem needs can be divided into two types (Maslow, 1970). The first group emphasizes self-respect and the inner desire for strength, achievement, adequacy, mastery, competence, confidence, independence, and freedom. This type of need is probably the greatest single reason why adults take courses and training. Tough's (1979) research provides insightful support for self-esteem as a wide-ranging impetus to adult learning. He found that almost all adults interviewed reported that their reason for learning was to *raise* the level at which they performed a task or action. These adults could have performed these behaviors at a minimum level without further learning, but they learned in order to perform them more successfully.

Although this type of self-esteem can be general, like reading faster or improving writing skills, for adults it is usually related to a role. Adults want to be effective in their positions of responsibility. They want to be good parents, able workers, and knowledgeable citizens. Because of this, the need for self-esteem permeates this book. In Chapter Four specific motivational strategies for developing self-esteem in the *adult as a learner* are considered. Chapter Eight comprehensively discusses competence as a major motivational factor with powerful influence at the ending of learning sequences. In this chapter, esteem needs will be treated in terms of what instructors can do in the beginning of a learning sequence.

The second type of esteem needs are more other-directed and related to respect from other people. These are prestige, status, fame, glory, dominance, recognition, attention, importance, dignity, and appreciation. Maslow (1970) cautioned that this set of esteem needs, although very powerful, under certain conditions can be dangerous to the person. These needs can lead to severe dependency on others and self-distortion, and make the person more prone to manipulation. He saw the most healthy self-esteem as based on *deserved* respect from others, which comes as a result of our *real* capacity, competence, and adequacy for the task. The following motivational strategies are in accordance with this perception and philosophy.

Strategy 31: Offer the opportunity for responsible attainment of knowledge, skills, and learning goals that relate to the esteem needs of the learners.

The number one priority for the instructor in the employment of this strategy is to fundamentally answer the question "How can I help the learners to be as vividly aware as possible, in the beginning of this learning sequence, of the ways in which these learning activities will make them more effective in the roles and goals that they value?" Functionally, this means the instructor stresses the *practical* and *applied* aspects of the learning experience as they relate to the learners' esteem needs. This means the adults will be able to "see" how their learning will be a concrete process of developing skills and knowledge that makes them more competent at what they regard as worthwhile. It is here that the use of felt and normative needs assessments can be extremely beneficial. Both the procedure and the resulting data are ways to create content and set objectives that help learners to realize they will be learning something that makes them realistically more effective in personally important areas of living and work. Like an architect showing slides of the construction and completion of a proposed building, we display to learners the content, objectives, and processes that will lead to their desired learning goals.

Strategy 32: When appropriate, plan activities to allow the learners to share and to publicly display their projects and skills.

When adults know from the beginning of a course or training session that their learning outcomes will be shared and available to their fellow learners, their motivation for the learning task is usually increased. Public attention means public evaluation. This activates one's need for esteem with its accompanying motivational influence. However, the emphasis is not to be on competition or showing off. Rather, the emphasis can be on sharing, gaining feedback, appreciating uniqueness, understanding personal differences, and learning from one another. Adults like to see how their peers solve similar problems, apply new skills, and evaluate their work. Since so much of what they learn will be used in their jobs and families, the learning environment has less crucial consequences and is an excellent testing ground for practice and refinement. "Respectfully learning from and with each other so that all of us can be more successful at what we value" is the spirit of this type of sharing. As long as the instructor engenders and maintains this tone of cooperation, most adults feel safe and appreciate such learning opportunities.

Some methods and activities for this strategy are as follows:

- Oral presentations and classroom demonstrations.
- Public displays on tables, walls, and bulletin boards.
- Discussion, role playing, and simulation.
- Duplication of papers and other written works.
- Fishbowl techniques (a small group of learners communicates, practices, or demonstrates among themselves, while the rest of the group is circled around them and observes them).
- A publication of a collection of the learners' works in a course book or magazine.
- Photograph collections of learners' activities or projects.
- Films, slides, and audio or audiovisual tapings of learner performances.
- Open-house activities that invite wider community participation and observation.

Self-Actualization Needs. These needs are found in a person's desire for self-fulfillment. They are the internal strivings within people for those activities that allow them to experience their potential and to be what they are or what they are capable of becoming. These growth needs are most readily met by learning that is intrinsically rewarding (the doing of the activity is in itself satisfying).

Even though Maslow believed that the previously discussed needs are to be met before self-actualization needs can fully emerge, the research has not supported this contention (Whaba and Bridwell, 1976). The need for self-actualization is often present on a full or partial basis in adult learning. "Learning for the sake of learning" is not uncommon among adults. Cross (1981) found a range of 10 percent to 39 percent of adults in various state surveys who listed *seeking knowledge for its own sake* as their *primary* motivation for learning. Tough (1979) found pleasure to be a major reason why adults start learning projects. Such pleasure had many different sources, but frequently included the joy that comes from possession of knowledge, satisfying curiosity, interesting content, practicing a skill, and spending time in the activity of learning— all very self-actualization-type behaviors.

Self-actualization needs can also have implications for the process of learning. For some people to find self-fulfillment in their learning, they need to explore, to be creative, and to be self-directed. It appears that many adults prefer these elements so strongly that they opt for independent learning over institutionally guided learning. Penland (1977) studied the reasons why adults choose to learn on their own instead of taking a course. The rank order of the first four reasons most often selected is particularly revealing:

1. Desire to set my own learning pace.
2. Desire to use my own style of learning.
3. Desire to keep the learning style flexible and easy to change.
4. Desire to put my own structure on the learning project.

The traditionally cited factors of cost and transportation were ranked last. There seems to be ample evidence that tells us as instructors that adults want options and regular course procedures that allow them to exercise their self-actualization needs to the fullest. When this is possible, their motivation to learn may be significantly enhanced.

Strategy 33: Provide learners with the opportunity to select topics, projects, and assignments that appeal to their curiosity, sense of wonder, and need to explore.

This means giving learners the chance to investigate and understand things they want to know more about. Many adults take courses with the awareness of related topics they find particularly interesting or appealing. Given the opportunity, they often would like to spend more time in full pursuit of better understanding or appreciation of such wonders and interests. In many instances, such individuals would benefit from learning activities that provide for this exploration, such as research papers or reports that allow for self-chosen topics.

Strategy 34: To the extent possible, and when appropriate, provide opportunities for self-directed learning.

In such instances, the learner will essentially plan, conduct, and evaluate a particular learning activity or project. Goal-setting and contracting strategies can be quite useful at this time. The role of the instructor is one of a consultant who gives guidance and feedback. Such a modality may be an appropriate choice when learner motivation is high, when the learner is assertive and has some basic knowledge of the topic to initiate planning, and when the relative complexity of the subject is manageable by the learner. For example, this would probably not be a very good means to learn a foreign language for the first time. An excellent reference for any instructor who wishes to consider this approach is *Learning How to Learn* (Smith, 1982).

Strategy 35: Challenge the learners.

Most adults who really want self-fulfillment desire challenges in their lives. They want to extend the boundaries of their capabilities and to develop their potentialities. Educational books abound with the imperative "Challenge the learner." Doesn't everyone seem to believe learners *should* be challenged? But this is easier said than done, for both the instructor and the learner. The essence of a challenge is risk and the possibility of failure. In fact, if there is no chance of failure in a task, there is no real challenge to the task. This is a delicate matter, not easy to structure in a learning situation.

To ask a learner to take a risk is to ask that person to make a deliberate personal encounter with the unknown. It will involve doing something in which the outcome of success is uncertain. The greater the challenge, the greater the probability of failure. This is where courage and learning meet, a very exciting encounter. The adult who *willfully* takes on a challenge will be a motivated learner.

The first step for the instructor is to offer some project or learning task that definitely will extend the learners beyond their current abilities. Normative needs assessments are helpful devices for this purpose. In general, the instructor has to have some awareness of the entry-level skills and knowledge of the learners.

The second step is directly from Maslow—minimize the real dangers of the task and enhance its attractions. One does not climb a mountain without a safety rope and the view at the top should be pretty good. Most adults are moderate risk takers and enjoy a challenge in which they have a reasonble probability of success. They just do not want to fall on their faces or lose all their options. Functionally, this means poor performance on the learning task should not mean complete failure and there should be some flexibility so that the learner can find an alternative means to learn if the challenging task becomes too difficult. For example, a learner might choose a project that demands a great deal of reading and the eventual synthesis of this material in a written report. After he begins the task, he realizes he will not have enough time to complete it. It is best if, at this point, there are other options available for his continued learning, such as an oral report, a written test on what has been read, an extension of time to complete the task, or some other more achievable assignment. At the very least, the consequences of failure on the challenging task should be fully discussed with the learners *before* they make their commitment to the task. On the attraction side of the ledger for challenging tasks, the instructor indicates the realistic and practical benefits. For example, "Complete this fitness program and you will be able to run two miles" or "Complete this curriculum and you will have a 90 percent chance of passing the licensing exam."

The third step is for the instructor to arrive at some degree of certainty that the learners *truly want* to participate in the learning activity or project. If the learners feel coerced or manipulated, they will feel more like they are in a struggle than a challenge. Their motivation will significantly suffer. In such situations their motivation will be for survival and will be tinged with resentment.

The last step is optional. Sometimes it helps both the learner and the instructor when there is either an oral or a written commitment to complete the challenging task. For the learner this adds the influence of a social contract and increases the dissonance felt when effort is not extended. Both of these factors should enhance learner motivation. For the instructor this is an indication of the serious intent of the learner that should increase the instructor's empathy and care for the learner during the challenging task.

Challenges are excellent opportunities for adults to affirm themselves and to build competence and confidence. They are invigorating experiences. However, they are not all fluff. Work during a challenging learning task can be filled with sweat, doubt, and anxiety. Instructor support is very important at this time. Also, challenges usually end. The instructor's role at the conclusion of challenging tasks is quite influential. This will be fully discussed in Chapter Eight.

6

Making Learning Stimulating

Against boredom even the gods themselves struggle in
vain.   —*Friedrich Nietzsche*

For centuries boredom has been a nemesis to the quality of life
almost everywhere. Rare is the individual who seems able to
continuously escape its oppressive grasp. Work and learning appear
to be two areas where people are especially vulnerable to the
spontaneous emergence of this vague but powerful emotion. Unlike
so many other predicaments of human existence, boredom's threat
lies not so much in the fear that something bad may happen but
in the realization that *nothing* may happen.

At first glance, boredom seems simple to define and easy to
explain. It is often considered to be an individual's emotional
response to an environment that is perceived to be monotonous
(Davies, Shackleton, and Parasuraman, 1983). However, when
adults are interviewed, their reasons for feelings of boredom include

135

constraint, meaninglessness, lack of interest and challenge, repetitiveness, and the never-ending nature of a task or job. Although so many possible causes make boredom a difficult concept to study, they also provide important understanding for developing motivational strategies to reduce boredom and increase stimulation. Only recently (Hockey, 1983) has more extensive research dealt directly with the problems of monotony and boredom. Smith (1981) reports that it is difficult to find more than forty scientific papers published on this topic within the last fifty-three years.

Although conventional wisdom would support the idea that boredom directly interferes with learning and performance, the research is far from conclusive on this issue (Hockey and Hamilton, 1983). There is a reduction in alertness but performance and memory do not appear to readily diminish in even prolonged work situations. Through means of personal will and flexible adaptation, adults seem amazingly capable of continued effort to concentrate when they want to. When we consider how much we have learned while in a state of boredom, this is not so surprising. Who has not passed a course, read a book, endured a class, or completed a homework assignment that was an exercise in tedium? Some successful adults would say that most of their formal learning experiences have been and continue to be a series of boring events. What the research and personal experience do seem to support is the finding that a host of negative influences on human performance appear to follow or accompany boredom—irritability, fatigue, strain, distractibility, and carelessness (Hockey, 1983). Boredom may not in and of itself decrease learning, but it is a fertile ground for those things that disrupt and diminish a person's ability to maintain effort and attention. At best, under conditions of continual boredom a person will learn while in a state of pain and stress. It does not require a great leap in logic to understand that such classical conditioning can erode the motivation of most adults to learn. In such situations, the instructor's quest for optimal performance from cooperative learners is a losing battle. Also, when adults work and learn in circumstances that are continually boring, their motivators tend to be fear, pressure, and extrinsic goals (paychecks, grades, job status, and so on). Obviously, for many people these work. However, their long-term human consequences—such as stress (Hockey, 1983), minimal competence, and negative attitudes (Deci, 1980), as well as lowered productivity (Peters and Waterman, 1982)—are distressingly formidable. In many ways, motivation while learning acts like a timed-release capsule. Its negative or positive consequences discharge into our psychological systems long after the learning tasks have been completed.

So what can we as instructors do about boredom? How do we prevent the common decay that this viral influence seems to so potently exert on learner motivation? By definition, the opposite of boring is stimulating, and it is the process of stimulation that appears to be the most effective antidote to boredom.

How to Stimulate Learner Participation

Since the "during phase" of learning is the longest and contains the highest number of instructional activities, our approach to stimulation is aided by motivational strategies that are flexible, creative, and constantly applied. Stimulation operates at many different levels. It varies according to what is done by the instructor and the degree of participation and quality of involvement that it influences within the learner. On this basis, motivational strategies that are employed by an instructor can be categorized according to three possible goals for learner participation—attention, interest, and involvement:

1. *Attention.* The learner becomes more alert and investigates what is occurring in the learning activity. This is very similar to the orienting response (Gage and Berliner, 1984) where the learner focuses attention to find out "What is it?" In this state, the learner is more ready to acquire information and to track and monitor the material presented by the instructor (Corno and Mandinach, 1983).

2. *Interest.* The learner consciously desires more information and is emotionally willing to participate in the learning activity, but the learner remains essentially *passive* in his experience with the learning material. The learner is open to "receiving" the learning experience. There is listening, watching, feeling, reading, note taking, and so on, with a desire to comprehend and remember. This is recipient engagement where the amount of mental investment on

the part of the learner remains modest (Corno and Mandinach, 1983).

3. *Involvement.* The learner is actively engaged in the learning activity (Levin and Long, 1981). The learner is searching, evaluating, constructing, creating, and organizing the learning material into new or better ideas, memories, skills, understandings, solutions, or decisions. Often there is a product created or a goal reached. This may be a novel insight applied, a new skill learned, a problem solved, a written piece completed, or a book finished. Numerous mental transformations have occurred. Considerable mental effort has been expended by the learner, with varying amounts of emotional and physical energy exerted as well (Corno and Mandinach, 1983).

One needs little experience as an instructor to realize that these three stimulation goals may overlap. What is attention getting may become interesting, and what is interesting may induce involvement. However, it is important to realize that the strategies that will be included according to each of these goals have limited possibilities. What may help someone to pay attention may never really get them interested and, unfortunately, as many an in-service trainer has found out only too quickly, passive adult interest does not easily transform itself into active learner involvement. These stimulation goals can help us to better understand the probable outcomes of the motivational strategies we employ. Also, the strategies that will be incorporated under these stimulation goals can be used on an "as-needed basis." For example, sometimes during an involvement activity we will notice that learner interest is waning. At such a time, we may employ an attention or interest strategy to arouse or encourage learner involvement. Humor is an intervention that can often be used in this manner.

But how stimulated do we want our learners to become? Is it wise to have adults excited when they are learning material that is demanding and complex? Research in arousal theory provides some helpful guidelines. Increases in stimulation usually lead to increases in arousal, which is the degree of energy mobilized in a person (Apter, 1982). A person's feelings of arousal reflect the intensity of motivation that a person is experiencing at a given moment of time. For many years it was thought that a person's level of arousal could be considered as optimal for particular types of learning (Hockey, 1983), with lower degrees of motivation being best suited to complicated tasks and higher degrees of motivation being best suited to simple tasks. However, it is now clear that arousal is a far more complex process than originally conceived (Hockey, 1983) and that the effect of a person's level of motivation on performance is not related in a simple, unidimensional way to task complexity. There are many people (airline pilots, surgeons, coaches, and so on) who excel at and enjoy performing very complicated tasks while under the influence of highly intense feelings of arousal.

There are many different theories of arousal, but Apter's (1982) theory of psychological reversals is especially helpful for understanding how to use stimulation to the best advantage of adult learners. According to this theory, how we interpret and how we are influenced by the degree of motivation we are feeling depends on the state of mind we are in. When we are in a state of mind where the goal to be achieved is seen as essential and unavoidable (survival, safety, obligation) with the process of performance less important than future consequences, we want our level of arousal to be low. In this *telic* state of mind we are anxiety avoiding and tend to interpret, and therefore feel, high degrees of stimulation as unpleasant and stressful. When we are in a state of mind where the goal to be achieved is seen as freely chosen and avoidable (pleasure, competence, interest) with the process of performance equal to or more important than future consequences, we want our level of arousal to be high. In this *paratelic* state of mind we are excitement seeking and tend to interpret high degrees of stimulation as pleasant and enjoyable (see Figure 4).

According to Apter's model (Figure 4) of arousal, when adults have a frame of mind that "sees" a learning task as imposed or forced on them with serious future consequences (such as promotion, grades, or certification), they will want moderate to low levels of stimulation so they can remain relaxed and alert in their pursuit of these important goals. When they interpret a learning task as something they have chosen to do and that involves a process that is at least as important as the related consequences (such as reading a particular book, solving a problem, or competently

Figure 4. The Relationship Between Arousal and Hedonic Tone.

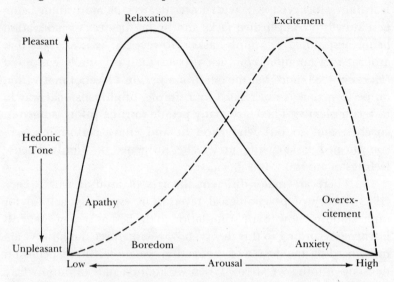

Note: The continuous line represents the anxiety avoidance system; the broken line represents the excitement seeking system.
Source: Apter, 1982, p. 102. Used by permission.

applying a skill), they will want moderate to high levels of stimulation so they can feel invigorated and challenged by the experience. This does not imply that learning goals are counterproductive. If the consequences of the learning task have no meaning for adults, they will feel apathetic. The issue for the instructor is how the consequences of a learning task should be emphasized. Also, learning tasks can become too stimulating. For example, asking a learner to perform a skill in front of a large group of adult peers may cause the learner to become too excited and impair the performance of the particular skill.

There is one more insight about human arousal that Apter's theory explains better than most other theories do. This is the "agony and ecstasy" of daily existence where excitement can become anxiety or vice versa. This switching back and forth can happen so rapidly because our state of mind can instantaneously change due to a memory or external circumstance. Our level of arousal remains relatively stable, but because our subjective interpretation of this feeling has changed, so has our emotional experience of it. For example, we receive a telegram from which we expect good news. Our state of mind is positive and we feel excited as we open the letter. The news is bad. Our excitement quickly turns into anxiety. In another example, more appropriate to learning, we are about to take a major exam for which we have studied and are well prepared. We feel confident and enthusiastic. However, the first item of the exam is a problem for which we have no readily available answer. Within seconds our feelings of enthusiasm have turned into anxiety and a palpable sweat. It is not uncommon to have experiences where there is a constant fluctuation between excitement and anxiety, as in the observation of a closely competed athletic event. Our state of mind has a similar influence on relaxation and boredom. For example, a relaxing conversation can easily turn into a boring one once the topic has waned or the point has been made. Another memory or distraction can easily turn a relaxing and stimulating lecture or film into a boring event. Having this understanding as instructors, we can readily see how unstable learner motivation is and how instructional stimulation depends on helping adults maintain the appropriate state of mind.

Apter's approach to arousal suggests a number of useful principles for instructors who wish to sustain optimal stimulation during adult learning activities. First, *stimulation tends to be phenomenological rather than behavioral.* What is stimulating is a subjective and unique experience for every individual, which is why stimulation is so difficult to maintain the more we increase the number or the heterogeneity of a learning group. The perception of an instructional experience is like the perception of music. What is exciting and interesting for one person may not be so for another person. Some people like jazz while other people are bored with it. The same can be said of rock, classical, or pop music. People respond to learning in a similar way because what is stimulating to a person is a function of the person's developmental stage, mood, cultural background, experiential history, and expectancy for the situation. With twenty adult learners, there are twenty possibilities. That is why the instructor's empathy, creativity, flexibility, and constant attention to learner reaction are necessary ingredients to sustain a stimulating learning environment. This principle also means that while reinforcement may dominate behavior, it is pleasure that dominates the mind. Most learning is a cognitive activity with instantaneous emotional consequences. To keep people stimulated means to keep them *emotionally involved*. Therefore, as instructors we must determine how the learning activity mentally and emotionally affects our learners. Is the activity novel, complex enough, interesting, and so forth? If we want an activity to be stimulating, we need to evaluate the learning process on the basis of how effectively it engages learners at their mental and emotional levels of perception. We know that success (reinforcing event-achievement of a desired goal) builds interest (Bloom, 1981). It is an essential partner to stimulation. Very few people will remain interested in something they cannot achieve. But success needs stimulation just as badly because it is stimulation that makes the moment-to-moment process of learning enjoyable. Stimulation puts the quality into a learning experience and makes the *entire* process worthwhile. It is like the taste in food that makes eating pleasurable, while success is more like the energy that is derived by our bodies from the food itself. If either the taste or the resultant energy were absent from a meal, it would be a far less vital experience. So it is with stimulation and success in learning.

Secondly, *the goal-state of the learners strongly influences the degree of stimulation they will experience as pleasant or unpleasant.* When adults feel pressured toward goals that have serious consequences for them, they will need lower levels of stimulation to remain alert and relaxed. When their learning goals are freely chosen and they feel confident about achieving them, they will need higher levels of stimulation to feel energized and involved in the learning process. There is not much chance for enjoyable learning when adults feel coerced toward learning goals that have grave outcomes. In such situations, they will want learning activities that are calm, not too challenging, and that are relatively short-lived. Their basic goal is to finish the process as soon as possible and to move on to other things. Choice is a critical factor here. The more adults feel they have chosen a learning goal and the more they feel they have some control over the learning process, the more they will feel relaxed and open to greater degrees of stimulation. Choosing assignments and style of learning, or even something as small as a few optional questions on an exam, can make an immense difference in what adult learners are open to experiencing. Anything we can do to increase the learners' feelings of confidence and security in arriving at the learning goal will help them to feel increased levels of stimulation as pleasant. In general, it is probably easier to influence a learner's state of mind than it is to influence a learner's arousal level. By providing choice, security, and removing the pressure of serious learning consequences, we increase the range and probability that stimulation will become enjoyable and exciting for the learner. In this respect, goal-states are like the mountaintop for any climber. The goal is desired, important, necessary, and gives definition to the processes involved. However, once the climber starts, the mountaintop takes a secondary position in the climber's state of mind. Now each pitch of the climb becomes the climber's focal point, with appropriate challenge, security, and attention being organized and planned by the climber for the most enjoyable ascent. Thus, as instructors, once the learning goal is accepted and understood by the learners, we begin to provide learning activities that are sufficient unto themselves with their own particular set of challenges, realities, and experiences that are within reach of the learners' abilities. Timewise, the learners focus on the present learning activity with the confidence that the final learning goal will be reached.

To some extent, learner performance and preference are influenced by the relationship of task complexity and learner arousal level. This may be true in only a very general way (Hockey, 1983). However, this understanding allows us to formulate a stimulation baseline for any learning activity. That minimum standard is that learners appear *relaxed and alert* for any learning experience. No matter how complex the task, we know that they must at least be relaxed and alert to perform adequately. With this approach, if we see boredom beginning to occur, we can increase either the stimulation level of the activity and/or the complexity of the activity to raise their alertness. Also, if we help learners to feel more excited and stimulated by the learning experience but see their performance begin to decrease, we have a choice to lower their stimulation level and/or to decrease task complexity until their performance is at a more optimal level but not below a level that is less than relaxed and alert. Furthermore, once learners are at least relaxed and alert, we can consider what we can do to positively influence their goal-states (diminishing pressure or awareness of crucial consequences) in order to help them arrive at a more excitement-seeking state of mind. For this principle to be effective, as well as all the strategies that follow, it is important *to match the learning process* (whether it be materials, activities, assignments, questions, or discussion) *with the cognitive, emotional, and physical-motor levels of the learners* (Hunt, 1961). When the learning process is not within reach of the learner's capacity, neither stimulation strategies nor task complexity will make a positive difference.

Finally, *any learning activity can become satiating.* It happens to everyone, often without any intention on our part. Satiation is what lies behind the "divine discontent" of human existence. Apter (1982) considers it an autonomous process, originating within the individual himself due to the needs of the body, largely unavoidable for any serious length of time. In instructional situations, what can keep satiation at bay are the context, sequence, and rhythm of learning activities. These qualities are what make the seasons stimulating, turn steps into dance, and elevate words into prose and poetry. Context refers to where something occurs, the environment or background in which something is seen, heard, felt, or performed. Giving a speech to a few friends is very different from giving the same speech to a group of one's professional peers or a national audience on a televised network. As instructors, where we present anything or where we ask our learners to perform anything will significantly affect the stimulation of these experiences. Sequence refers to the order in which different things are presented or performed. This order can be based on content and/or process. Presenting a lecture on a different topic each day of the week is an example of sequencing content. Asking learners to hear a lecture, participate in discussion about the lecture, and then to write a reaction paper to these two experiences is an example of sequencing different learning processes. Most instructional sequencing decisions are based on the logical flow of the information or the subject matter being dealt with (McLagan, 1978). However, motivational flow is just as important. Sometimes we want to start with a highly stimulating learning activity to help the learners become involved and committed to the topic at hand. Other times it is wise just to create an exercise to get learners active even before all parts of a given skill have been demonstrated. The guideline for us as instructors is to seek an *optimal merging* of the informational flow with the motivational flow of the learning experiences we sequence for our learners (McLagan, 1978). Rhythm is the pacing of the content, process, context, and sequencing of learning experiences—the timing, balance, and repetition of when we do what we do. Largely it is an intuitive and esthetic process that draws upon our sensitivity to ourselves, our learners, and our subject matter. Rhythm is the basis for instructional decisions that deal with when to start, end, vary, or repeat a learning activity; when to take breaks; and when to increase or decrease the stimulation during a learning activity. There is no strict formula for it just as there is no programmatic method for creating fine music. Although we cannot easily define rhythm, its axiom admonishes us to pay attention to it. Timing is everything.

The motivational strategies that follow are categorized according to the stimulation goals that they are most likely to achieve: attention, interest, or involvement. Their successful employment is significantly dependent on the context in which they are used, on the sequence they follow, and on the rhythm that paces their relationships. Please keep these qualities in mind as you read about them and consider them for instructional purposes. Three functional questions may help the application of these motivational strategies:

1. In which context will each of these strategies have the stimulation effect I want to achieve?
2. How can I sequence these strategies to enhance stimulation as well as to continually support learner understanding and performance during learning activities?
3. What is the optimal pacing of these strategies to achieve the most pleasant level of learner arousal on the continuum between relaxation and excitement?

How to Maintain Learner Attention

"Pay attention or you won't learn anything!" The words have an unsettling effect. They conjure up disquieting distant images of former teachers, harsh faces, and shrill voices. And whether we liked it or not, they were right. No attention, no learning. As instructors we know this dictum only too well. But demanding attention from adults is one of the least effective ways to get it. In fact, pressuring people to watch or to listen to us probably directly interferes with the three instructor characteristics that naturally enable adults to willingly give their attention to us. These are our *status, competence,* and *expertise* as perceived by adult learners (Gage and Berliner, 1984). By self-confidently assuming our roles as instructors who have important knowledge and skills that we can effectively convey, we have made the first step toward efficiently enlisting our learners' attention. Every instructor has this opportunity, and no matter what the course, seminar, or training session, we can give ourselves the best chance for a good beginning with this kind of realistic self-image. With this personal approach, the following strategies can be most helpful to maintain learner attention.

Strategy 36: Provide frequent response opportunities to all learners on an equitable basis.

Whenever people attend a learning situation, the amount they will publicly interact with their instructor or fellow learners will have an important effect on the attention they give to the learning activity (Kerman, 1979). If they know they are not going to respond or perform in a given learning session, these incentives for paying attention are absent with predictable results. They can literally afford not to be alert because lack of alertness has no immediate consequences. Since note taking, monitoring information, or listening to fellow learners has no imminent effect on their relationship to their instructor or peers, they have lost an important reason for concentrating on the task at hand. Also, if they see the same few people dominating the response opportunities within a given activity, they may become discouraged and resentful of the entire process.

Response opportunities are any chances provided by the instructor for learners to publicly participate or perform during a learning activity. These include answering questions, giving opinions, demonstrating skills, reacting to feedback, and so forth. Our goal as instructors is to instill within our learners a constant awareness that they will be receiving opportunities to respond or perform during the learning activity.

Before discussing specific techniques that enhance this process, there are four conditions that are important to establish with adult learners that will maintain an atmosphere that is humane and respectful for all parties involved. First, announce to the learning group that you intend to have everyone responding to the learning process during your instruction. This creates an expectancy that everyone can understand and use to make sure they are prepared and alert. People do not like to be caught off guard, and many adults will have had years of conditioning where if they did not volunteer to respond, there was no opportunity given. Secondly, make sure everyone does get an equitable chance to respond or perform. Seating charts can be invaluable for this process (and some minor record keeping may be necessary). Thirdly, random selection is best on a moment-to-moment basis. This form of unpredictability gives everyone the feeling they may be next. However, if the skill or response demands some degree of advance preparation on the learner's part, a more orderly process of selection is beneficial. Also, calling only on volunteers can be hazardous unless everyone tends to volunteer. We have all had the experience of the same few people in a group responding or performing over and over again because no one else seems to volunteer. It may be necessary to call a moratorium on voluntary responding (a few sessions may be all that it takes) in order to give everyone a chance. Fourthly, always dignify the learner's response. The real fear for most adults in public responding is embarrassment. They must know they will be treated respectfully and gently for their efforts. By consistently giving learners some degree of credit for their response and by using their responses to move toward further learning, we model this for everyone. A helpful mental attitude that enables an instructor to carry on this process is to remember that even the wrong answer is the right answer to another question. For example, if I ask who was the president during the First World War and someone responds, "Abraham Lincoln," I can still say, "Yes, he was president during a war—the Civil War. Now let's find out who was president during World War I." And I move on smoothly and respectfully. Most mistakes are not random (Gage and Berliner, 1984). They are usually logical and have a pattern. By giving learners the degree of credit possible for their participation and by helping them to learn from their errors while still respecting their integrity, we can reduce their fears. In all of these instances, our guiding frame of mind is to let learners know what they can competently do and then to as fluidly as possible help them to take the next possible step. In some cases this might mean further probing, a hint, a second chance, waiting a while longer, or help from ourselves or another learner. As long as we avoid a right/wrong attitude toward our learners, so much else is possible.

Some specific techniques enhance learner reaction to response opportunities:

1. When asking a question or announcing an opportunity for task performance, wait three to five seconds before selecting a respondent. This allows everyone to consider the possible answer or skill to be demonstrated. It gives learners a chance to organize themselves mentally and emotionally for their response. It also helps to focus everyone else's attention on the forthcoming answer or demonstration.

2. For voluntary situations, ask for a show of hands in response to your question or activity and wait three to five seconds after the first indication of a volunteer before selecting a respondent. This has the same advantages as no. 1 as well as increases the number of possible respondents to choose from. When we tend to call upon our first few volunteers, we often unwittingly "teach" the rest of our more hesitant learners not to volunteer.

3. While pausing before selecting a respondent, look over the group making eye contact with different adults throughout the group. This will tend to increase everyone's attentiveness because your survey encompasses the learners as an entire body.

4. For responses and demonstrations of some duration, alert nonperformers that they will be asked to respond in some

fashion to what they have observed or listened to. For example, "After Zachary has presented his case study, I will ask three of you to give him your evaluation of which sales techniques were critical to his success with his client." (Notice I have not indicated which three nonperformers will do this.) This method invests nonperformers in the task at hand and increases their responsibility to their fellow learners.

5. Sometimes use light humorous unpredictable methods of respondent selection. For example: "The next people to get a chance are all those with birthdays in February" or "Well, let's see who had toast for breakfast. Okay, we've got three volunteers." Or "Check in your groups to see who has the largest wristwatch. Good, because that's who's going to try the next problem for us."

6. During any task where learners are working on their own or in small groups, move among them as an available resource and observer. Depending on the situation, you can comment, question, react, advise, or simply quietly observe. Under such conditions learners are no longer isolated in their work and you have provided numerous response opportunities for them.

Strategy 37: Help learners to realize their accountability for what they are learning.

People tend to take seriously that learning for which they are held accountable (Good, 1983). There are times when paying attention takes real effort and determined resolve. Even under conditions that are normally stimulating, fatigue, satiation, and life's everyday problems can take their toll on the learner's ability to concentrate. For times like these as well as other learning situations, adults are more likely to find the willpower to remain attentive when they clearly know that knowledge and skills that they will have to demonstrate are directly dependent on these learning experiences. There is no doubt that learners are keener about learning material for which they are aware they will be evaluated. There is an almost automatic focusing of attention among learners when any instructor announces, "What we will cover next will be on the final exam." Although the majority of accountability schemes rely on testing, there are many other possibilities such as job performance, projects, target behaviors, and skill demonstrations. Whatever the form of accountability, adults will usually intensify their concentration on those aspects of their learning experience that directly bear upon what they or someone else holds them responsible for knowing. However, accountability often can be construed by adults as a coercive force for paying attention. When exams and final papers are mentioned as related to their learning tasks, they may easily feel threatened into becoming more attentive. Their anxiety is real. We have all felt it. Therefore, accountability is to be used to enlist learners' attention in a manner that is logical and necessary, not as a menacing manipulation.

The best way to ensure that accountability is used in an appropriate manner is to be certain that all components of the curriculum or program design are imperative and integrated for the learning goal and the means by which it is evaluated. In this way the learners know that *all* the learning activities are valuable and build toward the competencies or knowledge they must exhibit. There is no "busywork" or learning experience that does not vitally contribute to the end result. A good analogy for this approach is a recipe for a fine soufflé. Every ingredient and every process that mixes and prepares the ingredients is necessary to the final outcome. Once the instructor is certain that the learning activities are a concise and efficient body of requisite experiences for the learning goal, the following methods may help to encourage learner attentiveness:

1. Announce and demonstrate how your learning program is efficiently designed to build the requisite skills and knowledge for which the learners will be held accountable. Use syllabi, outlines, models, or diagrams to briefly but lucidly show the integrated plan of your program and related learning goals. Indicate how learner accountability will be conducted (tests, projects, job performance, and so forth) and how it is functionally dependent on the learning process and content. This will help learners to realize that their concentration is necessary every step of the way.

2. Selectively use *manding stimuli*. Mands are verbal statements that have a highly probable consequence associated with them (Skinner, 1957). When a person yells "Watch out!" people usually stop what they are doing and quickly check their surroundings for immediate information or action. Instructors have available to them many mands that can focus learners' attention and cue their concentration. Some examples: "Please note this . . ."; "Now listen closely . . ."; "It is critical to realize that . . ."; "It will help you a great deal to understand this if you remember that . . ."; "The point that brings this all together is . . ." Wise use of such mands can be a continual instructional resource for gaining learners' attention toward material that does make a difference in their training or education.

3. Selectively employ handouts. These can be outlines, models, diagrams, advance organizers (Woolfolk and McCune-Nicolich, 1984), key concepts, definitions, and any mixture of all of these. Essentially they help the learners to follow and focus on your lecture, presentation, or demonstration. Their value is that it is more likely that learners will pay attention to what is important when what is important is concretely noted, well organized, and literally within their grasp.

Strategy 38: Provide variety in personal presentation style, methods of instruction, and learning materials.

Variety has motivational effects (Gage and Berliner, 1984). It is stimulating and draws learner attention toward its source. People tend to pay more attention to things that are changing than to things that are unchanging. However, variety for the sake of variety is not a good idea. Concentration and learning often demand that a stimulus be held constant for further understanding and retention. That is why microscopes, photographs, and videotape replays are of such value to science as well as other people in the pursuit of further knowledge. Whenever we as instructors can change some element of the process of instruction without making that variance so extreme that it distracts learners from the subject at hand, we will probably help them to pay attention. Timing variety so that it can serve as a cue to important information or skills is probably one of the best ways to use it to the advantage of motivation and learning. It is also critical to remember that if there is any one factor of stimulation that closely adheres to the influences of context, sequence, and rhythm, it is variety.

First, there is *variety in personal presentation style*. At the physical level, every instructor is an instrument of stimulation. How instructors use their bodies and voices can be a constant source of variety for their learners. Following is a checklist of those categories of human characteristics that instructors can vary to stimulate their learners. Each category contains a series of related questions that can be used to evaluate a videotape of yourself during an instructional session.

1. *Body movement*. How often do you move? In what direction? Are you ever among your learners? Are you predictable in your movements?

   Some movement during instruction is desirable. Across the room as well as along the sides of the room are possible directions. Now and then "going in" among your learners is another variation. Such movement brings you temporarily closer to all learners and makes them more likely to pay attention to where you will be next.

2. *Body language*. Do you use gestures? If so, what kind? When? How animated is your face? How often do you smile? How does your body language change in relationship to learner questions, responses, and behavior?

   Body language reveals how you feel about what you are saying and how you feel toward your learners (Hurt, Scott, and McCroskey, 1978). It reveals the quality of your enthusiasm as well as your personal regard for the persons or topic being addressed. Being animated and friendly makes an instructor a more attractive stimulus to adult learners.

3. *Voice*. What is the tone and pitch of your voice? How often and when do these change? How is your voice used for emphasis, emotion, and support of your topic? If one could not see you, but only hear you, would your voice alone provide sufficient stimulation and variety?

Of all the aspects of personal presentation style, the voice is probably the most important. It is a constant *metacommunication:* communication about communication. It influences everything learners hear their instructors say. Adults will almost universally accept the vocal quality of a message as the correct cue when a person's words seem in conflict with the way they are spoken (Hurt, Scott, and McCroskey, 1978). For example: *"That* is a good job?" would not be a compliment to adults. Since so much of instruction is talking, creative use and variation of one's voice is a major asset to gaining learners' attention. With appropriate pauses the voice can be doubly effective.

4. *Pauses.* When and how often do you pause? How long do you remain silent? For what purposes do you use pauses?

According to Shostak (1977), pauses can greatly enhance verbal instruction. They can be used to break informational segments into smaller pieces for better understanding, capture attention by contrasting sound with silence, signal learners to listen, emphasize an important point, provide time for reflection, and create suspense or expectation.

5. *Eye contact.* While instructing, how frequently do you make eye contact? What percentage of the learners receives your eye contact?

Direct eye contact with learners communicates interest and attention (Hurt, Scott, and McCroskey, 1978). It adds intensity to the instructional process and encourages the learners' reciprocal interest and attention. The more such eye contact is widely distributed among the learners, the more they can feel they are being "talked with" rather than "spoken at."

By using these questions and related categories of personal presentation style along with the Enthusiasm Rating Chart found in Chapter Two, we have an excellent means to diagnose and build a more varied repertoire of stimulating skills for which we are the actual source.

There is also *variety in methods of instruction and learning materials.* Methods of instruction are the ways in which instructors interact with learners and the activities that learners can participate in while they are learning. Lecturing, discussing, showing a film, and playing a simulation game are four different methods of instruction. Learning materials are the physical resources used to instruct, such as films, books, tapes, chalkboards, and so forth. Using variety in either of these areas will usually stimulate adults. Some specific guidelines for this approach are as follows:

- Selectively change the channel of communication. For the majority of learners this means some variance in the auditory, visual, or tactile (manipulative) modes of dealing with learning. However, the greatest amount of information is usually processed through the auditory and visual channels. We hear and see most of what we eventually learn. By switching the channel of communication from auditory to visual, even momentarily, instructors can cause changes in the response patterns and attention mechanisms of learners. In fact, adults seem to prefer visual information (Gage and Berliner, 1984). By selectively using slides, graphs, pictures, chalkboards, overhead projections, and other visual media, we can stimulate greater learner attention. However, most research (Travers, 1973) emphasizes that the clearer and simpler the visual aid, the more effective it is. Parsimoniously using visual aids to draw attention to new or critical information increases their effectiveness (Levin and Long, 1981). See *How to Be an Effective Trainer* (Smith and Delahaye, 1983) for an excellent overview on how to construct and implement visual media. Also, remember varying the intensity of any stimuli (size, shape, color, loudness, complexity, and so forth) has been found to increase arousal and attract learner attention (Day, 1981).
- When making a change, vary the process of learning. This means that the learners are asked to think or act differently from what they have just been doing. For example, they move from listening to a lecture to solving a problem, or they watch a film and then discuss its contents, or they work alone and then they work in small groups. In each of these cases, different forms of thinking, acting, and/or communicating are involved. Every time an instructor alters the process of learning, learners must use different mental and physical resources. This prevents

fatigue and energizes the learner. As the old adage goes, "A change is as good as a rest" (Holding, 1983, p. 158).

Strategy 39: Introduce, connect, and end learning activities attractively and clearly.

Each instructional session usually has a number of learning activities within it. During this time learners might solve a problem, have a discussion, see a film, and practice a skill. This is analogous to a sporting event where each team receives clearly delineated opportunities to exercise its skills. While baseball gives a team three outs to score, football allows four downs to go ten yards. In sports these units of participation have obvious beginnings and endings to simplify transitions, to focus spectator and player attention, and to keep the game running clearly and smoothly. In a similar manner, a learning activity is significantly enhanced when it is distinctly introduced and evidently connected to previous and future learning activities.

Just as a kickoff tells the crowd to "pay attention, the action is about to begin," an attractive introduction gives learners the same message. Some stimulating methods beyond visual/auditory aids and shifts in personal presentation style (body, facial, and voice changes) are as follows:

- *Asking provocative questions.* "How many have ever . . . ?" "What do you think is . . . ?" "When was the last time . . . ?" "Did you imagine before you took this training that you were going to . . . ?"
- *Calling on learners to become active.* Ask them to help, to move, to observe, to evaluate, to remember, and so forth.
- *Creating anticipation.* "I have been looking forward to doing this exercise with you since our training session began." "This film will show the concrete advantages of applying the skills you have been learning." "This next set of problems is really tricky, but I have confidence you can handle them."
- *Relating the learning activity to pop culture and current events.* "You might say the next person we are going to discuss is the

Michael Jackson of the business world." "This case study has a Star Wars quality about it." "What we are going to take a look at next has been organized like an Olympic sporting event."

Connecting learning activities is a real art. Instructors make numerous transitions in any learning session. To "segue" automatically and fluidly helps to maintain learner attention and to maximize instructional impact. Some helpful techniques are:

- Using organizational aids such as handouts, outlines, models, and graphs that interrelate concepts, topics, key points, and essential information.
- Indicating what the new activity relates to, such as how it continues the building of a skill or how it further demonstrates a concept or how it may be helpful to a future learning goal.
- Making directions and instructions for the next learning activity as clear as possible. This technique applies to introducing as well as connecting learning activities. People often stop paying attention because they are simply confused about what they are supposed to do. By presenting accurate directions, instructors can avoid unnecessary distractions and misleading behaviors among their learners.

Closure refers to how we end a learning activity and help learners to feel a sense of completion. This not only focuses their attention but also gives them the feeling of satisfaction that naturally arises from the awareness that a learning task has been accomplished. Some helpful means to this end are:

- *Reviewing the basic concepts or skills achieved during the learning activity.* "Before we move on, let us review the main ideas we have discussed thus far."
- *Allowing for clarification at the end of the learning activity.* "Now that we have finished this section, are there any questions about what we have done?"
- *Allowing for feedback, opinions, or evaluation.* "Perhaps the best way to end this exercise would be to share with one another what we have learned from cooperating in this task."

- *Taking advantage of the spontaneous closure that can arise within the group dynamics of any set of learners.* The training group has just voluntarily applauded the response of a fellow learner. "I couldn't think of a better way to end this discussion. Let's take a break."

Strategy 40: Selectively use breaks, physical exercises, and energizers.

Most learning requires effort, and prolonged expenditure of effort usually produces fatigue. Also, adult learners often come to learning activities with large amounts of their energy already having been exerted in family and job situations. For them to become tired, even in the most stimulating environment, is a realistic probability. Once fatigue sets in, the stimulation value of any activity is seriously reduced and paying attention can readily decline. To avoid this dilemma, selectively allow for breaks or incorporate physical exercise and energizers into your presentations. A ten-minute respite can make a world of difference. When breaks are not possible or too inconvenient, give learners the chance to stand up and stretch or take them through a small set of physical exercises. Also consider the possibility of energizers (Weinstein and Goodman, 1980), which are very short adult games (ten to fifteen minutes) that can add enjoyment and social contact to the process of renewing learners' attention and energy. A final suggestion: Please do not let the clock solely determine when breaks are taken. Fatigue is not chronological. Your flexibility about such matters can greatly enhance the amount of attention you receive from your learners. By investing ten minutes of learning time into a break *when it is needed,* you may receive back as much as sixty minutes of quality attention from your learners.

How to Build Learner Interest

When our stimulation goal is interest, we want much more than adults who pay attention. We want learners who desire more information and understanding about what we have to offer and who willingly participate in the learning process. They may not expend a great deal of personal or mental effort, but they have psychologically joined with us to comprehend and remember the content of the learning activity. Interested learners are open and responsive learners who want to concentrate upon and retain what they are experiencing. They are also on the edge of becoming *involved* learners, more willing and ready to take the plunge into the perseverance and active engagement that will literally change how they think and act.

Most adults will be interested in learning activities that allow them to be successful learners who experience what they are learning as needed and stimulating. Chapters Four and Five have thoroughly discussed the strategies that help adults to be successful in learning processes that clearly meet their fundamental needs. This chapter provides those strategies that contribute to making a learning activity stimulating to the degree that learner interest is ensured.

Strategy 41: Relate learning to adult interests.

By embedding the learning activity and what we say and do as instructors in current adult interests, we provide learners with a constant stream of *relevant* material. By offering learning that generally pertains to adult goals and developmental tasks, we are exposing them to experiences that will naturally pique their curiosity and desire for understanding. The following adaptation of Cross's (1981) description of adult life-cycle phases is an age-related guideline for topics and examples that adults should find inherently interesting.

1. *Leaving home (age eighteen to twenty-two).*
    Establishing autonomy and independence from family.
    Establishing new living arrangements and friendships.
    Being successful at college, vocational training, or first full-time job.
    Clarifying identity and sex role.
    Establishing intimate relationships.
2. *Moving into adult world (age twenty-three to twenty-eight).*
    Getting married and establishing a home.

Becoming a parent and rearing young children.

Facing the reality of permanent work and planning career goals.

Entering into community activities.

Building the foundation for the dream that one holds for the future of one's life.

3. *Search for stability (age twenty-nine to thirty-four).*
   Establishing children in school.

   Reappraising satisfaction and progress in career, marriage, and other important commitments.

   Encountering possible separation, divorce, and remarriage.

   Striving for career success.

4. *Becoming one's own person (age thirty-five to forty-four).*
   Facing crucial career promotions.

   Confronting mortality and aging.

   Being responsible for adolescent children as well as aging parents.

   Reassessing personal priorities, values, and marriage.

   Becoming more independent of spouse, friends, and social influences.

   For women, encountering "empty nest" and possible new career or education.

5. *Settling down (age forty-five to fifty-six).*
   Completing career advancements.

   Launching children and becoming grandparents.

   Developing new interests, hobbies, and leisure activities.

   Experiencing physical limitations and menopause.

   Becoming more active participants in civic and community life.

6. *The mellowing (age fifty-seven to sixty-four).*
   Facing the possible loss of mate and friends.

   Adjusting to the aging process and health problems.

   Preparing for retirement.

   Accomplishing goals in the time left to live.

   Experiencing greater self-acceptance.

7. *Life review (age sixty-five and above).*
   Experiencing retirement and major shifts in daily routine.

   Adjusting to new living arrangements and reduced income.

Adjusting to death of friends and spouse.
Experiencing physical decline.
Preparing for death.
Searching for integrity versus despair.
Valuing of family and past accomplishments.

In addition to this approach, there is the possibility of using interest surveys (Smith, 1982) or selecting from interest areas that have been commonly found (McLagan, 1978) to exist among adults. Whether the learning activity deals with data processing, Dante, or delivering a baby, the more we can relate it to adult interests, the more likely it will be stimulating for them. In general, the most attractive and informative examples, analogies, supporting evidence, and current events are those that vividly touch upon what people already find interesting.

Strategy 42: When possible, clearly state or demonstrate the advantages that will result from the learning activity.

People usually want to know more about anything that offers them a real advantage. They often want to be better, quicker, and more creative in doing what they value. There are many things they want to save and gain such as time and money. Adults want to overcome their limitations in strength, physical vulnerability, intelligence, and speed. Any learning that offers the possibility of acquiring a significant advantage is not only interesting but can, indeed, be fascinating.

Following is a list of general items (McLagan, 1978) that adults want to gain to some degree:

Health	Security	Advancement
Time	Praise	(vocational or
Money	Comfort	social)
Popularity	Leisure	Enjoyment
Improved	Competence	Self-confidence
appearance		Personal prestige
Efficiency		

If anything we offer adults to learn can help them to acquire any of these items, they will probably consider that learning to be advantageous. This is not an exhaustive list. The most important questions for us are "What are the real advantages to adults that this learning experience offers?" and "How can I make them apparent and available to my learners?" If we can answer these questions clearly, we have a vital opportunity to increase adult interest. For example, which technician could easily remain indifferent to a trainer who introduced a new tool with the statement "Ninety percent of all malfunctions in this system can be repaired with this instrument."

Strategy 43: While instructing, use humor liberally and frequently.

Humor is many things and one of them is interesting. People love to laugh. They will be a little more interested in anyone or anything that provides this possibility. Humor offers enjoyment, a unique perspective, and unpredictability. All of these qualities are attractive and stimulating to most human beings. But how does one develop a sense of humor? Or better yet, how does an instructor successfully incorporate humor into learning activities? There is no guaranteed formula. However, Goodman (1981) has some helpful suggestions:

- People are more humorous when they feel safe and accepted.
- Laugh *with* people (includes), not *at* them (excludes).
- Humor is an attitude. Be open to the unexpected, insane, silly, and ridiculous that life daily offers.
- Do not take yourself too seriously. How easily can you laugh at yourself?
- Be spontaneous.
- Don't be a perfectionist with humor. It will intimidate you. No one can be witty or funny 100 percent of the time.
- Have comic vision: If you look for humor, humor will find you.

Strategy 44: Selectively induce parapathic emotions.

Parapathic emotions (Apter, 1982) are strong feelings (anger, delight, affection, sorrow, and so forth) that people undergo as the result of experiencing something that is essentially make-believe. For example, parapathic emotions are the intense sentiments we may have from watching a film, a debate, or a theater production. People tend to become interested in anything that can induce such emotions. Excellent speakers often use stories, anecdotes, and quotes to elicit parapathic emotions in their audiences. In colloquial terms, these "grabbers" act as magnets to attract audience interest at a high level. They are often used in the beginning of speeches and presentations for just this very purpose. Adults cannot easily turn their attention away from anything that has made them feel deeply. Whenever we as instructors can use such devices within the context of our learning activities, we will have an excellent means to arouse and sustain learner interest. Any medium that can induce powerful emotions, such as literature, drama, and music, is a fertile field to consider as a possible resource.

Strategy 45: Selectively use examples, analogies, metaphors, and stories.

This strategy may seem redundant. This book is filled with examples, and many of its motivational strategies discuss how to effectively use examples. However, I have such respect for the impact of appropriate exemplification that a direct discussion of its merits is included here.

Examples are the bread and butter of any good instructional effort. Not only do they stimulate, but perhaps more than anything else an instructor might easily do, they tell learners how well they really comprehend what has preceded them (Gage and Berliner, 1984). For learners they are the "moment of truth" for personal understanding—when the information, concept, or demonstration is clarified, applied, or accentuated. Good examples allow learners to focus new learning so that it is concretely illustrated within their own minds. A fine example reinforces learners for their concentration and mental effort. Most of all, it is difficult for learners to remain interested in anything they cannot understand. Examples are the refueling stations in any learner's journey to new knowledge. Choose them carefully, make them vivid, and use them generously.

Analogies and metaphors are examples that enhance interest by colorfully showing new ideas and information in already understandable form and context. Because adults are experientially rich learners (Knox, 1977) with considerable mental powers of abstraction and deduction (Flavell, 1970), they readily appreciate their use. For example, to say instructing unmotivated adults is difficult is logically clear, but to say instructing unmotivated adults is like teaching Attila and the Huns how to be polite adds zest to meaning.

Stories, especially when they are well told, imaginative, and unpredictable, are extremely interesting. Like a good picture, they are worth a thousand words. Used wisely and relevantly, they can literally captivate a group of learners.

Strategy 46: Selectively use knowledge and comprehension questions to stimulate learner interest.

Every time we pose a question to adults, we are providing a stimulus. Dewey (1933) wrote that thinking itself is questioning. Well-timed, quality questions are opportunities to spontaneously stimulate learners. Bloom's taxonomy (Bloom and others, 1956) is an effective system for classifying questions that enhance learner interest. *Knowledge* questions depend on rote memory and require learners to recall or recognize information. For example, "What do you check before setting up this machine?" *Comprehension* questions require learners to interpret, compare, or explain what they have learned. For example, "Could you now describe two ways to repair this typewriter?" Bloom has four other types of questions but these are more effective to encourage learner involvement and will be dealt with later in this chapter.

By selectively using knowledge and comprehension questions, we encourage learners to covertly or overtly respond to whatever is being presented to them. This enhances their participation by stimulating their thinking and making them more active in the learning process. These two types of questions may be identified by their *key initiators*:

Words knowledge questions usually contain		*Words comprehension questions usually contain*	
Define	Who?	Describe	Rephrase
Identify	What?	Compare	Reorder
Recall	When?	Illustrate	Contrast
Recognize	Where?	Interpret	Differentiate
		Explain	

Knowledge questions tend to be overused by instructors (Wlodkowski, 1984). Because their answers can so easily be categorized as right or wrong, they can intimidate adults. Also, they tend to promote remembering but not necessarily thinking. They are most effective when used infrequently and for the purposes of emphasis, practice, and focusing learner attention. For example, "Given this information, who do you think is the most appropriate client for this marketing approach?"

No matter what kind of questions we ask, there are a number of questioning skills that can increase learner responsiveness. Some of these have already have been discussed under the response opportunity section of this chapter. Other helpful questioning skills may be used:

1. Avoid instructor echo, repeating portions of learner responses to a question. This tends to arbitrarily conclude what the learner has said and dulls further reflection.
2. Avoid pressuring learners to "think" about what has been asked. Adults usually resent this form of indirect intimidation, which implies that they are not motivated or capable in the first place. The question asked should provide its own provocative stimulation.
3. Avoid frequent evaluative comments, such as "That's good," "Excellent," "Fine answer," and so forth. Even though these may be positive, they make us as instructors the judge and jury, deciding what is right and wrong. Acknowledgment, appreciation, and transition responses, such as "Now I see how you understand it," or "Thank you," or "Well, that must mean . . . [followed by a new question]," tend to have greater chances of continuing discussion, interest, and thinking.

4. Avoid "Yes, . . . but" reactions to learner answers. Essentially, this is a rejection of the learner's response. The "but" cancels out what precedes it and affirms what follows it. For example, "Yes, I think that might work, but here is a better way."

5. Probe answers to stimulate more thinking and discussion. Probes are questions or comments that require learners to provide more support, to be clearer or more accurate, and to offer greater specificity or originality. Some examples: "How did you arrive at that conclusion?" "What are some other possibilities?" "I don't quite understand." "Explain a bit more."

6. Insert questions into ongoing lectures and explanations. Sometimes these may be rhetorical or specific. Used in this manner, questions act much like examples. They refocus attention, bring learner comprehension to the surface, and stimulate further interest. For example: "Who do you think most benefited from this discovery?" "What do you imagine is the first question most potential buyers ask about this appliance?"

Strategy 47: Use unpredictability and uncertainty to the degree that learners enjoy them with a sense of security.

We don't want to act like psychotics, but we do want what and how we instruct to have some quality of the unexpected to them. Unpredictability is very stimulating. In fact, the more unexpected the event, the greater the arousal that is felt (Apter, 1982). Every form of entertainment, including sport, art, fiction, and humor, makes use of such properties as uncertainty and surprise within secure contexts. When our learners do not exactly know what is going to happen next or when it is going to happen, we have usually captured their interest and anticipation. This is the way learning can becoming an adventure. When adults feel safe and capable, unpredictability breeds a sense of enjoyable excitement. Being in a course or training session where anything might happen but no one will be hurt is exhilarating. Such instruction can occur when we:

1. *Plan the unexpected,* diagnosing our materials and methods for patterns of predictability and inserting the unpredictable.

For example, in a course where we have been assigning tasks, learning projects, learning partners, evaluation procedures, and so forth, we turn over some of these choices to the learners themselves. Or, in a situation where written materials have dominated learning, we choose to depart from them to real-life situations and more personalized learner interests. On a moment-to-moment basis we might make a mistake on purpose, lecture from a seat among our learners, act a bit out of character, tell a self-deprecating story, or affectionately tease a learner. In the context of good taste and proper timing, there are so many possibilities.

2. *Attempt instructional experiments.* In these instances, we do things that we have carefully considered and that seem effective to us but that we have no certainty about until we actually do them. Every creative instructor does this now and then because often new methods and materials can only be tested on the job. We may even tell our learners that what we are about to do is something quite new and enlist their support and feedback.

3. *Stay aware of the moment and trust our intuition.* Every learning situation is unique and our next best instructional process may be entirely dependent on circumstances we could not predict. A question, a cultural or political event, a learner's problem, or the mood of a group can create a learning opportunity that only our spontaneity and flexibility can take advantage of. Whether it is something like Watergate or the morning paper's headline, or the fact that one of our learners has lost a job, adults appreciate relevance and an instructor who can adjust instruction to the important matters that unexpectedly evolve in a human situation.

In all of these instances, the guiding rule of thumb is learner security. We may take a chance. We may even make a mistake, but as long as the integrity of our learners has been maintained, we can continue to learn from the process as professionals who know that creativity demands some degree of risk with consequences that are not totally predictable.

How to Develop Learner Involvement

The difference between interest and involvement is learner activity. During involvement learners are genuinely participating in the learning process. They are *doing something* mentally and/ or physically with the information and learning materials at their disposal. In a literal sense, the learning process cannot continue without their reactions and responses. They are exerting effort and concentration, and making mental and physical transformations that lead to new ideas, skills, and products. Often there is some degree of perseverance and self-discipline on their part to remain engaged in the learning process.

The same conditions of success, need, and stimulation apply to involvement as they did to interest. The difference is in the kind of processes we offer to stimulate learners. By nature, these are motivational strategies that directly invite, encourage, or allow for active, ongoing learner engagement and participation. The quality of these stimulating procedures is such that learners eventually readily "join in" with these strategies in order to make progress in new learning.

Some of the motivational strategies that follow will overlap to some extent. Some of their component parts will be found in other strategies. In order to avoid confusion, it is helpful to realize that by adding new elements to a strategy, it becomes structurally and systemically different. Therefore, its effects are qualitatively different as well. This is analagous to adding different instruments to a band. As each new instrument is included, a new sound evolves and a greater range of music is often possible.

Strategy 48: Use disequilibrium to stimulate learner involvement.

According to the eminent cognitive scientist Piaget (Sigel, Brodzinsky, and Golinkoff, 1981), people are self-motivated to adapt to the environment. Learning is the way we adapt, and we best learn in situations where we can actively participate and construct new knowledge. The essential functional need that motivates us is cognitive *disequilibrium,* which is the tension we feel when we experience something that does not fit what we already know. This tension causes us to involve ourselves with the new experience until we can understand or "fit" it into our repertoire of possessed knowledge and skill. When this occurs, we feel a sense of balance or equilibrium and the tension is reduced until the next new experience comes along. For example, when I first heard of micro-computers, I thought they were simply smaller computers. I had no idea how personally functional and inexpensive they were. However, when I heard a colleague had *purchased* one, I began to investigate them quite carefully. I now possess a great deal of new knowledge about microcomputers. Considerable mental transformations have taken place and equilibrium has been restored.

Adults are experienced purposive learners. They have a goal in mind. They want to solve a problem, gain a skill, or understand something. Whenever they are confronted with something new or different that they need to know, they will readily feel a tension to assimilate and accommodate the new learning. Whether it is a better way to discipline children or a faster method to get work done, if it truly seems original, unique, or different, it will usually enhance their participation for learning. The novel engages people as long as it is not so strange as to confuse or scare them. For instruction, this works for both content and process. New topics, unfamiliar insights, surprising research, and unique skills will encourage learner involvement. So will novel instructional methods and unusual materials, as long as they are effective. The guiding question for us is *how can we bring to our learners information or processes that are different, novel, contrasting, or discrepant from what they already know or have experienced?* This is what makes learning fascinating. There are also a few other ways to employ disequilibrium:

1. *Introduce contradictions or disturbing data and information.* According to Bigge (1982), learner involvement is at its best when learner perplexity is just short of frustration. When people feel a positive sense of dissatisfaction about what they know or have experienced, they will think harder and reflect more deeply. Their basic response is "How come?" and they will seek new learning to find an answer. Often this can be done with questions such as "If professors are such excellent scholars, why are so many of them such poor instructors?" or "If the United States is the land of opportunity, why is it that only 15 percent of adults enjoy their jobs?" Another way is to present disturbing information. For example, "The world can produce enough food to feed everyone, yet starvation and hunger run rampant even in countries that have the

highest standards of living" or "This training method is the most criticized but also the most widely used in business today." When selectively used, such information will intensify learner investigation of the material that follows it. Another possibility is to take learners mentally in one direction and then to completely switch directions. For example, "We have talked about all the advantages of this managerial system. Now let us take a look at some of its disadvantages." Excellent Socratic teaching is a method that constantly uses these forms of disequilibrium.

2. *Play the devil's advocate.* Now and then take the other side of an argument or the other point of view. This stimulates the learners' thinking and causes them to further develop and elaborate what they understand.

3. *Selectively use the Zeigarnik effect.* Zeigarnik (Jones and Gerard, 1967) demonstrated that learners tend to recall unfinished tasks better than completed ones. Much like disequilibrium, she theorized that a tension system builds up in the person until the task is finished. This is one explanation for why people wake up in the middle of the night with problems and other "unfinished business." It is also part of the reason why television serials and soap operas are so addictive. They never really come to an end. As instructors we can benefit from this understanding. Sometimes it is wise to take a break or end a class in the middle of a stimulating learning activity. Learners will be much more eager to resume their involvement when the next opportunity is presented to complete the learning task. "Always leave them wanting more" is an adage that may work just as well for instructors as entertainers.

Strategy 49: Selectively use application, analysis, synthesis, and evaluation questions and tasks to stimulate learner involvement.

These four categories complete Bloom's taxonomy (Bloom and others, 1956) in the cognitive domain. Each of them, whether given as a question or a task, will require learners to use their minds in such a way that mental effort and transformations have to occur. Learners cannot respond to them without some degree of involvement. Each category is briefly explained here and exemplified along with its key initiators:

1. Application questions and tasks. These require learners to use what they are learning to solve problems in particular situations. For example, "Using the two troubleshooting strategies you have learned, correct as many errors as you can on this completed tax form." Key initiators: apply, solve, classify, choose, select, use, and employ.
2. Analysis questions and tasks. These require learners to identify causes and motives as well as to infer, deduce, and generalize. For example, "Why do you think supervisors and employees respond differently to similar job frustrations?" Key initiators: analyze, conclude, infer, distinguish, deduce, detect, why, and *give* motives, causes, or reasons.
3. Synthesis questions and tasks. These require learners to think creatively and to develop something new by putting parts of different ideas, skills, or information together to make a unique whole. Synthesis activities involve learners in solving problems that have more than one answer or in producing something that has more than one possibility. For example, "Given this list of client needs, design an appropriate telecommunications system that is as economical as possible." Key initiators: predict, draw, construct, produce, originate, propose, plan, design, synthesize, combine, develop, create, and solve (more than one answer).
4. Evaluation questions and tasks. These require learners to judge or appraise anything they are perceiving. For example, "In your opinion, which president since 1960 has had the most effective relationship with Congress?" Key initiators: judge, argue, decide, appraise, evaluate, and any request for a person's opinion.

Strategy 50: Make learner reaction and active participation an essential part of the learning process.

In this strategy, the goal is to help learners to literally step into and to become a part of the learning activity. When learners are an inclusive element in the learning process and it cannot continue without their responses, a momentum can be created that keeps the learners active and involved. This is also one of the best forms of learning because it is *constructive* learning where the learners must translate the material into a form that is meaningful to them (Rosser and Nicholson, 1984). Principles and skills can be presented, but it is the learners' *performance* in activities such as outlining, problem solving, discussing, and experimenting that internalizes the learning for them. Another advantage is that most of the activities cited here, by virtue of their inherent structure, are quite stimulating, in and of themselves (Hoover, 1980). All of the following activities can also be used to operationalize the four categories of Bloom's taxonomy just described.

1. Create learning situations where learners are required to be active, such as games, role playing, exercises, discussions, team projects, simulations, and microcomputers.
2. Use active investigation methods, such as puzzles, problems, experiments, and case studies.
3. Encourage overt bodily activity by providing the opportunity for manipulation of materials or the construction of models, displays, and artworks.
4. For observation experiences, have learners actively record information, evaluations, or insights while they are watching.
5. When there is a great deal of verbal material, such as with long lectures and large amounts of reading, consider having activities where learners paraphrase and explain to someone else what they have been learning, or where they outline or write summary paragraphs about the material covered with the intention of sharing this information.

Strategy 51: Introduce minor challenges during instruction.

Most people enjoy taking moderate risks (Apter, 1982), especially when they are feeling confident. This is part of the reason why sports, games, and gambling are stimulating for so many adults. A challenge offers the opportunity to take a risk. There is some possibility of failure or mistake. Although challenge has been discussed at some length in Chapter Five, the focus here is on minor challenges that are smaller, more spontaneous, and do not demand serious personal commitment on the part of the learner. They are

flexible ways to create enjoyment and involvement in a learning
task by presenting goals or conditions that create a moderate degree
of uncertainty in the learners' beliefs about achievement. This can
be done by introducing time limits, criteria of performance, friendly
competition, and potential barriers. Some examples: "Let us see
how many people can type this document in less than five minutes,"
or "There are four possible ways to solve this problem. See if you
can come up with at least three of them," or "The group that
finishes this task first can present the next case study," and finally,
"See if you can complete this diagram without using your manual."
In addition to their stimulation value, such minor challenges
increase involvement on the part of the learner because they
introduce goals that relate to the self-esteem of the learner and
whose achievement usually requires greater effort and concentration. When such challenges are issued in a friendly and tactful
manner, they are usually appealing to adults.

*Strategy 52: Create opportunities and conditions for the flow
experience.*

This is one of the most enjoyable forms of involvement
possible in learning (Csikszentmihalyi, 1975). We have all had *flow
experiences* outside of an educational context. It is the feeling and
concentration that sometimes emerge in a closely contested athletic
contest, a challenging board game such as chess, or, more simply,
in reading a book that seems as if it were just written for us, or in
the spontaneous exhilaration that accompanies a long, deep conversation with an old friend. In such activities, we feel totally absorbed
with no time to worry about what might happen next and with a
sense that we are fully participating with all the skills that are
necessary at the moment. There is often a loss of self-awareness that
sometimes results in a feeling of transcendence, or a merging with
the activity and the environment (Csikszentmihalyi, 1978). Writers,
dancers, therapists, surgeons, pilots, and instructors report feelings
of flow during engrossing tasks within their repertoire of activities.
In fact, when interviewed, such flow experiences are considered by
them as one of the major reasons why they enjoy and continue to
do the work they do (Csikszentmihalyi, 1975).

Learners can have flow experiences as well. If we think of our best courses and finest instructors, we often can remember being captivated by the learning events we shared with them—challenging experiments, creative exercises, and exciting lectures in which our minds and skills participated at a level where a new depth and extension of our capabilities emerged. Time passed quickly during such experiences and our desire to return to them was self-evident. They were also not trivial. Effort and concentration on our part was necessary to gain what we did accomplish.

We can provide flow experiences for our learners, too. Probably the most important condition to establish them is our attitude toward play and work. Too often these two elements of reality are set against one another as a dichotomous split. To have fun and pleasure during work makes that work suspect, as though it were too hedonistic or superficial. Learning is equated with work and falls into the same categorical trap. Csikszentmihalyi (1975, p. 202) rectifies this artificial dualism with the following words: "One way to reconcile this split is to realize that work is not necessarily more important than play and that play is not necessarily more enjoyable than work. What is both important and enjoyable is that a person act with the fullness of his or her abilities in a setting where the challenges stimulate growth of new abilities." In this perspective, *flow* and its accompanying feelings of enjoyment mean a sense of fulfillment, an opportunity to grow, to develop new skills, and to maintain a self-concept as a fully functioning human being. To provide adult learners with flow experiences, Csikszentmihalyi's research (1978) suggests the following further requirements.

1. *Challenging.* The chosen activity has a demanding goal to achieve, or a difficulty to resolve, or a discovery to make.
2. *Meaningful context.* Some people other than the learner care about the activity. They are concerned about the quality of the learner's performance and will pay attention to it.
3. *Flexible structure.* The activity is structured so that the learner can increase or decrease the level of challenges being faced in order to match exactly his or her skills with the requirements for action (see Figure 5). This gives the learner a sense of control over the experience.

4. *Distinct area of performance.* It should be easy to isolate the activity at least at the perceptual level from other stimuli—external or internal—that might interfere with involvement in it.
5. *Clear criteria of performance.* The learner should be able to evaluate how well or how poorly he or she is doing at any time.
6. *Concrete feedback.* The activity should provide distinct information or signals so that the learner can easily know how well the criteria of performance are being met.
7. *Broad range of challenge.* The activity should have several qualitatively different ranges of challenge so the learner may obtain increasingly complex information about different aspects of the self (see Figure 5).

Figure 5. Flow Experience.

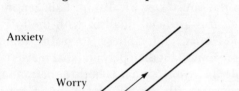

Action Opportunities (Challenges)

Anxiety

Worry

Boredom

Flow

Anxiety

Action Capabilities (Skills)

Source: Csikszentmihalyi, 1975, p. 49. Used by permission.

As Figure 5 illustrates, when learners believe their skills fall short of the challenges that are provided, they will usually worry. Also, if the challenge seems much greater than their capabilities, serious anxiety will probably be felt by them. However, if their skills are superior to the challenge, they will probably be bored. If there is an extreme discrepancy, with their skills far outdistancing the level of challenge, they will probably become anxious as a result of the continued frustration they cannot avoid. However, when their talents are equal or nearly equal to action opportunities, the stimulation process of flow is quite possible. Games are an excellent means for developing the flow experience. With their structure, feedback, flexibility, and clear criteria of performance, such activities as video games, racquet sports, and team contests like basketball are obvious examples. The microcomputer as an instructional device has excellent potential in this direction.

Two further examples are offered to illustrate the possibility of flow in both training and more conceptually oriented learning experiences. Word processing can be a flow experience. With a word processor and a long-term individualized goal (eighty words per minute) that is within the reach of the learner, the requirements of challenge, meaningful context, and distinct area of performance have been met. By employing short-term goals in the areas of initial speed, accuracy, and form, the requirements of flexible structure and clear criteria of performance are also met. The machine itself will provide concrete feedback. As instructors who vary the complexity of what we request the word processing trainee to do, we can creatively extend a broad range of challenges.

Designing a stimulating instructional plan could be a flow experience as well. By asking the learner to incorporate in the plan at least two strategies from each of the three stimulation goal states of attention, interest, and involvement, we have provided a challenge with a broad range of possibilities. By allowing the learner to select the type of audience, subject matter, and learning processes, we have provided the meaningful context. Flexible structure can be ensured by encouraging the learner to select strategies that are familiar and at a high level of skill development. Designing this plan during course time will give it a distinct area of performance. The criteria of performance could be that each strategy is accurately described as a learning activity or instructor behavior. Concrete feedback could be provided by comparing what is written to a model of numerous strategies and related activities that has been projected on a screen for popular viewing or by requesting feedback from the instructor and an assistant who are readily available during course time. Personal feedback could include information relative to performance in terms of accuracy, creativity, and perceived effectiveness so that the learner can realize different aspects of concept and skill development.

Any form of interaction can generate flow. Children do it all the time. To them, a few pieces of wood and a couple of rocks become space vehicles or the buildings of a small village and they are quickly at play. They turn boring car rides into opportunities for elegant games by challenging themselves to spot unique automobiles or by using road signs to stimulate various songs and word sentences. Grown-ups intuitively do this as well, more often than we might expect. Find any group of adults and you will find many people who have found a way to enjoy housecleaning, dishwashing, cooking, lawn care, automobile maintenance, and many more of life's mundane tasks. Instinctively, they have applied to work the principles that Csikszentmihalyi (1975) has discovered as basic conditions for enjoyment. Now this wisdom is available to us as instructors. The challenge and necessary effort are apparent. If we can create these conditions with adults, enjoyable learning is within reach.

When it comes to stimulation and adult learners, it seems important to have a criterion of feedback that can be used to estimate this quality of our instruction. If, for example, our standard is 90 percent of learners paying attention, and we notice that less than this amount is alert to us or the task at hand, we have an indication to do something about it. This may be as simple as taking a break or changing the learning activity. The important point is that because we have a standard (90 percent attention) and a means of feedback (observation), we have a built-in quality control factor for stimulation. Such a device can help us immediately or with future planning. It can act like a motivational altimeter to increase our awareness that learner responsiveness is falling below a level where more general boredom may contaminate the entire learning process. It can also lead to greater assistance for individual learners. Since there is no exact standard of learner attention that has ever been researched and found to be related to excellent instruction, we will have to apply our own criteria. I have used the 90 percent standard for learner attention in recent years and found it to be most helpful. Adults like it because it really is for their benefit. They want to become interested and involved and they know paying attention (being relaxed and alert) is often the first step. For the instructor, such a standard provides a constant challenge during instruction, and when successfully met, increases one's feelings of competence and flow. There is also the added benefit of having greater awareness and contact with the entire learning group most of the time. To actually know that what one has done has helped to create a group of vitally active and friendly adults who are enjoying learning can be quite a feeling.

7

Integrating Emotions
with Learning

One cannot explain things to unfriendly people.
—*Sigmund Freud*

People are always emotional (Zajonc, 1984). Their emotions may not be strongly felt at all times and they may be due to mood as well as to reaction, but people continuously have feelings. Although it is often thought that children are more emotional than adults, it is likely that the reverse is true. Because of their age and experience, adults have more emotional associations with what they encounter, but because their devices of control over feelings are more extensive and elaborate, we do not as easily perceive these feelings in them (Kidd, 1973).

When adults learn anything under any circumstances, their emotions will be involved. Recent brain research not only supports this assumption but also indicates the necessity of emotional engagement during learning to maintain motivation for learning.

178

Split-brain investigations indicate that ordinary language production is usually controlled by the left hemisphere while the right hemisphere adds the emotional and humorous overtones important for understanding the full meaning of oral and written communication (Levy, 1983). Both hemispheres are involved in thinking, logic, and reasoning. In the normal adult it is the integrated whole brain that contributes important and critical processing operations. The final level of understanding or output cannot be assigned to one hemisphere or the other. When learning achieves lasting value, it is an intimate synthesis of both sides of the brain. Adult learning can only operate at optimal levels when cognitive processing requirements are of sufficient complexity to activate both sides of the brain and provide a mutual facilitation between hemispheres as they integrate their simultaneous activities. With little or no emotional involvement, adult learners would easily become disinterested and lack the intense concentration necessary for sustained learning. Levy leaves little doubt about the importance of affect during learning with this summarization: "Considerable evidence now suggests that the right hemisphere plays a special role in emotion and in general activation and arousal functions. If this is so, if a student can be emotionally engaged, aroused, and alerted, both sides of the brain will participate in the educational process regardless of subject matter. With maximum facilitation of both hemispheres, the result will be an integrative synthesis of the specialized abilities of the left and right into a full, rich, and deep understanding that is different from and more than the biased and limited perspectives of either side of the brain" (p. 70).

Related to brain research, and partially as an outgrowth of it, is the field of educational endeavor that deals with cognitive and learning styles. A learning style can be defined as a person's characteristic ways of information processing, feeling, and behaving in and toward learning situations (Smith, 1982). Learning style (as synonymous with cognitive style) may help to regulate the direction, duration, intensity, range, and speed of learning performance (Messick, 1976). Adults do seem to have preferred patterns of perceiving, remembering, thinking, and problem solving. Some people are more emotionally responsive and show a preference for right hemisphere processing (Tucker, 1981). Therefore, it is quite

possible that learners who are involved in learning processes that
are matched to their learning styles can more easily adapt to them
as well as successfully perform their task requirements (Shipman
and Shipman, 1983). However, even though the general topic of
learning style has enjoyed sustained interest on the part of researchers and has generated extensive research that seems to be
promising, the data base is still limited and descriptive in nature
(Wang and Lindvall, 1984). At this time there are at least seventeen
different instruments that measure, to some extent, learning style
but there is no unifying concept or construct to integrate this field
of study (Smith, 1982). Also, there is evidence that higher levels of
learning style flexibility accompany higher achievement levels. For
optimal learning, people seem to have to employ as much of their
neuropsychological assets as possible. With this understanding, this
book takes the position advocated by Levy (1983): What is known
about learning style is useful as a method to *introduce* learning
processes and materials, but the aim of instruction is to guide the
adult to *a deep synthesis of both brain hemispheres* with all their
specialized abilities engaged and integrated to provide learning that
utilizes the *entire* brain and respects the *inseparability* of cognition
and emotion. See Smith (1982) for a comprehensive discussion of
learning style methods and instruments for adult instruction.

Since it has been established that emotions are always present
during adult learning and are an important influence on learner
motivation, a critical question immediately arises. Which emotions
are best for learning? In other words, which emotions have the most
positive motivational consequences for adult learners? Unfortunately, the study of human emotions does not provide an easy
answer to this direct and rational question. Like the stock market,
emotions are often unpredictable, complicated, and very mixed. Not
only are people capable of loving, hating, desiring, and loathing a
particular thing, but they are capable of feeling these emotions *all
at the same time*. Because emotions are so complex, it is difficult to
measure and pinpoint their exact relationship to learning and
behavior (Weiner, 1980a). Yet, there are some suggestions that can
be made regarding the types of emotion that are helpful to adult
motivation during learning. The previous chapter has dealt in some
detail with the emotions of apathy, boredom, excitement, anxiety,

relaxation, alertness, and enjoyment. These are the feelings most prevalent during the presence or absence of stimulation. What follows may also discuss some of these emotions but will deal with them for reasons in addition to or beyond stimulation. Also, with the exception of parapathic emotions, most of the emotional consequences discussed relative to stimulation are considered as mediated through cognitive interventions and individualistic efforts on the part of the instructor. In this chapter, strategies for enhancing affect are more directly focused on emotionally laden sources within the learners themselves and include the social relationships of learners as a means for increasing affective responsiveness and a positive emotional climate for learning.

Probably the most conservative, yet safest, generalization to make about emotions that are helpful to adult motivation during learning is that any emotion that can be described as pleasant is usually conducive to learner motivation (Hurt, Scott, and McCroskey, 1978). Simple classical conditioning makes this a sensible dictum. People tend to develop positive attitudes toward things they associate with pleasant feelings. To be a part of a pleasant instructional process with a pleasant instructor and pleasant peers makes for a pleasant learning experience. That is a lot of pleasantness. And pleasant is a word like *nice* or *good*. It lacks intensity, challenge, and passion. It has a quality of blandness about it. However, instructors should not be misguided. A pleasant learning situation is not necessarily an easy thing to achieve and it is certainly helpful to most adult learning. Mild joy, curiosity, optimism, affection, and confidence are all *pleasant* emotions. When adults have these feelings, they are in a positive mood for learning.

The next generalization is that threat, fear, powerlessness, rejection, and incompetence are emotions that are often, especially in the long run, disruptive to learner motivation (Schmuck and Schmuck, 1983). Threat and fear can be excellent motivators of adult behavior. This is genuinely the case when *reality* provides the basis for the threat. We fear bad weather and dress appropriately. We fear accidents and behave more carefully. We fear ignorance and want to learn. But when a person, such as an instructor, seeks to frighten us, it is an entirely different matter. The issue of fear has now become personalized and our basic integrity may be threatened.

If this is the case, we will tend to be resentful, resistant, and in some cases, vindictive. Unless we change our minds about the situation, at best we will learn with considerable stress and our goal will be to finish the learning task, not to achieve excellence. Under such conditions, learning on a long-term basis will produce within us a negative attitude and minimal competence (Deci, 1980). Also, if the fear permeates our performance with anxiety, we will be prone to make excessive errors (Combs and Taylor, 1952). Personalized threat and fear violate all the principles of andragogy, and it is unequivocal that they should be avoided during adult instruction (Knowles, 1980).

People need to feel some degree of influence in a group (McClelland, 1975). When they feel ignored, discounted, or impotent, their ability to achieve group goals suffers accordingly. Not only do feelings of alienation and powerlessness disrupt their attention and energy for group tasks, but the potentially powerful influence of group norms has little impact on their behavior, because with no power to affect the group, they have, for all intents and purposes, lost their sense of relationship to the group. In learning groups as well as almost any other kind of group, people who feel powerless will tend to act either overtly hostile or covertly devious because these are usually their only remaining means to influence the group (Schmuck and Schmuck, 1983). Also, because they feel so little group support when called upon to perform or cooperate, such learners feel intense anxiety with its consequent debilitating effects. Much the same could be said for adults who feel rejected in learning groups. All people want to be liked, even though the ways they go about achieving it may sometimes seem to indicate the opposite desire (Knowles, 1980). This need for affection causes people to be willing to do things to please others that in some cases may even demand personal sacrifice. Feeling friendship in a group with the opportunity to share emotions and experiences is extremely nurturing and beneficial to people's psychological health. However, when people feel generally disliked in a group, they usually feel extremely frustrated, lonely, and sometimes even betrayed. In learning groups, adults who feel rejected tend to become withdrawn or to act insecurely and passively. They are not likely to volunteer, initiate cooperation, or perform at their best. And when learning is not stimulating or extrinsically rewarding, there is little that can be positively done to hold their attention and maintain their perseverance.

There is no question that feelings of incompetence lead to serious motivational problems for adult learners (Knowles, 1980). Competence is a motivational factor of such power and magnitude that much of the next chapter is devoted to its discussion and strategic elaboration. Given the outlook of this chapter toward pleasant emotions as beneficial for adult learner motivation, one might easily think that unpleasant emotions have a balanced opposite effect and are a negative influence on learner motivation. This is frequently *not* the case. Motivated adults often feel doubt, anxiety, worry, apprehension, and even physical pain in their efforts toward learning and nonlearning goals. The creativity, risk, and perseverance that new learning and greater achievement demand cannot, by their very nature, leave us free of such emotions. Scientists, artists, athletes, and learners know that striving for excellence and accomplishment includes passage through and endurance of many unpleasant feelings. But wanting something, believing in its value, and having the self-confidence to achieve it makes discomfort an acceptable and bearable reality. Without the willingness of human beings to endure pain and painful emotions, the world would not know its greatest accomplishments, nor would people be capable of the effort necessary to reach the simple achievements that make life worth living. Therefore, the goal of instructors is not to make learning painless but to make learning *worthy* of the discomfort it may require and to provide those motivational influences, emotional and otherwise, that support and nurture people through the difficulties inherent to excellence in achievement.

With this goal in mind, affective responses of adults during learning can be seen as having at least four different sources: (1) emotional reactions influenced by personal mood, (2) emotional reactions influenced by the instructor, (3) emotional reactions influenced by the learning process and materials, and (4) emotional reactions influenced by the learning group. Although these four sources of emotional influence have been listed separately for purposes of discussion and strategy, they operate as a holistic ensemble (Watzlawick, 1977). This means they have a *combined impact* on learner emotions *all the time* during learning. One cannot completely ascribe a particular feeling to a singular source. Learners may think they feel happy because of what an instructor has just said, but that feeling is to some extent also due to the emotional climate of the group, the learning task they were participating in, and the mood they were in at the moment the remark was made. A humorous anecdote made to a group of adults who are in a bad mood because of some external crisis could easily fall flat. For the instructor, this means keeping these four sources of emotional influence moving in the most positive direction possible during learning so that they systemically enhance one another for optimal learner motivation. Adults who are in a good mood when they enter a cohesive, supportive learning group led by an empathic, competent instructor are much more likely to feel optimistic about the learning task they receive and, therefore, motivated while they work on it.

Personal mood as it is used in this discussion is considered in a very specific restricted sense. It refers to the emotional state of an adult upon entering the learning situation and it is primarily caused by events and physical conditions outside of the sphere of influence of the instructor. In this interpretation, a learner's personal mood may be caused by family and work experiences and/or physiological factors such as hormonal shifts and blood sugar level. These kinds of things do significantly influence how learners feel when they participate in learning situations but there is very little that instructors can realistically do about them. Because adults have so many crucial responsibilities outside of the learning environment (family, job, and community), the emotions that result from problems due to these obligations may impinge on their motivation during learning. Realizing this can be helpful to instructors in three ways. First, there is a limit to what we can do to positively affect the emotional state of our learners. Knowing this can to some extent lessen our confusion and potential guilt about those adults who seem hostile, negative, or uncooperative for reasons that are not apparent from the learning situation. For example, there are times when people have had a bad day and there is little else that can be done about it. Secondly, appreciating the potentially powerful effects of a negative personal mood on learner motivation can help to increase our patience and compassion for adults who learn with us. And thirdly, respecting the strong influence of personal mood can help us to understand that there are some problems with learner motivation that can only be resolved with help *outside* of the learning environment. Where appropriate, this knowledge can enable us to confer with particular adult learners to encourage them to seek assistance from resources more amenable to their work and family situations. Sometimes it is simply good sense to recognize that a doctor, a minister, a counselor, or a spouse can do much more to help an adult learner's motivation than anything we could do or say as instructors.

Fortunately, the remaining sources of emotionl influence (the learning group, the learning process and materials, and ourselves as instructors), are much more manageable in the learning environment. There are many ways to organize, plan, and communicate through these sources to ensure emotions that enhance learner motivation. The rest of this chapter will detail conditions, skills, and strategies that help to create positive affective responses during learning.

Using Personal Communication Effectively

As instructors, we are probably the single most important influence on communication in the learning environment and, therefore, the dominant influence on how emotions are expressed and dealt with during learning. Chapter Two was an extensive discussion of those essential characteristics that make a person a motivating instructor and an effective communicator. Also, Chapter Four dealt in depth with those strategies that create positive learner attitudes toward the instructor. What remains for further discussion is a more specific breakdown and elaboration of those particular communication skills necessary for the enhancement of emotions during learning.

It is not possible to not communicate (Watzlawick, 1977). People may misunderstand us, dislike what we have said, or distort our message but if we have had an exchange with someone, that person takes away a meaning from the interaction. And since feelings enter all messages, there will be some degree of emotional response as a result of our communication. This awareness of the continual effect of communication becomes even more crucial when we realize that some communication experts have found that as much as 70 percent of what we communicate may not be understood in the manner we intended it to be (Robinson, 1979). *Effective* communication is reciprocal, with each sender and receiver alternating roles and understanding the particular message as it was intended to be understood (Schmuck and Schmuck, 1983). Effective communication is mandatory for competent instruction and the enhancement of emotions conducive to motivation during learning. McLagan's seminal study (1983) of competencies for the field of training and development lists nine skills as critical to the role of instructor. Five of these are communication-related: feedback skill, group process skill, presentation skills, questioning skill, and relationship versatility. In a parallel sense, excellent companies are like excellent learning environments—their members tend to be motivated, productive, and continuously increasing their achievements. Peters and Waterman (1982) found such companies to be characterized by intense communication that tended to be informal and rigorously supported at the managerial level. All of this is to say that to be an effective instructor of adults who can both deal with emotions as well as enhance their motivational influence requires a competent repertoire of communication skills.

The following list of these basic skills has been compiled from a variety of books and studies on communication. No central or "core" list that all the experts can agree upon seems to be available. Each skill listed has been chosen because it is commonly supported in the literature and because it bears some relationship to developing and demonstrating *empathy,* the most important psychological process inherent in human communication. Following each skill is its definition and an applied example. Take a few moments after reading each skill to check your understanding of the skill and to reflect on your ability to use it. If you are dissatisfied with your comprehension or ability to utilize these skills, consider further training in communication skills development. While these skills may appear simple, they are difficult to effectively execute on a continuous basis. Learning them well takes practice and interaction with other people. It is worth the effort. Many instructors fear emotions and withdraw from them, not because of the feelings they engender but because they do not know how to deal with them. These skills are one of the few means that we have to effectively communicate about feelings and to exercise their power as a constant positive influence on learner motivation.

1. *Paraphrasing.* Paraphrasing is the skill of repeating the essence of what another person has just said in one's own words. It emphasizes the cognitive or central idea of what has been communicated. It demonstrates understanding to both parties and, if necessary, increases the chances for dialogue about the issue. Example: Having just given a problem as an individual assignment a few moments ago, you see a learner who seems confused. You go up to the person and ask, "Would you like some help?" The learner responds, "Not really. I think I can take care of it myself. This work is a little tricky for me, but I can do it." You respond (paraphrase), "Okay, at this time you're pretty confident you can do it without any help from me." The learner replies, "That's right, but thanks for the offer."

2. *Checking impressions.* Impression checking involves describing in a tentative fashion the emotional state of the learner, based on words and actions that have just been communicated. It is similar to paraphrasing but focuses on the feelings rather than the ideas of the learner. Impression checking must always be tentative. Its goal is to open communication channels so that the learner will describe his or her feelings more directly and communication can continue. Example: You are having an intense discussion with your learners. You state an opinion about the federal government. A learner responds, "That's a bunch of bull! I don't believe that at all!" There is a deadening silence among the group. You respond (check impression), "You seem quite angry about what I just said." The learner responds, "That's darn right . . ." and goes on to issue a strong viewpoint that is counter to your own. (The important point here is that dialogue has continued and emotions supportive of motivated involvement have not been cut off or thwarted. Skillful impression checking is invaluable to exciting learning. Adults have a right to get emotional about what they are learning. The question is can we, as instructors, handle it?)

3. *Describing feelings.* This is the direct communication of the instructor's own feelings. Instructors are often cautious with this communication skill because to state one's true emotions places one in a vulnerable position with whomever receives the message. However, when this skill is used with appropriate timing and tact, it can be beneficial. Example: You are in the middle of one of your favorite lectures. You are enthusiastic and the learning group seems very interested in the material that is being presented. For no apparent reason you make a Freudian slip and state a word that has a highly sexual connotation, which is further magnified by its contextual placement in your sentence. You know the group has heard it because no one looks like they did a moment ago. You stop and comment, "Did I just say what I think I said?" Some learners in the group nod in agreement. With a slight smile you respond, "I am really *embarrassed*. Please accept my apologies." You begin to laugh and the rest of the group good-naturedly joins in with you. You recover the moment and move on with the lecture.

4. *Describing others' behavior.* A behavior description clearly and specifically notes some of the overt actions of the learner so that the person can understand precisely what behaviors are involved (and in the case of problematic behavior, comprehend you with less of a tendency toward defensiveness). Behavior descriptions neither impugn motives nor imply unalterable generalizations about the actions of the learner. Inferring beyond behavior for psychological interpretations is a common cause of interpersonal friction between instructors and learners. Example: A learner hands in a revised composition assignment that has a significant number of spelling and grammatical errors in it. You decide to confer with the learner and begin the dialogue with a behavior description. "This is your second attempt at this assignment and it contains five spelling errors and four grammatical mistakes. I'm concerned and thought we should talk about it." (Notice there has been no inference about carelessness or lack of ability. The news is not good for the learner, but it is straightforward and respectful.)

5. *Assertive statements.* Assertive statements are a means to resolve a situation where learner behavior is having a problematic effect on the instructor. Sometimes they can be a simple request such as "Could you please give me your attention?" or "Could you

return my book by Friday?" At other times they may be more complex, involving describing behavior, describing feelings, listing possible effects, and making a request. Assertive statements are one of the most advantageous means possible to avoid anger and resentment toward a learner in a manner that helps to solve the instructor's problem as well as treats the learner with respect. Example: You are conducting a discussion during which two learners continuously talk between themselves. It is not unlikely that they may be talking about the discussion topic but their behavior is becoming a distraction. You have tried using silence and looking at them, but this action on your part has had no apparent effect. You stop your conversation and calmly issue an assertive statement to them. "Excuse me. I'm not sure what your conversation is about, but when you continue to talk while the rest of us are involved in this discussion, I find myself becoming distracted and losing my concentration on the topic at hand." (You could add a request, "I would appreciate it if you would stop." But this may not be necessary. Your assertive statement allows these two learners to act responsibly once they know the effect of their behavior.)

As can be seen in these examples, how we handle our own as well as our learners' emotions is a constant process in the learning environment. Emotions occur not only in reaction to subject matter issues but also emerge relative to how we manage, evaluate, and respond to the everyday business of human interaction. Skillful communication is so important because the learning environment is first of all a human environment and no motivation plan or strategy can supersede or diminish the influence of this reality.

Enhancing Affect During Learning

Emotions put life into learning. In a figurative sense, when people are encouraged to feel as well as to think while learning, both their hearts and minds are actively involved. This kind of unity means whole-brain functioning with all of its resources and capacities more available (Levy, 1983). It is rare to meet renowned scientists or scholars who are not deeply emotional about their work. As indicated earlier, people's feelings will be present to some degree while learning no matter what we as instructors do. The following strategies are a means to promote emotional involvement on the part of adults so that their entire neuropsychological resources are more positively available during learning. With the strategies for stimulation they form a potent arsenal of methods to enhance emotional responsiveness in adult learners.

Strategy 53: Selectively emphasize and deal with the human perspective of what is being learned, with application to the personal daily lives of the adult learners whenever possible.

This strategy is based on the assumption that *anything* that is taught somehow bears a relationship to a human need, feeling, or interest. Otherwise, why else would we instruct or train for it? For us as instructors the question is "What are the human ramifications of what we are helping learners to know or do?" Once we have an answer to this question, the emotional aspects of what we instruct will be clearer and we can decide how to integrate them, generally or specifically, into the learning process. Whether it is how to wire a circuit, or how to speak a foreign language, or how to write a complete sentence, there are human purposes that these skills or knowledge serve. If we can understand these qualities, especially as they may relate to the daily lives of our learners, we have some guidance in selecting those emotional aspects of the learning experience we may wish to emphasize.

Giving a human perspective to a learning experience infuses it with value beyond the technical requirements of the task and changes it from an expendable, isolated activity into a potentially valued source of personal satisfaction for the learner (Peters and Waterman, 1982). For example, "We are not just studying how to use a telecommunications device; we are learning a dynamically more effective and efficient way to communicate to the mutual benefit of ourselves and our clients." If this viewpoint is sincerely portrayed by the instructor and accepted by the learner, the instructional activity has a transcendent meaning that will induce more positive emotional responsiveness in the learner. In plain words, this makes learning special. In fact, the sentence structure of the previous quote can be used to help glean the human ramifications for any specific learning objective: "We are not just *(specific topic or skill)*; we are learning *(human purpose)*."

When human beings are in any way the topic of study, do their morals, values, decisions, problems, feelings, and behavior bear a relationship to similar qualities in our learners? If this is so, it may be worth the time to ask our learners to deal with these through reflection, discussion, writing, or any other learning process. When our topics lie more in the realm of such physical and natural sciences as biology, chemistry, physics, and geology, showing how this knowledge relates to solving human problems, aids in the development of civilization, or brings about technology that makes life easier and more enjoyable helps to bring about more affect-laden reactions in learners. For skills from math to medicine, using human problems to illustrate and practice these useful tools increases emotional responsiveness in learners. In the technological fields such as data processing, computer programming, and mechanical drawing, accentuating and illustrating the advantages and contributions that these processes make to human endeavors can help to diffuse their mechanistic isolation and humanize the learning process.

The previous examples have emphasized the human perspective toward what is being learned so learners can more easily identify with the topic at hand and therefore have their emotions more available to the process. Probably more emotionally powerful is any learning situation where what is being learned has an immediate relationship to the *personal daily lives of adults* (Brown, 1971). If an instructor is conducting a seminar on alcoholism as a community problem, what are the implications of this information for the communities of those adults present and, more important, for their own families? In a similar vein, when an instructor is demonstrating a sales technique, why not demonstrate it with the type of client most often encountered by those sales personnel who are learning the technique? Consider a basic education instructor teaching the difference between a circle and a square. This may seem to be a highly abstract concept, but if the instructor, as a point of discussion and illustration, asks the learners to think of important circles and squares in their own lives, an emotional flavor is now introduced to the concept. The closer we bring our topics and skills to the personal lives of our learners in the "here and now," the more available and fluid will be their emotional involvement.

Strategy 54: When appropriate, relate content and instructional procedures to learner concerns.

One of the developmental dimensions of maturation during adulthood is a fuller awareness of deep concerns (Knowles, 1980). Concerns are especially provocative of adult emotions. They are more profound and more persistent than interests because they contain an inner uneasiness. For people they usually represent a gap between some ideal and reality. They usually indicate some fear or worry about people's aspirations. Parents and teachers are not *interested* in discipline; they are *concerned* about discipline. In like manner, business owners are not *interested* in profits; they are *concerned* about profits. If anything in learning can be helpfully related to adults' concerns, their emotions will be quickly present and readily felt. The question for instructors here is "Does anything about this topic or skill relate to adults' concerns, and, if so, can I constructively deal with it?" For example, a seminar on human relations would very likely instigate learner concerns if the issues of racism and sexism were used as a basis for skill development. However, the instructor has to be able to constructively deal with these issues for optimal motivation to continue.

Strategy 55: Selectively relate content and instructional procedures to learner values.

Concerns often relate to human values that represent the important and stable ideas, beliefs, and assumptions that consistently affect a person's behavior (Fuhrmann and Grasha, 1983). Someone who values politics does not merely vote. That person probably also joins or supports a political organization, donates some amount of money to political causes, writes or telephones political representatives about selected issues, reads about political matters, acts on behalf of certain political candidates at election time, and frequently talks about politics with friends and colleagues. Every adult has some strong values and when these are integrated with a learning experience, the adult's emotions will be easily available (Kidd, 1979). When learning events correspond to people's values, they will usually feel reassured or joyful. People are pleased to hear their political beliefs supported and to know they are rearing their children soundly and appropriately. But when the instructional process or content does not mesh with adults' values, there is a good chance for a value collision and they may feel frustrated, tense, and sometimes angry. The following topics are areas with which many adults will associate firmly held values (Simon, Howe, and Kirschenbaum, 1972):

Politics	Friends	War/peace
Religion	Money	Authority
Work	Aging	Love
Leisure time	Death	Sex
Education	Health	Culture (art, music,
Family	Race	literature)
Material possessions	Ethnicity	Personal tastes
		(clothes, hair
		style, manners)

When these topics become any part of the learning experience, adults' emotional responsiveness is likely to increase. However, there are some guidelines for instructors who wish to successfully incorporate adult values into the learning process. The first is *not to be dogmatic or to moralize about value-laden topics* unless there is an exceptionally good reason to do so. Taking a rigid position on any value may conflict with the viewpoint of some of the adults present, which may threaten them and lead to hostile reactions. Arguing, denial, withdrawal, and dismissing the authority of the instructor are possible consequences. Another more constructive approach is for the instructor to offer a value position as a personal opinion with appreciation for the fact that the learners' opinions may vary and that their right to their own decision about such matters is acknowledged. For example, "The area of discussion we are getting into now will probably reflect some of my political beliefs. I'm fully aware that those opinions may differ with some of yours. Let's use this as an opportunity for dialogue and greater understanding, with the recognition that the outcomes of such a discussion are a matter of personal choice that everyone has a right to." A second guideline is for the instructor to introduce the topic as one that reflects differing values and to serve as a moderator with no particular advocacy. For example, "There is no doubt that the sex education program we're about to study is controversial. Let's take a careful look at it, understand it, and leave some time for discussion, realizing that everyone has a right to their own opinion." This approach can be effective because it encourages mutual respect of differing values and leaves the final opinion with the adult learner as an individual right. The third guideline is to present a concept or a skill at the *value level* of learning, with personal acceptance and application at the prerogative of the individual learner. For example, "Use of the childrearing practices I have introduced to you is to a large extent dependent on your family situation and value system. Let's take some time to analyze these skills, using these two criteria to point out their strengths and weaknesses for each of us. I realize the final choice will be yours but I think hearing some different perspectives would be informative for all of us." Such an approach could be used for a variety of learning processes that might include applied, analytical, creative, interpretive, or evaluative activities. In general, value-oriented learning seems to have the greatest probability for successful emotional involvement when instructors encourage an atmosphere of mutual respect and allow each adult personal choice in matters of opinion, selection, and application.

Strategy 56: When appropriate, deal with and encourage the expression of emotions during learning.

An instructor of any type of course can encourage learners to express how they feel or to indicate what their emotional response is to what is being learned. Important emotional reactions on the part of learners can relate to aspects of learning such as progress, evaluation, application, understanding, or a given assignment. To discuss learners' feelings usually enhances their emotional responsiveness when those feelings are readily apparent and *not to deal with them* would lessen learner motivation. For example, a controversial speaker, film, or topic has just been presented and the learning group has a strong but mixed emotional response to the process. Having a chance for reactions and dialogue at this time can promote clearer understanding, relieve tension, and allow for closure to take place. In a more positive vein, a small group of learners may have just completed an exercise or role-playing session and appear "emotionally charged" by the experience. Giving them a chance to say how and why they feel the way they do can be informative for themselves as well as the rest of the learning group. Both of these instances stress how important the instructor's communication skills will be for an adept handling of these matters and a constructive outcome.

Strategy 57: When appropriate, help learners to directly experience cognitive concepts on a physical and emotional level.

This strategy means helping learners to engage their physical senses such as touching, hearing, and seeing to understand and to incorporate what is normally an abstract concept. It also means emphasizing the physical and emotional properties of ideas so that they become the more salient and direct avenues through which understanding is channeled. This was a popular notion in confluent education (Castillo, 1974), but has recently received further scientific support in studies dealing with imagery (Sheikh, 1983). Singer and Pope (1978) contend that as events are encoded in language, they become abstracted and lose their immediate impact on experience. Thus, as concepts are transmitted and integrated verbally, there is further lessening of their emotional quality and nonverbal meaning for us. When ideas become images, they seem to have a greater capacity for the attraction and focusing of emotionally loaded associations (Sheikh, 1983). In a general way, using images and the physical senses to experience concepts gives them greater descriptive accuracy and a more holistic quality that is theoretically more likely to engage the whole brain. There are a number of different ways to do this.

• *Let the learner experience the physical and emotional properties of a concept or idea before it is more cognitively considered.* It is one thing to talk about mental retardation. It is quite another experience to discuss the concept after a visit to an institution for the profoundly and severely retarded. This rather intense example is not meant to encourage sensationalism during instruction. It is just that to allow a truer picture of reality to precede related instruction often enhances the motivation of people to learn the concepts and skills we use to describe and deal with that reality. In this same line of thinking, I once knew two trainers who enacted a very realistic argument just prior to initiating their workshop on conflict resolution. Another variation of this approach would be to bring a video game to a seminar and have each participant play it before starting a presentation on feedback.

• *Use memory, imagination, and imagery to vitalize conceptual understanding.* For example, the concept is excellence. Having learners remember what they did and how they felt reaching a previous excellent achievement in their lives can enrich and increase the vividness of what this concept really means. In a similar vein, the concept could be dehydration. Using imagery (see Chapter Five) to have learners see themselves in a hot, dry, sunburnt desert with nothing but rocks and sand for miles while the wind mercilessly blows stinging dust into their faces and every orifice of their parched and brittle bodies makes the effects of thirst a bit more palpable. Literally, if instructors using their memory, imagination, or imagery can see a concept, hear a concept, or feel a concept and help their learners to do likewise, they can substantially increase positive emotional responsiveness for learning.

• *Have learners enact the concept.* This means that learners carry out or become a representation of the concept or idea. For example, an instructor is conducting a seminar on communication skills. This person wants the learners to understand how superficial many communication exchanges really are. In order to accomplish this, the learners are instructed to pick partners and to have a three-minute "trite" conversation. Only things that are trite (what they had for breakfast, yesterday's weather, and so on) can be addressed. Afterwards, the learners will discuss their reactions and what implication this experience has for the conversations they usually have. In another example, an instructor might be dealing with the concept of disability. Having learners go through a number of activities using their opposite hand (from the one they normally use) can bring the concept of disability to a fuller realization. An adult basic education instructor conducting a course in geography might have learners take physical positions within the classroom that represent the planets and their movements in the solar system in order to increase their understanding of systemic relationships. There are a myriad of possibilities with this approach.

Maintaining an Optimal Emotional Climate

The word *group,* as used in this section, refers to a collection of interacting people with some degree of reciprocal influence over one another (Schmuck and Schmuck, 1983). This definition excludes aggregates of people in mere physical proximity such as persons at a football game. Most organized learning takes place in groups because of the greater efficiency of operation afforded by dealing with people in collective sets and because of the richer resources and motivations for learning provided by a group (Knowles, 1980). There are more adults learning in group settings than there are people involved in all of elementary, secondary, and higher education combined (Robinson, 1979). However, although the number of adult learning groups continues to grow at a rapid pace, their participants often criticize them as being cold, hostile, and indifferent learning environments (Kidd, 1973). That is, indeed, unfortunate because learners who view themselves as being disliked or ignored by their learning peers often have difficulty in performing up to their potential. Such people experience anxiety and reduced self-esteem, both of which interfere with learning and performance.

Every learning group is as unique as a fingerprint. It develops its own internal procedures, patterns of interaction, and limits. To some extent, it is as if imaginary lines guide and control the behavior of learners in a group. Each learning group has *formal* and *informal* aspects (Cooley, 1956). The formal aspects of a learning group deal with the role of each person as a learner and the work to be done in that capacity. The learning tasks and goals, the structure of procedures and rules, and the information and decisions relative to them are examples of the formal aspects of a learning group. The informal aspects of a learning group involve the ways in which each member relates to other members as persons. The feelings, attitudes, and friendships that develop as people relate to one another are examples of the informal aspects of a learning group. In the research on group dynamics there are many terms in tandem that stand for the formal/informal dichotomy such as external-internal, task-psyche, task-maintenance, and instrumental-experience. The important point is that informal processes are present in all the interactions of a learning group and do make a difference in the accomplishment of its formal goals (Luft, 1984).

The emotional climate reflects the formal/informal aspects of a group and consists of the degrees of tension and harmony felt within the group. A *positive emotional climate* means members of a group like and are committed to the group. The most frequently used term to describe this state of affairs is *cohesiveness* (Johnson and Johnson, 1982). Group cohesion is the extent to which the influences on members to remain in the group are greater than the influences on members to leave the group. It is the sum of all the things influencing members to stay in the group. When learning group members like one another and wish to remain in one another's presence, the group is cohesive.

When the norms and goals of a group are learning and achievement, cohesiveness is a powerful force to sustain learner motivation. Johnson and Johnson (1982) are ebullient in their description of the positive effects of group cohesiveness:

> As cohesiveness increases, members also become more committed to the group's goals, accept assigned tasks and roles more readily, and conform to group norms more frequently. Members of cohesive groups put a greater value on the group's goals and stick more closely to the group's norms than do members of groups lacking cohesion. They are also more eager to protect the group's norms by putting pressure on or rejecting those who violate them. They are more loyal to the group and more willing to work toward a common goal. Unlike members of loosely assembled groups, members of cohesive groups take on group responsibilities more often, persist longer in working

toward difficult goals, are more motivated to accomplish the group's tasks (if for no other reason than to
live up to the expectations of their fellow group
members), and are more satisfied with the work of the
group. When the norms of a group favor productivity,
those groups that are highly cohesive are more productive in accomplishing goals and in completing
assigned tasks. Moreover, group members communicate more frequently and effectively in highly cohesive
groups. Their interaction is more friendly, cooperative and democratic. They are more likely to influence
one another in making decisions, to be more willing
to listen to other members, to be more willing to
accept the opinions of the other members, and to be
more willing to be influenced by other members. They
are also more willing to endure pain or frustration on
behalf of the group and more willing to defend the
group against external criticism or attack. Finally,
they are more satisfied with the group. (p. 373)

Johnson and Johnson are enthusiastic but not misleading.
There is enough research evidence available now to persuasively
argue that the achievement of at least a minimal level of group
cohesiveness can enhance learner motivation and performance, and
that, therefore, our attempt as instructors to establish this condition
is worth our effort, skill, and strategy (Schmuck and Schmuck,
1983). Also, the methods and conditions that establish a cohesive
learning group strongly correspond to the salient recommendations
for an adult-oriented learning environment (Knowles, 1980). Furthermore, if working and learning are considered as parallel activities (Brophy, 1983), where each might benefit from similar group
processes, it is important to emphasize that Peters and Waterman
(1982) found work productivity and excellence where group cohesiveness was well developed.

For a group to be cohesive, it must successfully meet the
personal needs of its members (Johnson and Johnson, 1982).
Chapter Five details the means to achieve this end for learning
groups. In terms of the informal aspects of members' needs such as

mutual inclusion, influence, and affection among themselves, the
sections of Chapter Five that deal specifically with safety, belongingness, and esteem needs are particularly instructive for the beginning
phase of the instructional process. Exhibit 6 is a self-diagnostic
inventory to check your leadership behavior as it influences your
learning group's cohesiveness *during* learning. This inventory
reflects those behaviors on the part of an instructor that would
maintain conditions in a learning environment where learners
could adequately have their informal needs met.

There is another possible use for the Cohesion Behavior
Inventory. By changing the personal pronoun "I" to "My instructor" with appropriate alterations of subsequent verbs and pronouns
in each statement, the Cohesion Behavior Inventory can become an
instrument that provides feedback from the learners' perspective.
For example:

1. My instructor tries to make sure that everyone enjoys being a
    member of the group.
    Never 1 : 2 : 3 : 4 : 5 : 6 : 7 : 8 : 9 Always

With this information used in conjunction with your own diagnosis of your cohesion behavior, you can make a comparison to see
what you think you do and how your learners perceive the results
of your actions. This may pinpoint any inconsistencies or flaws in
your leadership behavior that may need further refinement or
improvement.

In addition to the direct behavior of the instructor, the *norms*
of a learning group can do a great deal to maintain a high level of
cohesiveness among its members. Norms are the group's common
beliefs regarding appropriate behavior for its members (Johnson
and Johnson, 1982). These *shared expectations* guide the perceptions, thinking, feeling, and behavior of group participants and
help group interaction by specifying the kinds of responses that are
expected and acceptable in particular situations. All learning
groups have norms, set either formally or informally. For a group
norm to influence members' behavior, they must recognize that it
exists, be aware that other group members accept and follow the
expectation, and feel some internal commitment to the norm.

Exhibit 6. Cohesion Behavior Inventory.

The following questions should help you reflect upon how your behavior influences the cohesion of your learning group. Answer each question as honestly as possible.

1. I try to make sure that everyone enjoys being a member of the group.

   Never 1 : 2 : 3 : 4 : 5 : 6 : 7 : 8 : 9 Always

2. I disclose my ideas, feelings, and reactions to what is currently taking place within the group.

   Never 1 : 2 : 3 : 4 : 5 : 6 : 7 : 8 : 9 Always

3. I express acceptance and support when other members disclose their ideas, feelings, and reactions to what is currently taking place in the group.

   Never 1 : 2 : 3 : 4 : 5 : 6 : 7 : 8 : 9 Always

4. I try to make all members feel valued and appreciated.

   Never 1 : 2 : 3 : 4 : 5 : 6 : 7 : 8 : 9 Always

5. I try to include all members in group activities.

   Never 1 : 2 : 3 : 4 : 5 : 6 : 7 : 8 : 9 Always

6. I am influenced by group members during instruction with respect to their specific needs and opinions.

   Never 1 : 2 : 3 : 4 : 5 : 6 : 7 : 8 : 9 Always

7. I take risks in expressing new ideas and my current feelings.

   Never 1 : 2 : 3 : 4 : 5 : 6 : 7 : 8 : 9 Always

8. I express liking, affection, and concern for all group members.

   Never 1 : 2 : 3 : 4 : 5 : 6 : 7 : 8 : 9 Always

9. I encourage group norms that support individuality and personal expression.

   Never 1 : 2 : 3 : 4 : 5 : 6 : 7 : 8 : 9 Always

These questions focus upon several ways of increasing group cohesion. The first question describes a general attempt to keep cohesion high. Questions 2 and 3 pertain to the expression of ideas and feelings and the support for others expressing ideas and feelings; such personal participation is essential for cohesiveness and for the development of trust. Questions 4 and 8 also focus upon support for, and liking of, other group members. Question 5 refers to the inclusion of other members, and question 6 takes up one's willingness to be influenced by other members. Questions 7 and 9 center on the acceptance of individuality within the group. All these factors are important for group cohesion. Add all your answers together to get a total cohesion score. Keep your responses to these questions in mind as you instruct your learning group.

Source: Adapted from Johnson and Johnson, 1982, pp. 375-376.

There are several ways in which norms can be implemented in a group. One frequent method is to simply state them as the rules that govern the behavior of the group. In learning groups this is commonly done for such issues as attendance, participation, assignments, and evaluation. Norms can also be initiated through modeling. Thus, the instructor's formal and informal behavior toward learners has a powerful effect on the norms of the learning group. Another method is to incorporate the cultural norms of the group members into the learning group. In business and institutional settings this is commonly done. Learners often assume that the norms that govern their behavior in a particular institution will transfer to learning events sponsored by that institution. Some norms can occur through group selection. For example, learners might offer suggestions for which topics need specific discussion or which skills necessitate further practice. The instructor can then lead the group through a decision-making process to gain the group's consent for acceptable recommendations. Two group skills extremely important for appropriately handling this process are conflict negotiation and consensual decision making (Johnson and Johnson, 1982). Generally, members will more actively support and accept norms that they have helped to set up. Ownership gives members a sense of personal choice, understanding that the norm reflects their values, and better awareness of the need for their backing to maintain the norm. Finally, the more clearly the members see how a group norm aids in the accomplishment of a salient group goal to which they are committed, the more readily they will accept and internalize the norm.

Most instructors will probably use several means to implement and maintain norms that are conducive to a learning group. Whichever methods are chosen, the following norms are strongly supported by theory and research in adult development (Knox, 1977). They provide the kind of shared expectations that can functionally create and increase group cohesiveness during adult learning (Knowles, 1980; Johnson and Johnson, 1982).

• *A people-centered learning environment.* It is caring, warm, informal, respectful, and trusting. The instructor's behavior and learning activities reflect a concern for the development of persons, a deep conviction as to the worth of every individual, and a faith that people will make the right decisions for themselves if given the necessary information and support. It gives precedence to the integrity of people over the accomplishment of things when these two values are in conflict.

- *A high level of trust.* People are generally *open*. They offer information, ideas, thoughts, feelings, and reactions to the issues the group is pursuing. Members *share*. They offer their materials and resources to others in order to help them move toward greater learning. People are *accepting* and express regard for other learners and their contributions to the group's work. Members *support* one another by recognizing the strength and capabilities of other learners and showing confidence that they can help themselves. People have *cooperative intentions* and are willing to work together to achieve the group's learning goals. In a group with a high level of trust, members do not fear that if they openly express themselves, that information will be used against them.

- *An ease of communication.* People listen attentively to one another. They are accessible to one another for conversation and dialogue. Feelings are expressed and opinions reflect sincerity and authenticity. Agreement may not be achievable but mutual understanding is.

- *A collaborative atmosphere.* Cooperation overrides competitiveness as a dominant group value. People want to achieve their best, but that does not put them in a winning or losing attitude toward the performance of their peers. They are willing to share what they know or can do without fear of holding back because other members might take advantage of them or achieve more by comparison.

- *An acceptance of personal responsibility.* People hold themselves accountable for their individual choices and behavior. They are not likely to blame or offer excuses for the results of acts they have chosen to do. They accept the natural consequences of their behavior and keep the commitments they have made. Members can trust each other's word and agreement.

- *Clear and accepted learning goals.* Members understand and desire the learning objectives of the group. This allows them to coordinate and motivate their behavior in the proper direction. With clear learning goals that are operationally defined, measurable, and observable, members are able to contribute as well as to evaluate the efficiency and usefulness of their behavior. Explicit and wanted learning goals reduce group conflict and make the resolution of group problems accessible because they provide understanding of the group's actions needed to achieve them.

One of the major reasons why the norms just cited often remain in the realm of platitudes and good intentions for adult instruction, rather than becoming actualized and building group cohesiveness, is because instructors do not use a structure for learning that promotes the kind of learner interaction that would make such norms a dynamic reality. Without an organized means of learning that encourages people to demonstrate their trust and to openly communicate and collaborate with one another, there is little opportunity for the kind of interpersonal contact where these norms can develop and flourish. The following strategy is a functional form of learning that has proven to be exceptionally powerful in creating group cohesiveness and learner motivation.

Strategy 58: Use cooperative goal structures to develop and maximize cohesiveness in the learning group.

Deutsch (1962) conceptualized three types of goal structures for social situations: cooperative, competitive, and individualistic. A *cooperative* goal structure is one in which the goals of the separate individuals are so linked that there is a positive correlation among their goal attainments. Under this cooperative condition, an individual can attain the goal if and only if the other participants can attain their goals. Each person seeks an outcome that will be beneficial to all other group members; an example would be a mountain-climbing team where the primary goal is to reach the summit, and if one climber excels in helping the team to climb to the top, every other member of the team also benefits. A *competitive* goal structure is one in which the goals of the separate participants are so linked that there is a negative correlation among their goal attainments. An individual can attain the goal if and only if the other participants cannot attain their goals. Each person seeks not only to succeed but also to cause the other participants to fail; an example would be an automobile race where when one driver wins the race, all other race car drivers have lost. In an *individualistic* goal structure, there is no correlation among the goal attainments of the participants. Whether an individual accomplishes the goal has no influence on whether other participants achieve their goals. Each person seeks an outcome that is personally beneficial, without regard to the goal attainment of other participants, such as in a typing class where one person learning how to type has little to do with how well any of the other class members learn how to type.

Considerable research during the pasty thirty years has found that each goal structure promotes a different pattern of interaction among group members (Johnson and Johnson, 1982). While cooperation provides opportunities for positive interaction among group members, competition promotes cautious and defensive member interaction (except under limited conditions), and individualistic situations encourage group members to work by themselves with far less interaction with other group members. The evidence indicates that a cooperative goal structure, compared with competitive and individualistic ones, promotes more exchange of information, more helping and sharing of resources among members, more peer influence toward productivity, higher incidence of creative and risk-taking thinking, higher emotional involvement in and commitment to productivity by more members, higher acceptance and support among members, more of a problem-solving orientation to conflict management, and a lower fear of failure by members. A recent meta-analysis by Johnson and others (1981) of 121 research studies on the topic of instructional goal structures found that cooperation was considerably more effective than were competition and individualistic efforts in promoting learner achievement. Another meta-analysis by Johnson, Johnson, and Maruyama (1983) of 98 research studies on the topic of instructional goal structures found that cooperative experiences promote more positive relationships among individuals from different ethnic backgrounds, between handicapped and nonhandicapped individuals, and among more homogeneous individuals than do competitive and individualistic experiences.

Cooperative goal structures are not miraculous. They build group cohesiveness because their interaction patterns create seven variables that have a high probability of increasing interpersonal

attraction among group members (Johnson, Johnson, and Maruyama, 1983):

1. People tend to like people whose best effort toward a goal helps
    them to achieve their own goal.
2. People tend to like people who support them in the achieve-
    ment of their goals.
3. People tend to like people who understand their perspective.
4. Realistic, dynamic, and differentiated interactions break down
    stereotypes and increase interpersonal identification.
5. Higher self-esteem lessens the tendency toward prejudice.
6. The greater one's successful learning, the more one likes those
    who have contributed to that success.
7. The more one expects future interaction to be positive and
    productive, the more one likes the people involved in that
    process.

When learning is the goal of a group that is highly cohesive,
it seems more possible, more valued, and more supported. That
makes learning more likely to be intrinsically motivating because
it is more pleasurable to learn with people one likes and respects,
and who will help and support one's effort toward a mutually
valued goal. Building a cooperative goal structure creates these
circumstances and involves the following steps:

1. *Group size.* Once there is some degree of certainty that the
learning goal is clear and desirable, the instructor must decide
which size of cooperative group is optimal. For learning tasks,
cooperative groups have the best chance for successful interaction
when they range in size from two to six members. Exceptions to this
guideline are larger groups where the purposes of interaction might
be discussion, brainstorming, or some form of team game. This
means that most learning groups will have to be broken down into
smaller groups with individual, cooperative assignments or responsibilities. Mutual communication and problem solving become
quite difficult once a group's size exceeds six members. Even groups
ranging in size from four to six require that members have adequate
interpersonal and organizational skills in order to be successful.
Also, the shorter the period of time available, the smaller the

cooperative group should be because a smaller size will allow for quicker organization and more efficient operation.

2. *Assignment of learners to groups.* In general, the more heterogeneous the groups, the better the depth of understanding, the quality of reasoning, and the chances for building cohesiveness across the entire learning group. Random selection procedures such as having learners count off and placing the ones together, the twos together, and so forth should be adequate for this purpose. However, sometimes practical reasons may override heterogeneity as the best approach. Interest in a specific topic, institutional memberships (a learning group from a particular company), accessibility for cooperation outside of the class, and limited skills or resources might predicate a different selection process or the possibility of self-selection. Also, it is important to consider changing cooperative group membership for different learning tasks and goals. This builds a stronger positive feeling of collaboration across the entire learning group and increases group cohesiveness.

3. *Structuring interdependence and cooperation.* It is important that the learners realize that the activity is a cooperative one and that they need each other's contributions and support. In most instances, the organization of the learning experience will make this self-evident. However, when appropriate, the instructor may be wise to make a few statements encouraging everyone's contributions and participation. For example, "The reason I've organized this lesson in this manner is so that everyone can participate and give and receive feedback. This form of cooperation will give us a chance to learn as much as possible from each other as well as to practice our skills. I trust you'll do your best and I know we can be a real help to one another." Words of this sort probably serve their best advantage when cooperative activities are being initiated for the first or second time in a learning group. Some ways to structure cooperation are as follows:

- *Materials interdependence.* Give learners a limited number of materials, instruments, or machinery so that they must share in order to successfully reach their learning goal. Interpersonal communication and working together become much more automatic under such conditions.

- *Information interdependence.* Each cooperative group member may be given or offered the opportunity to select different books or resource materials to synthesize with fellow members. For example, the learning goal might be to find common techniques among excellent coaches. Each learner might pick a different sport and study a famous coach's methods within that sport. Each member brings that information back to the learning group and shares it with them. The learning group then analyzes the material looking for techniques that are similar across different sports. In fact, any large body of reading or research material can be divided in this manner with each member taking responsibility to teach a portion of it to fellow group members. Such procedures require that every member participate in order for the group to be successful.

- *Interdependence with other groups.* the entire learning group is divided into subgroups with each smaller group investigating and reporting on some aspect of an individual topic or problem. For example, a learning group might be studying the causes, treatment, and prevention of juvenile delinquency. Each subgroup could take responsibility for a particular component within the topic with one group reporting on causes, a second group reporting on treatment, and a third dealing with prevention. Furthermore, after the presentations are made, people with similar role responsibilities (parents, educators, business people) can gather in small groups to discuss implications for their particular responsibilities. There are many variations of this overall process with greater interdependence as a common outcome.

- *Role interdependence.* Each member of a cooperative group is assigned a particular role that is complementary, interconnected, and essential to the roles of the other group members. For example, the learning goal is some form of skill development. One person is the *skill practicer.* Another person is the *recipient of the skill.* And a third person is the *observer/ evaluator.* In this manner each person has an essential contribution to make in terms of either skill practice or feedback. Roles can easily be rotated as well. Again, many variations of this condition are possible. For instance, the final goal is a paper or project. One person can be the *researcher,* another the *writer,* another the *editor,* and another the *typist/duplicator.* All of these possibilities contribute to group interdependence.

- *Positive goal interdependence.* Each group is requested to produce a single product, report, or paper. The process can be oriented toward comprehension, analysis, creativity, evaluation, skill development, or any combination of these. Outcomes could be a research report, a skill demonstration, a media project, an evaluation summary, a problem solution, an administrative plan, or just about anything that leads to greater learning and that a group can produce. The key issues are individual accountability and equal opportunity for learning. Individuals cannot let other members do all the work, nor can other members leave certain individuals out of the learning process. When necessary, two ways to ensure this are to make the group small enough so that contributions are more easily forthcoming and to ask for some kind of task accountability report so that each person's role and responsibilities are publicly acknowledged. The most important internal and interrelated messages in a group with a cooperative goal structure are "Do your part—we're counting on you" and "How can I help you to do better?" If there is a reward or evaluation for the group product, it should be equal for all group members. This emphasizes the necessity for collaboration and affirms the group members' interdependence. They do not count playing time in the championship game when they hand out those Super Bowl rings. Every team member receives one, and wisely so.

Any combination of the five forms of cooperative interdependence just cited is possible to structure within a learning group, depending on the learning goal, type of members, resources available, and time permitted. The following learning groups are defined and offered as examples where cooperative interdependence among adults may be a fruitful means for building group cohesiveness (Knowles, 1980).

- *Special-interest groups.* Groups organized according to categories of interests of participants for the purpose of sharing information, experiences, and exploring common concerns.
- *Problem-solving groups:* Groups organized to develop solutions to substantive problems of any nature.
- *Planning groups.* Groups organized to develop plans for activities such as field trips, guest speakers, resource utilization, and so forth.
- *Instructional groups.* Groups organized to receive specialized instruction in areas of knowledge or skill. The instructional task cannot be taught on a large group basis such as in a science laboratory, human relations seminar, or machine operation training course.
- *Investigation or inquiry groups.* Groups organized to search out information and report their findings to the entire learning group.
- *Evaluation groups.* Groups organized for the purpose of evaluating learning activities, learner behavior, and any issue that requires feedback or decision making on the part of the learning group or instructor.
- *Skill practice groups.* Groups organized for the purpose of practicing any set of specified skills.
- *Tutoring or consultative groups.* Groups organized for the purpose of tutoring, consulting, or giving assistance to other learning group members.
- *Operational groups.* Groups organized for the purpose of taking responsibility for the operations of activities important to the learning group such as room arrangements, refreshments, materials preparation, equipment operation, and so forth.
- *Learning-instruction groups.* Groups that take responsibility for learning all they can about a particular content unit and instructing themselves and/or the rest of the learning group.
- *Simulation groups.* Groups organized to conduct some intergroup exercise such as role playing, a game, or a case study review to increase knowledge or build skills.
- *Learning achievement groups.* Groups organized to produce a learning product that develops their knowledge, skills, or creativity.

4. *Monitoring and assisting.* Once the cooperative learning group starts working, the role of the instructor is one of observer, adviser, and consultant. If possible, and without being obtrusive, it pays to watch cooperative groups, especially as they *begin* their tasks. Sometimes we can see that certain groups need clarification or guidance. Otherwise, we are available to provide information, mediation, and assistance when it seems needed and desirable to the cooperative group members, always keeping in mind that it is the learners themselves who are the major resources for support and assistance to one another.

5. *Assessment.* For the learning product of a cooperative group the normal guidelines for effective evaluation remain intact. However, if the cooperative learning process has been of long duration with a major learning product and an obviously intense experience for participants, some time devoted to discussion or evaluation of the group process itself can be quite beneficial. Learners may want to share what they have learned in this regard and the instructor may benefit in terms of the value of this cooperative process for future groups of learners. This assessment should focus both on members' contributions to each other's learning and on how the maintenance of effective working relations occurred among group members. A questionnaire and/or discussion may be used for this purpose. Recommendations for improvement as well as an opportunity to indicate both negatively and positively contributing factors should be included in the assessment.

Research indicates that cooperation can be more effective than competition and individualistic efforts in promoting achievement and productivity in problem solving, creative tasks, concept attainment, retention tasks, motor performance, and relatively ambiguous assignments where learners have to estimate, judge, and predict as they investigate (Johnson and others, 1981). This is not to say that competitive and individualistic goal structures should be abandoned in adult training and education. For drill practice and enjoyment, when the stakes are not very high, individual and intergroup competition can be quite effective. Also, for any learning task where individual differences and abilities are significant, an individualized approach as in math or writing may be more helpful to the learners. In addition, cooperative groups can take considerable time to structure and operate. What matters most is that cooperation should dominate adult learning in the actual norms and the subjective atmosphere of the experience, with full realization on the part of the instructor that this cannot happen without some learning processes that are cooperatively structured. Furthermore, because cooperative learning builds and maintains cohesiveness with all its positive emotional consequences, the chances for more complete adult whole-brain functioning become ever present when such collaboration is a reality. Life's most important goals usually demand cooperation. The nurturing of our children, the quest for peace, and the search for our greatest discoveries have energized our mutual sharing and brought us together. Learning can serve this same purpose.

8

Building Learner Competence and Maximizing Reinforcement

CRGRGRGRGRGRGRGRGRGRGRS

> At the same time that we are almost too willing to yield to institutions that give us meaning and thus a sense of security, we also want self-determination. With equal vehemence, we simultaneously seek self-determination and security. This is certainly irrational. Yet those who don't somehow learn to manage the tension are, in fact, technically insane.
> —*Thomas J. Peters and Robert H. Waterman, Jr.*

Adults want to be competent and often seek learning as a means to this end. But competence is not just the resulting benefit of a learning achievement. It is, quite importantly for motivation, the personal feelings and beliefs that the process of learning can enhance or decrease in the learners themselves while they are learning. In learning, competence is seldom experienced without some external indicator of success whether that be feedback, test scores, praise, or rewards. These sources of information are often under the control of an instructor and the manner in which they are given has a significant impact on the degree of competence felt by learners. The effectiveness of these success indicators can also be explained by two rather opposing theories of motivation: cognitive evaluation theory and operant conditioning (reinforcement). To avoid endless theoretical debate and to move toward clearer issues of adult instruction, the question that seems most important at this point is should instructors of adults continuously guide what they do to build competence in learners on the basis of reinforcement theory? In general, the response to this question is a qualified no.

Operant conditioning is a major, significant, extremely well-researched theory. However, it does not seek to explain motivation in terms of the subjective cognitive and emotional states of human beings (Karoly, 1980). Competence is an internal experience for people. Adults feel degrees of competence in learning activities. Also, the developmental process and needs of adults are strongly oriented toward seeking competence both within learning activities and as an outcome of learning achievement (Cross, 1981; Knowles, 1980). Adults want to feel effective while they are learning and want to be more effective in their families, jobs, and communities as a result of what they have learned. Cognitive evaluation theory (Deci and Ryan, 1985) and its theoretical counterparts, personal causation theory (de Charms, 1968) and effectance theory (White, 1959), deal much more directly and comprehensively with the motivational influence of competence both during and after learning. While these theories view competence as a primary need and force in human behavior, operant conditioning explains competence as the result of applied and scheduled reinforcers.

Finally, and maybe most important, are the differences as well as the interaction between intrinsic and extrinsic motivation (Berlyne, 1960). Intrinsic motivation refers to the pleasure or value associated with an activity itself. In intrinsic motivation the "doing" is considered the primary reason for the performance of the behavior. There is good evidence that many learning activities involving manipulation, exploration, and information processing provide satisfaction in and of themselves. Many adults read because it is enjoyable, and many also write, compute, and think for the pleasure those processes provide. Extrinsic motivation emphasizes the value an individual places on the ends of an action and the probability of reaching those ends. In extrinsic motivation the goal rather than the "doing" is considered as the reason for the performance of the behavior. Therefore, to say that a learner acquired a skill or performed a task in order to receive a higher grade, or to advance in a job, or to receive praise from an instructor is to account for the learner's behavior primarily on the basis of extrinsic motivation. Serious questions have been raised about the influence of extrinsic rewards on learning behavior. One such criticism emanates from the research that has found that behavior that is well learned and controlled by extrinsic reinforcers often does not transfer to natural and uncontrolled environments (Kazdin and Bootzen, 1972). The concern here for adult instructors is does behavior that is learned through the application and control of carefully monitored extrinsic reinforcers become less likely to occur in natural settings outside the training environment? A second criticism is that extrinsic reward systems interfere with and decrease intrinsic motivation for learning (Ryan, Mims, and Koestner, 1983). Is it possible that using extrinsic rewards to enhance learning in adults actually undermines their interest and value for what is being learned? A third criticism comes from research that shows that when a learning-type activity (problem solving) is undertaken explicitly in order to attain some extrinsic reward, people respond by seeking the least demanding and most perfunctory way of ensuring reward attainment, even if that means doing the task becomes less interesting (Condry and Chambers, 1978). This tendency is described as the *minimax principle*—people are motivated to maximize reward with a minimum of effort (Kruglanski, Stein, and Riter, 1977). Do extrinsic rewards encourage learners to take shortcuts and to produce inferior learning performances and products?

These are grave and sensible questions. And, although it must be admitted that most of these studies have been done in laboratories with college students and do not measure long-term achievement, they do caution us about the uniform merit of applying external reinforcers to enhance adult learning. There is also another vantage point from which to judge these studies, our common experience as adult learners. How many courses and seminars have we entered with interest and anticipation, and left bored and apathetic? How many courses and seminars have we completed knowing full well we would apply very little of what we learned? Confessions aside, I myself claim more than a few. It seems reasonable, and in some instances quite memorable, that the emphasis on extrinsic reinforcers had more than a little to do with some of those outcomes. That is why, for reasons related to adult development, personal experience, and research, this chapter will be more oriented toward a competence viewpoint than a reinforcement perspective.

Unlike operant conditioning, motivational theories that accept the need for competence as inborn see this need as one that is not to be *acquired* but as one that already exists and that can be *strengthened or weakened* through learning experiences. Therefore, these theories and their related research have many more subtle and intricate ideas to enhance adult competence and to prevent its deterioration. In fact, in more than a few instances, these ideas are not oppositional to reinforcement theory but contain qualifications and suggestions that guard against the possible detrimental effects of a more simplified application of extrinsic reinforcers. Some reinforcement theorists might even argue that the competence theorists have simpy developed better ways to make reinforcers more rewarding. But that is not an issue for this book to settle. With this understanding, this chapter will first discuss all those motivational strategies that can be applied toward the end of a learning activity from a competence perspective before it deals with those strategies that seem to more exclusively belong to the domain of operant conditioning.

How to Help Adults to Be Self-Determined Learners

As discussed earlier (Chapter Five), most adults are experienced self-directed learners (Tough, 1979). When they do learn on their own in preference to taking a course, their ability to self-determine such issues as learning pace, style, flexibility, and structure seems to play a large part in their selection of this option (Penland, 1979). Also, most people who voluntarily undertake a learning project do so usually to solve a problem. Their desire to be effective in doing things they value seems to be a strong component in their motivation (Cross, 1981). This is exactly as cognitive evaluation theory would predict (Deci and Ryan, 1985). People have an innate need to be competent, effective, and self-determining. These strivings form the psychological basis for their intrinsic motivation and lead them to seek out and conquer challenges that are optimal for their capacities. Knowles (1978) and his theory of adult andragogy would offer an almost identical interpretation. However, when people take courses and training under the guidance of an instructor, the quality of their motivation and behavior may appear to be strikingly different. Many instructors have worked with adults who enter educational and training situations who are dependent, lacking in self-confidence, and often unmotivated for the learning tasks that lie ahead of them. Cross's (1981) Characteristics of Adults as Learners (CAL) model would explain this type of dependency as a function of the personal characteristics of the adult and the situational characteristics of the learning experience. For example, some adults, no matter what their age, are not very mature learners who would feel especially insecure in a compulsory learning situation. The CAL model is probably a more realistic perspective for such matters than the one that andragogy provides. Cognitive evaluation theory would explain this type of dependency as probably due to the lack of personal control in learning that is already felt by the adult learner that is intensified by the controlling or noncontingent events in the learning environment. From this perspective, some adults see the locus of causality for learning as outside of themselves or unpredictable. The learning situation they are in confirms such expectancies leading to further apprehension or passivity.

Such an analysis helps to focus on a singular quality that is essential to adult motivation for learning. *When adults see themselves as the locus of causality for their learning, they are much more likely to be intrinsically and positively motivated.* Adult self-directed personal learning projects have this important ingredient in their natural structure. But once adult learners come face-to-face with instructors in courses, seminars, and training programs, especially if they feel pressured into taking them, the locus of causality may shift away from themselves. Along with that shift goes intrinsic motivation and a sense of self-determination. And here is the rub—for reasons of *personal security,* this is likely to frequently happen to many adults. They need courses and training, in many instances, not so much because they want them, but because they need the jobs, the promotions, and the money for which these learning experiences are basic requirements. That is their reality and for many adults it may be one about which they feel little choice or sense of volition. In their eyes, they are merely surviving, holding on, stopping the downward spiral, and making themselves less expendable. Unemployment is not a figment of someone's imagination. And yet, even within the actuality of such a grim existence, human beings still have an innate need for self-determination. Anything we as instructors can do to maximize the perception of adults that the actions they take as learners are their own will meet this need and has the potential to enhance intrinsic motivation.

Building competence and self-determination go hand in hand. No one wants incompetent, self-determined adults. They make a lot of trouble and blunders. But what about the reverse? A competent, other-determined adult. That's a robot, not a very appealing choice for most of us. According to cognitive evaluation theory, competent, self-determined people are aware of their needs and feelings, make choices on the basis of these, and are effective in dealing with their environments (Deci and Ryan, 1985). Helping adults to take ownership of their learning and to make learning experiences worthy of adult choice, in the beginning and during phases of learning activities, has been dealt with in the previous four chapters. The following motivation strategies will consider what instructors can do to enhance the locus of causality within adult learners as well as to increase their feelings of competence at the ending of a learning activity.

When learners are concluding learning activities, most instructor interventions address some quality of their progress, mastery, or responsibility in the learning task. According to cognitive evaluation theory, these events can be seen as *informational* or *controlling.* Informational transactions tell learners something about their effectiveness and support their sense of self-

determination for learning. Controlling transactions tend to undermine self-determination by making learner behavior appear to be
dependent on implicit or explicit forces that demand, coerce, or
seduce the learner's compliance. They encourage the learner to
believe the reason for learning is some external condition outside
of the learner or the learning activity itself, such as a reward or
instructor pressure. When verbally communicated, they often contain imperative locutions such as *should* and *must*. For example, an
instructor might say to an adult learner, "Your performance was
excellent. As soon as I made the feedback concrete, you were really
able to apply your skill" (informational). Or the same instructor
might say, "Your performance was excellent. As soon as I made the
feedback concrete, you did exactly as you should do" (controlling).
The difference between these two series of statements may seem
subtle but is, nonetheless, very important. The former encourages
self-determination while the latter places much more of the emphasis for learning performance in the direction of the instructor's
control. The following competence strategies will always emphasize
the informational approach. It is andragogically sound, builds
learner responsibility, and has a greater chance to maintain and
increase intrinsic motivation.

Telling adults they learn for extrinsic reasons may, indeed,
be true. But in many ways this can deny the reality of what they
really want—to enjoy learning as well as to reap the benefits of its
achievement. By stressing that learning is a means to an end, we
gradually make the means less desirable. We create an expectancy
that this must be so. We discount the act of learning itself. That is
like cutting off the branches of a tree to get its fruit. We destroy the
beauty and diminish the possibility of the tree's future harvests.
Most adults want motivating learning for motivating rewards. The
same is true of work and family life. Emphasizing their personal
ownership in learning will not make the rewards for it any less, and
it will create a better chance for self-determination and intrinsic
motivation. It also increases the chances that future learning will
be more nurturing and attractive, and in a civilization where
lifelong learning is a reality, that literally means an enhancement
in the quality of adult life.

How to Provide Effective Feedback

Feedback is information that learners receive about the quality of their performance on a given task. It usually comes at the end of the learning behavior or at the completion of the learning activity. Knowledge of results, comments about skill performance, notes on a written assignment, graphic records, and an approving nod are forms of feedback that instructors often use with adult learners. Feedback appears to enhance learners' motivation because it allows them to evaluate their progress, to understand the level of their competence, to maintain their effort toward realistic goals, to correct their errors with little delay, and to receive encouragement from their instructors. Since adults have such a prominent need for effectiveness, their persistence in learning tasks is strongly enhanced when they can obtain feedback about the extent and type of change in their competence that results from an educational activity (Knox, 1977). This is especially true for adults who lack confidence as learners (Cross, 1981).

Strategy 59: Provide consistent feedback to learners regarding their mastery, progress, and responsibility in learning.

In general, feedback is probably the most powerful intervention that an instructor can regularly use to affect learner competence. It can also be far more complex than a few words about a learner's progress on a given assignment. The following characteristics are elements an instructor can consider in designing the most positively influential structure and style for feedback distribution.

• *Informational rather than controlling.* Generally, the more the learner is likely to interpret what the instructor says as pressure to achieve a particular consequence or outcome, the less likely it is that the learner will be intrinsically motivated to perform that activity (Ryan, 1982). On the other hand, feedback that does not imply pressure to attain particular consequences or outcomes and that does convey positive mastery information is more likely to enhance interest in the learning activity. Thus, feedback that implies improvement, progress, or correction in order to please the instructor, or for the sole purpose of gaining consequent rewards, goals, or grades, is generally to be avoided. Feedback that relates to the learner's increasing mastery and personal ownership of that mastery is to be emphasized. For example, "You've cut your error rate in half. You're making significant improvement in skill performance" rather than "You've cut your error rate in half. I'm glad to see you're going to meet the standard I set for skill performance." (Where possible, all further examples will demonstrate the informational approach.)

• *Based on performance standards.* Whenever possible, give feedback to learners based on how well their performance met the preset performance standard. This clarifies for learners the criteria against which their performance was judged and more explicitly indicates what needs to be done for further effective learning so the learners can more accurately guide their future attention, practice, or performance. Under these conditions, learners will be less likely to feel that the feedback merely represents the instructor's bias or personal opinion. For example, "We agreed that any project containing more than six errors would be returned for revision. I've indicated where those errors are located as well as some explanatory references you might want to consider if you need them."

• *Specific with suggested corrective procedures.* Bruner (1968) emphasizes that learning depends on knowledge of results "at a time when and at a place where the knowledge can be used for correction" (p. 50). Learners cannot correct mistakes unless they are informed concretely of their errors and, in most cases, are directed toward more appropriate responses. It is difficult to correct performance when a person is told only in general terms how well that person did. It is much better to describe the behavior in very specific terms and to suggest something the person could do to improve. For example, "Your left front wheel hit the sidewalk when you turned the car. Try to turn the steering wheel another half turn to the right next time." Implied in this characteristic is that learners receive adequate opportunity to correct their mistakes or to improve their performance. In general, the juxtaposition between corrective feedback and opportunity for learner application of this information should be quite close and efficient. This significantly improves learning as well as learner motivation and avoids learner frustration.

• *Supportive of self-evaluation and self-correction.* In terms of the adult needs for self-determination and self-direction, these are ideal feedback characteristics, but they are not easily achievable for every instructor. Self-evaluation means the learners are capable of measuring and judging their own performance. Functionally, this may mean something as simple as self-scoring answer sheets or as complex as a cooperative group evaluation based on comparison with an evaluation model. Self-evaluation saves instructor time, ensures that everyone gets feedback without delay, and strengthens the learners' awareness of personal responsibility for learning. When employing self-evaluation procedures, the instructor will have to be certain the learners know how to evaluate their performance, have the proper materials for self-evaluating, and regularly spot-check the work of a few learners to make sure everyone is maintaining a high standard of accuracy. Self-correction means the learners take over the corrective functions themselves. They understand the performance standard, know what to do to get there, and can evaluate the evidence that they have arrived. When learners can do this, their self-confidence is significantly enhanced. They have learned how to instruct themselves. For example, a learner writes a report, uses an exemplary model of another report to edit it, and hands in the finished product.

• *Quantitative.* There are some researchers who believe that feedback is most effective when it is given in numerical terms (Van Houten, 1980). This may not always be possible, but it does have some definite advantages. It is certainly precise and it can effectively show small improvements. And small improvements can produce large changes in the long run. One way to understand learning behavior is by *rate,* which is to indicate how often it occurs over a fixed time. For example, learners are told they completed thirty laps during a one-hour swimming practice. Another way is to decide what *percent* of learning behavior is correct or appropriate. Correct percentages are calculated by dividing the number of times the learning behavior occurs correctly by the total number of times the learning behavior occurs. Someone learning how to appropriately package a given product might be told 80 percent of the boxes were effectively wrapped and sealed (forty out of fifty attempts were correctly performed). Another common form of quantitative feedback is *duration,* which is how long it takes a learning behavior to be completed. For example, a lab technician might receive feedback on how long it takes that person to complete a particular chemical analysis. These are not all the forms of quantitative feedback that are possible, but they are a representative sample. Whenever learning appears to be slow or difficult to ascertain, quantitative feedback can be an excellent means to enhance learner competence.

• *Prompt.* This characteristic is carefully chosen in preference to *immediate* because it means that feedback should be ready, and quickly given as the occasion demands, rather than as soon as possible. There is good evidence that sometimes a moderate delay in feedback aids retention and enhances learning because such delay allows learners to more easily forget incorrect responses and, therefore, to have less cognitive interference with learning the appropriate or correct response (Surber and Anderson, 1975). This is probably more true of conceptual than physical skill learning. Also, none of the studies that support prompt over immediate feedback waited longer than twenty-four hours to administer the feedback, and some only waited as long as a fifteen-second delay. So, in general, it is best to be quick with feedback but to carefully pay attention to whether any delay might be beneficial, remembering that excessive delay of feedback decreases learner motivation, causes feedback to lose its effectiveness, and increases learner anxiety.

• *Frequent.* Some studies have found that the more often feedback is provided, the more rapidly people seem to learn (Van Houten, 1980). Frequent feedback is probably most helpful when new behaviors are first being acquired. In general, feedback should be given when improvement is most possible. Once errors have accumulated, learners will see improvements as more difficult and be less motivated to change. Also, once multiple errors become more established, the new behaviors encouraged through feedback seem more foreign and confusing to learners, making further progress seem even more remote. Therefore, if possible, it is not unwise to consider giving feedback each time a new learning task is performed until a reasonable standard of performance has been achieved.

• *Positive.* Positive feedback places emphasis on improvements, progress, and correctness rather than on deficiencies and mistakes. It is an excellent form of feedback because it increases learners' intrinsic motivation, feelings of well-being, sense of competence, and positive attitude toward those who have given this information. People prefer positive feedback because when they are trying to improve, emphasis on errors and deficiencies (negative feedback) can be discouraging and punishing. Even when learners are prone toward mistakes, as long as an instructor can show a *decrease* in errors, this may be considered positive feedback. Also, positive feedback can be given with corrective feedback. For example, an instructor might say to a learner, "You're making fine progress. You've been able to solve 85 percent of these problems without any errors. Let's take a look at the remaining 15 percent to see what can be done about them."

• *Personal and differential.* Differential feedback focuses on the increment of personal improvement that has occurred since the last time the learning task was performed. In skill or procedural learning, such as writing, operating a machine, or learning a particular sport, emphasizing small steps of progress can be very encouraging to learner motivation. This procedure also has the advantage of using self-comparison for improvement gains rather than comparison with other members of the learning group. This reduces feelings of competitiveness or pressure from evaluation based on how other members of the learning group are performing on the same task. Almost everyone can succeed at bettering themselves and have a chance for more frequent success when their own learning progress becomes the basis for measuring gains in learning. Also, the time allowed before such differential feedback is given can become quite important. For example, by reporting improvement based on a daily or weekly schedule rather than after each performance, learners may see greater gains and feel a larger sense of accomplishment.

In addition to the specific characteristics of feedback just listed, some refinements in the composition and delivery of feedback may be helpful, depending on the circumstances of instruction. Sometimes *graphing or charting* feedback can be encouraging to learner motivation because it makes progress more concrete and shows a record of increasing improvement. When effort is in question (the learner may lack confidence or interest), the *shorter the interval before feedback is given,* the more likely the learner will participate in order to receive feedback. For example, doing one problem with the knowledge that feedback will then be given may seem much more attractive than doing ten problems before feedback is initiated. Sometimes *asking adults what they would like feedback on* can be beneficial. Their needs and concerns may be different than ours as instructors, and the knowledge from such interviewing procedures can make the feedback we give more relevant and motivating. Adult *readiness to receive feedback* can also be important. If people are not ready to hear what we have to say, they are not likely to learn as much. For example, for instructors this may mean holding off on feedback until a personal conference can be arranged or until learners are more comfortable with the learning situation. There are times when *checking to make sure our feedback was understood* may be important. This is certainly true for complex feedback or situations in which learners seem very anxious. Also, everything that has been said about feedback thus far could also apply to *group feedback.* Whether it is a team, a cooperative group, or an instructional class, feedback on their total performance can influence each individual and help to enhance group cohesiveness and esprit de corps because group feedback consolidates their mutual identification. This is as true for a team batting average as it is for an adult typing class where the average number of words typed per minute for the entire class is posted weekly. Finally, sometimes the best form of feedback is to simply allow learners to move forward to the next more challenging learning task after successful performance on a prior task. They know they have done it correctly and any further information would only be an impediment to their progress. Computer-assisted instruction uses this technique on a regular basis (Hofmeister, 1984). To fluidly proceed through learning activities with a constant sense of forward movement builds a sense of accomplishment and enhances feelings of competence as well. This is also the purpose that much *simple positive feedback* serves, such as "Right," "Correct," "Fine," "Continue," "Proceed," or "Okay." In many learning situations that are not complex or that do not require further precise elaboration or correction, such feedback is desirable and works effectively to enhance learner competence and achievement.

Strategy 60: When necessary, use constructive criticism.

Constructive criticism is similar to negative feedback, but with a few more qualifications. It does emphasize errors and deficiencies in learning, but unlike basic criticism it does not connote expressions of disapproval, disgust, or rejection. In general, criticism does not have to be used as often as we may think. Instructors may have a tendency to overuse criticism when they do not know how to properly use feedback and/or work with learners who do not have proper entry-level skills for the learning task they are required to perform. The latter condition can often be alleviated through more appropriate selection and guidance procedures, such as pretesting and interviews. However, there are still circumstances where constructive criticism may be a necessary instructor strategy at the end of a learning activity.

1. When the learning process is extremely costly or involves a threat to human safety, mistakes cannot be afforded. Training with a particular machine, weapon, chemical, or medical procedure are examples of this type of situation.
2. When the learning performance is so poor that to emphasize success or improvement would be ridiculous or patronizing.
3. When the learning performance has significant errors and there are only a few remaining chances for improvement in the training or course situation.
4. When a learner directly requests criticism.

Constructive criticism may be a helpful and motivating way to deal with these situations. Like feedback, constructive criticism has the following qualities: informational, based on performance standards, behaviorally specific, corrective, prompt, and, when possible, it allows for efficient opportunities for improvement. In addition, where appropriate, constructive criticism has the following characteristics:

1. It helps the learner to see performance in the context of overall progress and not momentary failure. For example, "This science unit has really been tough for you. Your exam indicates

that 70 percent of the concepts are still unclear to you. I hope you keep in mind that you've already progressed through four units, and although this one seems difficult, that's a pretty good indication that you can do it. Let's go over the material."

2. It respectfully informs the learner of the conditions that lead to the emphasis on mistakes or deficiencies. For example, "This machine can be quite dangerous. For your own safety, before you get another chance to operate it, I think we'd better take a look at any mistakes you might have made" or "You've got only one more chance to practice before you meet with the review committee. I think the best use of our time would be to check your performance on the last case study and to concentrate on any mistakes that show up."

3. It acknowledges learner effort. For example, "There's no doubt you've put a great deal of work into this report. Just the number of references you cite testifies to the effort and comprehensive research that went into this project. The trouble is with its organization. There's no unifying theme that ties all this evidence together. What generalization could you think of that might serve this purpose?"

4. It provides emotional support. For example, "Your work with this client was not successful. In fact, you may have tried too hard. You put on too much pressure and didn't respond adequately to the client's stated needs. We can analyze the videotape to see just where this happened. However, you did very well with the other two clients you worked with. Since you have only one more chance to practice in this seminar, let's be as careful as possible to understand what might have gone wrong. I have considerable confidence that you'll be able to improve."

In both feedback and constructive criticism situations, it may be helpful for learners to know that more effort on their part can significantly contribute to their progress. This is, of course, done in an informational manner rather than as a pressuring tactic. The strategy that explains why and how to do this attribution is found in Chapter Four.

Using Praise and Rewards Wisely

In this book, the term *praise* has the same meaning and connotations it usually has in everyday language: to commend the worth of or to express approval or admiration (Brophy, 1981). It is an intense response on the part of an instructor going beyond positive feedback because, along with some indication of the degree of success of the learner, it includes such positive emotions as surprise, delight, or excitement and demonstrates real value for the learner's accomplishment ("That's a remarkable answer. It's comprehensive, insightful, and extremely precise."). Although instructors use praise as a strategy to enhance adult learner motivation, many researchers do not favor praise. Some see it as having the potential to reduce intrinsic motivation (Lepper and Greene, 1978). Others are critical of praise because it may contribute to a differential status between learners and instructors. Instructors distribute praise because they are the judges and experts who deem learners as praiseworthy. This may diminish their chances for a more egalitarian relationship. Although praise can be reinforcing, there is considerable research that shows that it does not always or even usually serve this function. Much of the evidence and suggestions regarding praise that follow are based on an analysis by Brophy (1981) that largely used studies done with children and adolescents. However, this work is heavily supported by research conducted with young adults (Ryan, Mims, and Koestner, 1983; Weiner, 1980a). Also, nothing is reported or recommended that does not receive substantiation from my experience as an adult instructor and from the principles of andragogy as a theoretical foundation (Knowles, 1980).

Praise is often ineffective because it is not related to exemplary achievement, lacks specificity (the learner does not know exactly why it was given), and is not credible. For example, sometimes it is given because learners elicit it themselves. They seem happy and enthusiastic about their work, show it to us, and we do not know what else to say. Other times we may give it because we feel sorry for learners who are having difficulty and use it to boost their morale. Such actions on our part as instructors devalue the currency of praise and depreciate its influence. Also, many competent adults do not want or expect praise. They want clear, positive feedback about their progress and may experience praise as annoying or patronizing. Furthermore, praise given too frequently and indiscriminately may begin to seem perfunctory and predictable to learners, encouraging them to interpret it as a form of instructor flattery or "jabber." The focus of praise on form rather than substance can cause a problem as well. Praise for when assignments come in or how learning responses agree with instructor values and directives may seem controlling and manipulative. In some instances, praise has even been used to terminate learner behavior. A learner-initiated discussion is, perhaps, in our opinion, going on a bit too long. We toss out a compliment on what has been said to provide pleasant closure and move on to something else.

In general, instructors who want to praise effectively need to praise *well*, rather than necessarily *often*. The same could be said about rewarding effectively. In fact, praise is often considered to be a verbal reward (Pittman, Boggiano, and Ruble, 1983). Whether verbal (praise) or tangible (money, promotions, privileges, and so forth) or symbolic (grades, trophies, awards, and so forth), there are guidelines that can be followed to more closely ensure the positive effects of these rewards on learner competence and intrinsic motivation (Brophy, 1983). Rewards for learning have the same vulnerability to being cast in the eyes of adult learners as controlling, indiscriminate, unfair, insincere, and invalid, just as praise itself might be regarded (Morgan, 1984; Lepper, 1983; and Ryan, Mims, and Koestner, 1983). The following strategy and its related guidelines will be discussed in detail to minimize the possible liabilities and to maximize the possible benefits of praise and other rewards for learning (Brophy, 1983).

Strategy 61: Effectively praise and reward learning.

In general, praise, like feedback, can be given frequently during learning and tends to come at the end of a particular behavior or activity. Other rewards (tangible or symbolic) tend to be given at the completion of a series or longer unit of learning behavior in adult learning situations. This distinction is mentioned because praise and feedback probably act more as a constant force during overall learning, with tangible or symbolic rewards (grades, awards, money, and so forth) becoming more salient at the completion of the general learning activities (Spence and Helmreich, 1983). There should be no interference among the three components if the following guidelines are respected. For purposes of clarity, rewards will be discussed in their more terminal sense because in adult educational settings (token economies are relatively rare), that is where they normally occur. Characteristics of effective praise and rewards are as follows:

1. Given contingent on noteworthy effort or success at challenging (for the particular learner) tasks. This makes the reward or praise informational and testifies to the competence of the learner. It implies some difficulty was overcome and the learner deserves the recognition that has been received. If the task was not challenging, then the praise would be indiscriminate and a reward, if given, would tend to be seen as likewise, or as a form of pay for participation rather than as a reward for excelling. Such indiscriminate distribution pushes the reward more toward the controlling end of its influence, with more potential for the minimax principle to take effect. In general, it is more accurate and helpful to adult learners to call rewards by another name when they are given for reasons other than special achievement or effort.

2. Given based on the attainment of specified performance criteria (which can include effort) that indicate the particulars of the accomplishment. This means a standard, whether normative or individual, has been achieved and the learner can clearly understand what specific personal behaviors are being acknowledged. This not only makes the reward or praise informational but significantly increases the person's chances of learning exactly which behaviors are desirable and important. For example, "Nice job," written on a paper is not as helpful as, "This paper has not a single spelling or grammatical error in it. I appreciate the meticulous writing and editing it obviously reflects."

3. Given attributing success to the personal effort and/or ability of the learner, with some indication whenever possible of the value of the accomplishment for its own sake. Emphasizing the learner's effort and/or ability increases the learner's sense of internal causality and implies the learner can continue such accomplish-

ments in the future as well. Combining this attribute with indication of the value of the accomplishment for its own sake confirms
such ownership because the learning task is admittedly worthy of
personal effort and/or ability in its own right. If the ability/effort
component is missing, the learner might more likely think the
accomplishment was due to some external factor like luck or
instructor favoritism. If the value component is missing or shifted
to external reasons, the learner might more likely think that
personal effort or ability was exercised because of pressure from
instructor surveillance or need for the extrinsic reward. When
external factors beyond the person or the accomplishment itself
seem to account for learning, a sense of competence and intrinsic
motivation are less likely to be enhanced. For example, note the
difference in the two forms of praise that follow. The first contains
both components (ability and accomplishment value). The second
shifts the reason for personal ability to an external cause. It doesn't
feel the same. (1) "Your design of this model is excellent. It meets
all the criteria for strength, durability, and esthetics. I'd like to share
it with the rest of the team. I think we could all learn from it." (2)
"Your design of this model is excellent. It meets all of the criteria
for strength, durability, and esthetics. I'm glad I was able to
influence you to take on this project." (For a general use of
attribution methods with any successful outcome, see Chapter
Four.)

4. Given with sincerity, spontaneity, variety, and other signs
of credibility. This may be a bit more true for praise than for other
rewards. Rewards are often known ahead of time and given with
more uniformity. However, the affect with which a reward is given
is critical to its impact on the learner. An insincerely given reward
or form of praise is really an insult to an adult. (A personal note:
I have conducted hundreds of workshops in which I have asked
instructors to volunteer the guidelines for effective praise. Without
exception, sincerity has been listed as the number one guideline.)

5. Adapted to the preference of the individual. Again, this
may be a bit more true for praise than for other rewards. Rewards
are often given in a regularized or ritualistic manner, such as award
ceremonies and merit systems. However, one would certainly want
rewards to be attractive and valued in relation to the learner's

personal preferences. When it comes to praise, this guideline often refers to the public or private manner in which it is given. Some people cringe in response to public praise but appreciate such sentiments expressed privately. A rule of thumb: When in doubt, it is probably best to give praise privately.

6. Adapted in sufficiency, quantity, and intensity to the specific accomplishments achieved. Rewards that are less than merited can be insulting and demeaning. Rewards that are too much for what has been accomplished are excessive, disturbing, emphasize external causality, and have some probability of diminishing intrinsic motivation if it exists (Morgan, 1984). There are common expressions in everyday language that reflect adult sensitivity and possible embarrassment in response to undeserved or inadequate praise: "No gushing over trivia" (too much praise) and "Damning with faint praise" (too little praise). They are sufficient guidelines unto themselves.

There is a mnemonic device to remember these six guidelines—"3S-3P," which stands for Sincere, Specific, Sufficient, Properly attributed, Praiseworthy, and Preferred. In sentence form, it would be stated as: *Praise (or other rewards) should be Sincere, Specific, Sufficient, and Properly attributed for genuinely Praiseworthy behavior in a manner Preferred by the learner.* It is also important to remember that the subjective viewpoint of the learner and the context in which praise and other rewards are given will immensely influence their effect (Morgan, 1984). As of now, there are no ways to accurately prescribe these conditions, except to encourage instructors to remain continually sensitive to their impact. Blanchard and Johnson (1982) recommend the use of touch and silence in giving praise. However, these techniques have not been widely researched and, for the time being, appear to be possible options, but not necessary requirements for communicating effective praise.

Using Evaluation Procedures and Tests to Support Motivation

Feedback, criticism, praise, and other rewards are usually based on some form of evaluation. How evaluation is structured and delivered can be supportive or detrimental to learner motivation.

The major purpose of evaluation in most educational situations is to find out how much change and growth have taken place as a result of educational experiences. Adult learners have a pressing need to know in what ways they have changed (Kidd, 1973). Since so much of their new learning may be soon applied, they are very interested in the evidence of these educational changes. Also, because they engage in most learning activities with some specific purpose in mind, their awareness of progress toward desired educational goals is vital to their personal motivation. However, they may be quite apprehensive about both the conditions and the results of evaluation procedures. Adults tend to undergo much more stress than youths in testing situations (Smith, 1982). They often feel awkward and anxious taking exams. Test anxiety is a serious and widespread problem among adults (Sarason, 1980). There are many reasons for their uneasiness. Among them are fear of revelation of ignorance, negative comparison with peers, and inability to meet personal standards and goals. (See Smith, 1982, for some helpful suggestions for training adults to cope with exams.)

Any evaluation procedure is likely to influence the learning behavior of adults. Because time and effort are limited commodities, evaluation procedures will tend to increase the proportion of time and effort people spend learning what they expect the evaluation procedures to measure (Frederiksen, 1984). Beyond the opportunity to provide feedback and rewards, evaluation procedures challenge learners to achieve certain standards and goals. The quality of that challenge and its influence on learner motivation is directly linked to how well the evaluation procedures measure desirable and important learning, as well as how effectively they communicate what is measured. The following two strategies are based on the assumption that the learners are clearly aware of the preset standards of performance that accurately reflect their educational needs (see Chapter Five).

Strategy 62: Use formative evaluation procedures to measure and communicate learner progress and mastery.

Formative evaluation procedures are generally diagnostic progress measures that determine whether or not the learner has mastered what is to be learned and what, if anything, the learner must still do to achieve mastery (Scriven, 1967). They are used essentially as part of the instructional-learning process to give continuous feedback, to assess strengths and weaknesses in learner performance, to diagnose areas of learning for progress and improvement, and to enhance instruction. Formative evaluation procedures pace the learning of adults and help motivate them to put forth the necessary effort at the appropriate time. They correspond to a well-defined content or skill portion of a course or training unit and help to ensure that each set of learning tasks is thoroughly mastered before subsequent learning tasks are started. For example, in an adult basic education course dealing with fractions, this may mean formative evaluation procedures are used to measure learner mastery of simple fractions before beginning work on more complex fractions. For any type of learning that is organized on a hierarchical basis where mastery of a specific area of content or skill is a prerequisite for continued mastery of more complex content or skills, formal evaluation procedures are excellent strategies to enhance learning and motivation. For those learners who have thoroughly mastered the particular unit of study, the feedback from formative evaluation procedures should confirm their sense of competence and assure them that their present mode of learning and approach to study is adequate. This should also reduce their anxiety about course achievement. For those learners who lack mastery of a particular unit of study, the formative evaluation procedures should reveal particular points of difficulty and indicate the specific ideas, skills, and processes that they still need to improve upon with the necessary corrective procedures to do so. This may not totally reduce their anxiety about achievement but should prevent them from feeling helpless and mitigate their feelings of frustration and worry that can often occur when people find themselves falling hopelessly behind in a learning task. Formative evaluation procedures can also provide feedback to the instructor to identify particular points in the instructional process that are in need of modification.

Formative evaluation procedures are most effective when they are separated from grading processes and not used as part of a judging or classification function. This assures learners that mistakes are not counted against them but are part of the learning process. This also maintains their motivation for higher achievement in the particular learning task because once a grade or classification has been "set" for a particular unit of study, it confirms closure for the task as well as tends to create self-fulfilling expectancies. For example, the learner might think, "Since I've already received two average ratings, I can't expect to do much better in this course." Also, when learners do well on or improve as a result of formative evaluations, they will generally be more confident when summative evaluations are finally given. Measuring what a learner has achieved at the completion of a course or training period (summative evaluation) is, no doubt, important to find out and to appraise. Mistakes and lack of improvement will have to be noted at such time. There are scores of books on evaluation that deal with this issue. However, the main point being made is that formative evaluation procedures can positively contribute to and enhance adult learning and motivation until such final assessments are necessary.

In general, adults become more competent, feel more confident, and look forward to evaluation procedures when these assessments meet these guidelines:

- Clearly related to goals and objectives that they understand and want to achieve.
- Reflective of progress in learning.
- Diagnostic and point out ways to improve learning without penalizing them.
- Expected.
- Returned promptly.
- Permeated with instructor comments that are informative and supportive.
- Used to encourage new challenges in learning.

See Knowles (1980) for an excellent discussion of self-diagnostic models of evaluation for adult instruction.

Strategy 63: Whenever possible, use performance evaluation procedures to help the learner realize how to operationalize in daily living what has been learned.

Performance evaluation procedures are one of the oldest forms of assessment. They are the construction of situations in which the learner actually performs a sample of the behaviors with which a given learning experience is concerned (Knowles, 1980). It is important to add that this strategy should resemble as closely as possible the ways in which what has been learned will ultimately be expressed. This may be a real situation in which an actual learned behavior, such as operating a machine or carrying out a procedure, is performed and the performance is rated by observers, timed, or otherwise measured. Also, it may be a simulated situation, in which conditions as much like those in real life as possible are created for demonstration of performance. If we want to measure how well a person has learned to repair TV sets, we can present TV sets needing repair. If we want to measure medical diagnostic procedures, we can provide simulations of medical problems or even live simulated patients (Elstein, Shulman, and Sprafka, 1978). The closer evaluation procedures come to allowing learners to demonstrate what they have learned in the reality where that learning will eventually be used, the greater their motivation to do well, and the more they can understand their competence and feel the self-confidence that emerges from effective performance. Whether formative or summative, a performance evaluation procedure is one of the best ways to conclude a learning activity because it promotes transfer of learning, enhances motivation for related work and learning activities, and clarifies learner competence. It also directly meets the adult need to use and apply what has been learned for more effective daily living. With such performance evaluation procedures, there is far less chance that adult learners will view what has been learned as too idealistic or unimportant.

When reality is too dangerous, difficult, or expensive to construct, then performance evaluation procedures may take the form of simulations, critical incident cases, games, exercises, role playings, and response-inviting computer, video, audio, or written materials. Where advisable, such procedures can be used on a pretest-posttest basis. Knowles (1980) is a fine source for further ideas and references that elaborate performance evaluation procedures.

Further Means for Affirming Learner Competence and Responsibility

There are more than a few important things that can enhance adult competence that do not easily fit under the categories of feedback, praise, or other rewards. They may also not come as the result of any standard evaluation procedure. They may be things that the learners know about but we as instructors do not. They may also be elements that were not included in the performance standards but are critical nonetheless, such as creativity or cooperation. In some instances, they may be part of the human experience that learners and instructors share because they have worked and accomplished something together, and now know each other as unique individuals. The following strategy provides for these less easily categorized outcomes of learning and helps to place them in a framework that can enhance learner competence, responsibility, and ownership.

Strategy 64: Acknowledge and affirm the learners' responsibility and any significant actions or characteristics that contributed to the successful completion of the learning task.

There are a number of ways to do this depending on time, situation, and learner needs. The idea is this: If there is anything significant that the learner has done or exemplified that has contributed to that individual's successful achievement, consider those means that can be used to reflect this back to the learner. This implies that the standard means of providing feedback, praise, or other rewards were not appropriate, preferred, available, or sensitive enough as methods to effectively have the impact on competence desired by the instructor. Or the instructor may believe that some means to further accentuate these competence indicators is merited. Some specific ways to do this are as follows:

1. *Interview learners for their opinions as to how and what were the critical processes that helped them to achieve successful*

completion of the learning task. This method is especially useful with self-directed individual and small group learning projects. Simple and direct questions such as the following can intensify and broaden learners' awareness of their personal competence: What did you do that made this task achievable? How were you the prime reason for your own learning? What do you think was most significant in accomplishing this task? Which choices did you make that led to this accomplishment? What have you learned about yourself from doing this?

Any questions directed to the various aspects of learner responsibility for learning can help learners to focus their attention on their personal effectiveness in bringing about their own learning. A more formative approach to competence in self-directed learning that is still progressing might be this set of four questions asked at an appropriate interval: What is your evaluation of what you have done so far? How can you still improve? How can you help yourself? How can I help you?

2. *Acknowledge the risk taking and challenge involved in the learning accomplishment.* As discussed in Chapter Five, when adults deliberately choose a challenging learning goal, the process of learning becomes even more special because they have knowingly placed themselves under the risk of failure. This condition adds to what they can learn about themselves. With further reflection, they can build their self-confidence and experience the merit of their abilities and effort. On the other hand, nonachievement of the learning goal can be a lesson in reality testing that encourages self-appraisal and further decision making. When there is success, there is good reason for jubilation and self-affirmation. When there is failure, the related issues can be explored through these questions: What has been learned from attempting to achieve the goal? Does the goal remain worthwhile? Is it reasonable to continue to strive for the goal? If not, what is the next best step?

In either success or failure, we help the learner to acknowledge what has been risked and how the acceptance of and striving toward a challenge have benefited the learner. This is best done through personal discussion. Taking on learning challenges that are reasonable and personally valued is a form of courage—the courage to persevere, the courage to extend personal boundaries, the courage to embrace learning for its own sake. These are not spontaneous human qualities. They are cultivated and evolve. As instructors, we can help them to grow in adult learners by reflecting where they occur and by acknowledging their substance and value.

3. *Affirm the strengths and assets of learners that contribute to their own achievement or the accomplishment of others in learning.* When instructors and learners work together for a period of time, they begin to recognize in each other various qualities that are beneficial to learning and interpersonal cohesiveness. Many of these characteristics may not be easily classified as effort or ability under the performance standards being applied. Also, they may not be praiseworthy in an absolute sense or on a comparative basis. However, they are significant enough to be recognized and influential enough to be appreciated. Helping learners to be aware of these assets in themselves will raise their self-esteem and make these strengths more available for competent use in future learning and work situations. We want learners to know about them as a general resource and, therefore, we do not have to relate them to a specific behavior or performance standard. For example, a statement such as "I just wanted you to know that I really enjoyed your sense of humor in this course" could suffice. This can be done on an informal one-to-one basis or as a concluding group exercise where each learner and the instructor are allowed two statements of appreciation to anyone about anything that has occurred during the course. Otto (1975) describes more formal and comprehensive methods to actualize this technique.

The following are some strengths and assets that learners often possess and can benefit from knowing:

Writing skills	Thinking skills
Physical skills	Experience
Planning skills	Cooperativeness
Personal traits	Creativity
Verbal skills	Math skills
Knowledge base	Sense of humor
Organizational skills	Helpfulness
Significant actions	Leadership skills

This list is more suggestive than exhaustive. The main point is that if we only follow the guidelines that have been previously set for feedback and praise, we may miss giving important information to learners that often results from the total human experience of the learning situation. Also, this approach provides for learner-to-learner feedback, which may not always follow strict guidelines but sometimes may have as much or more of a positive impact on the learner than anything an instructor might communicate.

Effective Use of Positive Reinforcement

One of the insights that Peters and Waterman (1982) make about the use of positive reinforcement is that it is an excellent means to help people move in directions where they are already headed. Positive reinforcement can be a gentle and precise way to develop and maintain adult motivation for learning. Rather than push, prod, or pull adults toward desired learning, it can invite, encourage, and confirm what they are capable of doing and achieving. If we have provided learning that meets their needs (and everything in this book supports this notion), then we can logically assume they want to learn and with reasonable support and effective instruction, they will do so. Positive reinforcement can be part of that support, the finishing touch that maintains and enhances their motivation. Feedback, praise, and other rewards have been discussed in a manner that maximizes their value to learner competence and intrinsic motivation. The remaining strategies will follow the more traditional guidelines of operant conditioning but will also be cast in a context and with a purpose that are supportive of adult development and self-determination.

Strategy 65: Use incentives to encourage adult participation in learning activities that are initially unattractive.

An *incentive* may be defined as an anticipated reinforcer (Hill, 1981). It serves as a goal we expect to achieve as a result of some specific behavior. Incentives take many forms, such as recognition, money, relationships, and privileges. Adults' lives are filled with incentives that are often the goals for which they strive and work. It is possible for something such as a particular job to become an incentive through learning or reading about it. When a series of behaviors becomes linked into a goal-seeking unit because of an incentive, the incentive may be considered to be a motive. This is often the function of bonuses and promotions in work settings.

There are three conditions when incentives may be an effective and inviting means to encourage adult participation in a learning activity:

1. The adult has had some experience with the learning activity and is not interested in or attracted to it. People will engage in almost any task if the incentive is perceived as equitable (McGraw, 1978). There are many adults who would not participate in particular workshops or seminars unless they were paid to do so. Payment for participation in such learning programs is common in business, industry, and education. And that is exactly what it is—payment. Not bribery, because nothing inherently immoral or illegal is being requested of the participants. In this culture, adults have a right to accept payment or other incentives for doing things they regard as unpleasant. In fact, incentives may allow them to maintain their integrity and to avoid the more damaging effects of pressure and threat. On a more positive note, incentives, by attracting learner participation, provide opportunities for instructors to incorporate strategies from the other five general motivation factors (attitude, need, stimulation, affect, and competence), and to have a chance to eventually enhance adult motivation for the learning activity itself.

2. The adult has had no experience with the learning activity. Maybe the training or instructional program is very new or unique. Ignorance prevents attraction and may induce caution and apprehension. It could be learning how to use a new machine, or how to apply a different auditing process, or how to work with a recently invented electronic device. Under such circumstances, incentives could actually contribute to the awakening of intrinsic motivation in the learner because there is no prior negative experience to lead the learner to believe that the incentive is being used

as compensation for participation in an unpleasant learning task (Lepper and Greene, 1978). The learner is more likely to see the incentive as reinforcement for "trying out" or becoming involved in a new learning opportunity.

3. The adult has to develop a level of competence before the learning activity can become enjoyable or interesting. Sports such as tennis and swimming are good examples of this situation. But the same could be said for learning a foreign language, or how to use a word processor, or how to play a trumpet. There are so many things that are just not that appealing to do until a basic level of competence has been achieved. In such situations, incentives usually will not prevent intrinsic motivation from developing within the learner and may be the only means positively available to sustain effort until the necessary level of competence is gained to allow the learning activity to provide its own pleasure and satisfaction (Lepper and Greene, 1978). That is why parents applaud vigorously and unashamedly for their children at those, to say the least, imperfect music recitals and why an instructor might have to give extra attention and recognition to a struggling foreign student in an adult basic education course.

There is one thing to stress about incentives as they are recommended in this strategy. They are considered to be *task-noncontingent rewards* (Ryan, Mims, and Koestner, 1983). This means the reinforcers are given for participation without respect to the completion or quality of performance in the learning activity. The adults will receive the incentive for taking part in the learning activity but not under the conditions of how well or to what extent they progress in the learning task. Thus, they have agreed to be involved in the learning activity but do not see their behavior within that activity as controlled or pressured by the incentive. This allows the learning process itself to have a greater influence on their intrinsic motivation and keeps the ownership for learning with the learners themselves. In some ways, this type of incentive is like unconditional positive regard. Adults receive something desirable for being in the learning situation no matter what the outcome. But let me quickly add, they must participate. If they do not give any attention or effort to the task, the entire learning situation is a sham.

Strategy 66: Consider the use of extrinsic reinforcers for routine, well-learned activities, complex skill building, and drill-and-practice activities.

Routine, well-learned activities are situations where the learner has the basic skill but there is a need to improve the speed, rate, or persistence of the skill. Such learned behaviors as typing, monitoring instruments and machines, and various sport skills are representative examples of routine, well-learned activities. How to repair electrical equipment or how to operate high-tech machinery are illustrations of complex skill building. Drill-and-practice activities run the gamut from shooting free throws to solving a series of math problems. All of these learning activities have one thing in common—they usually follow some form of set sequence and process for effective learning and application. Operant conditioning has been a very effective means to teaching such skills (Cross, 1981; McGraw, 1978; and Harper and Stewart, 1983). Extrinsic reinforcers are, therefore, commonly used in these learning situations. They are usually given immediately as positive feedback or rewards for successful completion of each step in the appropriate sequence. These extrinsic reinforcers take such various forms as money, attention, positive comments, correct indicators, points, tokens, and tones and graphics on computers. The reason they are so effective is that they are very adaptable as a modality to precisely monitor, prescribe, and reinforce complex skill building in a sequential manner. Because they so obviously confirm to learners that they are modifying their behavior toward a desired outcome, they tend to be seen as informational rather than controlling. Biofeedback is a good analogy and metaphor for how they should be used. Since they are frequently contained in self-instructional units and computer-assisted instruction programs and because their immediacy is vital to the learning process, they may not provide proper attribution or prescriptive corrective procedures. Nonetheless, they can be quite effective and can be considered as an appropriate means to enhancing adult learning and motivation. Also, routine, well-learned activities have little intrinsic motivational value and extrinsic reinforcers are one of the few means available to help learners want to improve their performance in these tasks.

Two further comments are warranted about using extrinsic reinforcers in such activities. The first is make sure the reinforcer is effective. One person might consider money to be an insult while another person might see it as highly desirable. Whenever possible, it is probably best to individualize reinforcers (Alberto and Troutman, 1982). Secondly, reinforce small improvements in learning and motivation. Probably one of the most frequent errors made by instructors is to expect too much before reinforcers are provided. This discourages learners and subverts the learning process. It is better to start with a realistic first step and to reinforce the best of what a learner can immediately do. Standards of performance can be raised as skills and motivation increase.

Promoting Natural Consequences and Positive Endings

The concept of natural consequences is reinforcement theory's interpretation of intrinsic motivation. According to Vargas (1977), natural consequences are stimulus changes that are produced by (and dependent on) the behavior of the individual who experiences them. Natural consequences are contrasted with extrinsic reinforcers that are provided by (and dependent on) the behavior of others. Walking has the natural consequences of moving us toward certain goals and allowing us to see and experience new things. Reading a book has the natural consequences of producing new insights and expanded awareness. Thus, we say that we are interested in and enjoy reading. In this manner, reinforcement theory accounts for intrinsic motivation. However, the emphasis remains more on the product or the result of learning than on the process (doing) of learning. Whether the performance of the learning behavior is a more powerful influence on learner motivation than the intrinsic product of that performance is a debatable issue. For example, is a person more motivated to solve a problem for the joy of the process of solving it, or is that person more motivated by simply getting the solution to the problem? In other words, is it the trip or the destination that is more important? This book takes the position that both of these elements are intimately related and that they cannot be arbitrarily divided. That is why stimulation and affect are carefully considered during a learning activity and why competence and reinforcement are emphasized at the ending of a learning activity. Cognitive evaluation theory supports this position as well (Deci, 1980). By employing the following strategy, instructors can emphasize natural consequences to their best advantage for learner motivation.

Strategy 67: When learning has natural consequences, help learners to be aware of them as well as their impact.

Helping adults realize the natural consequences of their learning behavior is an excellent motivational strategy for many reasons. It is definitely supportive of feedback (especially self-evaluated feedback) as discussed in this chapter but is much broader in its implications. Theoretically, that means natural consequences include *every* consequence that the learner can perceive as a result of personal learning behavior. This encourages instructors to *make learners active as soon as possible* so that the learners can quickly have natural consequences to increase and maintain their motivation. The remarkably successful Suzuki violin method does this for children, but so might any instructor of adults teaching any skill ranging from sports to computers. Natural consequences also imply that if the learner *only* concentrates on the performance standard as a means of appreciating the results of learning, some other very important consequences may be missed. Take, for instance, dieting. A person is learning how to lose weight. The program includes an exercise regimen, control of eating habits, and a nutritional guide. The progress is measured in terms of weight loss and the performance standard is set at a loss of twenty-five pounds. Each week the person calculates weight loss and eventually meets the performance standard. That is commendable and the person will probably feel terrific about successfully losing twenty-five pounds. However, there are many more natural consequences as a result of this achievement that may include feeling physically more fit, sleeping better, wearing a greater range of fashionable clothing, increased self-confidence, improved self-concept, more activity in sports, money saved from decreased spending on food, and new culinary tastes. It is quite possible that the person's motivation to learn how to lose weight and to demonstrate that learning was to an equal or greater extent enhanced by the consequences that were not included in the performance standard. The entire point is this: Important natural consequences due to a learner's behavior but not included in the performance standard can be emphasized and accentuated as well.

Many learning activities will have natural consequences for adults that are not included in the performance standard. To miss these is a shame. It is like serving a cake without the frosting. It is also what often makes learning so sterile. Motivating instructors allow and encourage important natural consequences to become conspicuous for their learners. People often do not realize many of the consequences of their learning. In these situations, instructors can act as revealing mirrors or powerful magnifying glasses to clarify and focus on significant consequences that may not be readily apparent. The guiding question is "As a result of this learning activity, what else does the learner know or what else can the learner do that is important and worth pursuing?" For example, an adult takes a course in technical report writing. The standard of performance is based on a readability index that is precise and provides excellent informational feedback. The adult achieves the standard of performance and successfully completes the course. It is also possible that due to the learning in this course, the adult is more confident as a writer, enjoys writing in general more than ever before, can more clearly communicate verbally, sees improvement in personal letter writing, and will now pursue jobs in which writing is a functional component. For the instructor of this course to take some time at the end of the course to discuss what other outcomes may have been achieved by the learners in the course would be a motivating ending that could enhance intrinsic motivation as well as transfer of learning. One last example: A woman took a basic swimming course as an adult at the local YWCA. The standard of performance was swimming a certain number of laps at the end of the course, which she successfully did. On the last day of class, the instructor took some time to discuss "what else" people may have learned in the course. There were people who were now interested in sailing, who would now get into a boat and never did before, who wanted to teach their children how to swim, who were going to swim regularly as a physical fitness regimen, and one person who made a down payment on a cottage near a lake that was directly attributed to success in the course. In this woman's opinion, it was a splendid ending that added much to the course in general.

Discussion is not the only route to revelation of natural consequences. Performance evaluation procedures and exercises often show much more than the specific learning that is expected. So do video and audiotapes that record progress and demonstrate "before and after effects." The creation of any personal product by the learner has this potential. And finally, there is the possibility of the instructor pointing the way by sharing examples in which a given skill or concept is applied outside of the expected context, such as when an instructor demonstrates how a communication skill might be used with one's own family as well as on the job.

Reinforcement theory emphasizes the idea that how a learning experience ends can play a major role in how likely the learner will be to remember and use what has been learned. The following strategy supports this important understanding as well as indicates when positive closure is a more vital influence on learner motivation.

Strategy 68: Encourage or provide a reinforcing event for positive closure at the end of significant units of learning.

A significant unit of learning can be determined by length or importance. In terms of length, when any entire course, seminar, or training program is terminating, a significant unit of learning has occurred. Within longer courses there may be segments based on content or skill that run for a few weeks with each component having a clearly delineated beginning and ending. For example, a course in marketing might be divided into units on promotion, sales, and contracts. In terms of importance, any segment of learning that has some characteristic that makes it special qualifies it as a significant unit of learning. Such characteristics could be level of difficulty, cohesiveness, or creativity; type of learning situation, structure, or process (special equipment, materials, location, grouping, or task); or presence of such prominent individuals as an esteemed audience, lecturer, or evaluator. The basic idea is that something notable is coming to an end. At such times, positive closure enhances learner motivation because it affirms the entire process, reinforces the value of the experience, directly or indirectly acknowledges competence, increases cohesiveness within the group, and encourages the surfacing of inspiration and other beneficial emotions within the learners themselves. Positive closure can be a small gesture, such as thanking learners for their cooperation, or something much more extravagant, such as an awards ceremony. Some ways to achieve positive closure are as follows:

- *Forms of celebration.* Festivals and merrymaking have for centuries been the joyous social means to acknowledge the ending of seasons, religious periods, and harvests. There is no valid reason to avoid this in learning. Savor with learners their moment of triumph and accomplishment. This can be a pleasurable discussion, a party, a round of applause, sitting back and reliving the experience through "remember when" statements, or mild congratulations. But let the moment linger and enjoy it together. It is a happy occasion, not to be taken for granted. Celebrations are a wonderfully inclusive metaphor. They allow people to feel pleasure for whatever they personally accomplished or valued during the entire learning situation.
- *Forms of acknowledgement.* These can be simple statements of gratitude and appreciation or more formal and ritualized awards. The goal is to recognize any learner contributions or achievements that were noteworthy during the span of the learning event. This can be done by the instructor and/or the learners as the situation permits.
- *Forms of sharing.* This is anything the instructor and learners might do to show their caring and sensitivity to the special quality of the learning experience and those involved within it. Some instructors have gone as far as to cook dinner for their learning group. Others have brought in personal collections or demonstrated such unique talents as musical and artistic abilities. More frequently, this type of sharing takes the form of a poignant final statement that may include an eloquent poem or an inspirational quote. When something has gone well, it deserves an equally fitting form of closure.

9

Incorporating
Motivational Strategies
into Instructional Plans

You've got to be very careful if you don't know where
you are going, because you might not get there.
—*Yogi Berra*

When it is very good, instruction is technical excellence under the
command of artistic expression. For no matter how many fixed
rules, precise definitions, and logical strategies we establish in
learning, the process remains embedded in a human context that is
open-ended, phenomenological, unique, and constantly changing.
For this reason, instruction remains a science within an art, more
akin to communication than engineering. In fact, instruction may
never be a sure thing, because what makes people learn is beyond
guarantee or total prediction. Therefore, it will always need the
timeliness, sensitivity, and vision that any effective relationship
with human growth and individuality demands. Among the many
important aspects of instruction, none seems more deserving of this
perspective than those that deal with motivation.

For our current understanding, human motivation in learning is too complex and indomitable to lend itself to easy panaceas. But one can plan for it. A logical and seductive assumption is that if instruction itself is well planned and efficient, motivation for what is being learned should neatly and nicely come along as well. In some instances this is true, especially when adults feel a strong need for what they are learning and the instructional process is stimulating with adequate informational feedback. However, the longer the instructional sequence or the more complicated the human factors within it, the easier it is for motivation to diminish, which it seems to do with regularity. If this were not so, motivation would not be the epidemic concern it is for instructors. Industry and business are filled with well-designed, efficient instructional programs that are not very motivating. Part of the problem is efficiency itself. Motivation takes people-to-people skills and time. Like a good conversation, it cannot be rushed. The best way to see a motivational strategy is as an investment. It pays dividends but often not immediately. Also, because what motivates people is often beyond the inherent structure of the knowledge or skill they are learning, it means instructors have to plan for motivation in its own right. It cannot be taken for granted. If we look at the motivational factors and strategies that have preceded this chapter, most of them address the internal human influence in learning, such as attitude, need, affect, and competence. Logical arrangement of, or adequate information about, concepts and skills do not automatically address these issues. Yet, they are vital to motivated learning, and planning for them, at the very least, seems sensible.

The Time Continuum Model of Motivation is an organizational aid for motivation planning. It is a systemic structure for introducing or applying motivational strategies throughout a learning sequence. Instruction is a complex network of influences and interactions whose results are produced by the total system of such influences, not by its individual parts (Sanders, 1981). *Motivation planning* is designing and organizing instruction so that the development and enhancement of learner motivation is an essential part of it. The Time Continuum Model of Motivation helps instructors to programmatically combine a series of motivational strategies from the beginning to the end of an instructional sequence so that a network of motivational influences is formulated. In this way, a continual motivational dynamic is established to enhance adult motivation for learning for the entire learning sequence. It may help to review this model in Chapter Three before reading further sections of this chapter.

Increasing Motivational Self-Awareness

In preparation for effective use of the Time Continuum Model of Motivation, there are a few considerations that you can make to increase your sensitivity to where and how it will be most helpful to you. The first is to conduct an analysis of yourself as an instructor and of your instructional situation relative to motivation. Many times instructors apply new methods in education and training without reflecting on how well these approaches fit their philosophy, style, and professional environment. This can be a mistake because, rather than fluidly integrating the new approach, there is a forcing or uncomfortable placement of the new process among other professional habits and circumstances that seriously limits its effectiveness. Exhibit 7 lists five areas that significantly affect an instructor's approach to learner motivation.

Having conducted the analysis outlined in Exhibit 7, it is to your benefit to review all the strategies that have been discussed in this book before proceeding on to the more specific motivation planning section of this chapter. Table 4 is a summary of the motivational strategies contained in the five previous chapters. Each major motivation factor is indicated within it, followed by a listing of specific related strategies and the purpose that they serve. The strategies preceded by an asterisk are those that are flexible enough to be used in other time phases (beginning, during, or ending) in a learning sequence. Although these designated strategies have been previously discussed relative to a particular time phase, because my experience and theoretical assumptions have indicated that their maximum impact appears to occur with such timing, they are still a potentially positive motivational influence at other times.

There are a number of things that can be accomplished in this review. The first is a more immediate sensitivity to all the

Exhibit 7. Instructor Self-Evaluation Regarding Motivation.

Evaluating and reflecting on the five areas listed below can help you to be more aware of how much and to what extent motivation planning and the strategies offered in this book can be of help to you. Take a few minutes for each section and give yourself time to answer the questions and to reflect on how you think and feel about your responses. Writing out responses to each section can clarify your thoughts and make the entire process more concrete and applicable.

1. *Your perception of your learners' motivation.*
    a. Do you see them as intrinsically motivated and capable of self-direction and self-determination in learning activities? If so, list two instructional behaviors on your part that allow them to exhibit these qualities. If not, what sequence of your instructional process would allow for development of these qualities?
    b. Specifically, which needs (educational or general) seem to strongly influence your learners' motivation in learning activities? In your estimation, list the three most important among them.
2. *Your perception of your instructional situation.*
    a. How much freedom do you have for flexibility in the instructional process? In which areas are you most capable of change and the introduction of new methods? In which areas are you most restricted?
    b. In what part of your instructional program do you feel a need for more creative approaches to learner motivation? Has any of the information in the previous five chapters helped in this regard? If so, how?
3. *Your objectives as an instructor.*
    a. What do you specifically want to happen as a result of your instruction? List and rank your three most important objectives as an instructor.
    b. How successful are you in the accomplishment of these? Any dissatisfaction with these? If so, where?
4. *Your assumptions about learner motivation.*
    a. After reading this book, what does motivation really mean to you? List three observable behaviors of motivated learners.
    b. How often do you see these among learners in your instructional situation.
5. *Your perception of yourself as a motivating instructor.*
    a. List the three things you most often do to enhance learner motivation.
    b. What particular behavior or characteristic do you possess that you see as a strength for helping adults want to learn? What strategies have you read that align themselves with this strength?
    c. Complete this sentence as often as you can, as you believe your learners would: "My instructor helps me to feel motivated because he. . . ."

---

possible strategies that can be used for motivation planning. The second is to utilize this summary as a checklist for all the strategies that you are currently employing as an instructor. Most instructors are not aware of all the things they do to functionally enhance adult motivation for learning. This kind of inventory will give you a concrete awareness of those strategies that are part of your repertoire. It will also indicate those that are not. You may consider these as possible new strategies to incorporate into your instructional efforts. If you find more than a few motivational strategies that you would like to initiate, rank these strategies according to those that seem to have the most personal value as well as the greatest probability of being successful. The use of these criteria for selection will increase the chances that the new strategies you finally choose will be effective and adaptable to your instructional situation.

Constructing a Specific Motivation Plan

Now that you have reviewed the sixty-eight strategies found in Table 4, the next step is to consider some ways to develop a motivation plan that can either be incorporated within your instructional plan or used to support your instructional plan. The first step is to clarify your instructional objective. Knowing as clearly as possible what you want your learners to do, perform, or achieve will indicate the sequence of instruction or the unit of learning to be considered. When needs assessments are used to develop instructional objectives, they can be a prior or inclusive step in motivation planning. After the instructional objective is well understood, the next consideration is the amount of time available to help learners to achieve it. This determined length of time will have a strong influence on the kind and the amount of motivational strategies that are chosen. The next consideration is the inherent structure of the material, knowlege, or skill to be learned. This structure itself may determine an order of content or sequence of steps that must be followed if the material is to be adequately learned, as is the case in math or a foreign language. There may also be an established programmatic or curricular design that must be followed. In those instances, when the structure of the material, in order to be effectively taught, must follow a strictly defined se-

Table 4. Summary of Motivational Strategies.

Major Motivation Factor	Purpose	Strategy
Attitudes (Beginning Activities)	To create a positive attitude toward the instructor.	*1. Share something of value with your adult learners. 2. Concretely indicate your cooperative intentions to help adults learn. *3. To the degree authentically possible, reflect the language, perspective, and attitudes of your adult learners. 4. When issuing mandatory assignments or training requirements, give your rationale for these stipulations. 5. Allow for introductions.
	To build a positive attitude toward the subject and learning situation.	*6. Eliminate or minimize any negative conditions that surround the subject. *7. Ensure successful learning. 8. Make the first experience with the subject as positive as possible. *9. Positively confront the possible erroneous beliefs, expectations, and assumptions that may underlie a negative learner attitude. 10. Associate the learner with other learners who are enthusiastic about the subject.
	To develop a positive learner self-concept for learning.	*11. Encourage the learner. 12. Promote the learner's personal control of the context of learning. 13. Help learners to attribute their success to their ability and their effort. *14. When learning tasks are suitable to their ability, help learners to understand that effort and persistence can overcome their failures.
	To establish learner expectancy for success.	15. Make the learning goal as clear as possible. 16. Make the criteria of evaluation as clear as possible. 17. Use models similar to the learners to demonstrate expected learning. 18. Announce the expected amount of time needed for study and practice for successful learning. 19. Use goal-setting methods. 20. Use contracting methods.

Needs (Beginning Activities)	To ensure that instruction is responsive to learner needs.	21. Use needs assessment techniques to discover and emphasize the felt needs of learners in the learning process. 22. Use needs assessment techniques to discover and emphasize the normative needs of learners in the learning process.
	To relate instruction to important adult physiological needs.	*23. When relevant, select content, examples, and projects that relate to the physiological needs of the learners.
	To satisfy and respect adult safety needs within the content and process of the instructional situation.	*24. When relevant, select content, examples, and projects that relate to the safety needs of the learners. *25. Use imagery techniques to help learners clearly remember specific problems or tasks that are relevant to the knowledge or skill being taught. *26. Reduce or remove components of the learning environment that lead to failure or fear. *27. Create a learning environment that is organized and orderly. 28. Introduce the unfamiliar through the familiar.
	To satisfy and respect adult belongingness needs within the content and process of the instructional situation.	*29. When relevant, select content, examples, and projects that relate to the love and belongingness needs of the learners. *30. Create components in the learning environment that tell learners they are accepted and respected participating members of the group.
	To satisfy and respect adult esteem needs within the content and process of the instructional situation.	31. Offer the opportunity for responsible attainment of knowledge, skills, and learning goals that relate to the esteem needs of the learners. 32. When appropriate, plan activities to allow the learners to share and to publicly display their projects and skills.
	To satisfy and respect adult self-actualization needs within the content and process of the instructional situation.	33. Provide learners with the opportunity to select topics, projects, and assignments that appeal to their curiosity, sense of wonder, and need to explore. 34. To the extent possible, and when appropriate, provide opportunities for self-directed learning. 35. Challenge the learners.
Stimulation (During Activities)	To maintain learner attention.	36. Provide frequent response opportunities to all learners on an equitable basis. 37. Help learners to realize their accountability for what they are learning. *38. Provide variety in personal presentation style, methods of instruction, and learning materials.

Table 4. Summary of Motivational Strategies, Cont'd.

Major Motivation Factor	Purpose	Strategy
	To build learner interest.	39. Introduce, connect, and end learning activities attractively and clearly. *40. Selectively use breaks, physical exercises, and energizers. *41. Relate learning to adult interests. *42. When possible, clearly state or demonstrate the advantages that will result from the learning activity. *43. While instructing, use humor liberally and frequently. *44. Selectively induce parapathic emotions. *45. Selectively use examples, analogies, metaphors, and stories. 46. Selectively use knowledge and comprehension questions to stimulate learner interest. 47. Use unpredictability and uncertainty to the degree that learners enjoy them with a sense of security.
	To develop learner involvement.	*48. Use disequilibrium to stimulate learner involvement. 49. Selectively use application, analysis, synthesis, and evaluation questions and tasks to stimulate learner involvement. *50. Make learner reaction and active participation an essential part of the learning process. 51. Introduce minor challenges during instruction. 52. Create opportunities and conditions for the flow experience.
Affect (During Activities)	To encourage and integrate learner emotions within the learning process.	*53. Selectively emphasize and deal with the human perspective of what is being learned, with application to the personal daily lives of the adult learners whenever possible. *54. When appropriate, relate content and instructional procedures to learner concerns. *55. Selectively relate content and instructional procedures to learner values. *56. When appropriate, deal with and encourage the expression of emotions during learning. *57. When appropriate, help learners to directly experience cognitive concepts on a physical and emotional level.

Phase	Purpose	
Competence (Ending Activities)	To maintain an optimal emotional climate within the learning group. To increase learner awareness of progress, mastery, achievement, and responsibility in learning in a manner that enhances the learner's confidence, self-determination, and intrinsic motivation.	*58. Use cooperative goal structures to develop and maximize cohesiveness in the learning group. *59. Provide consistent feedback to learners regarding their mastery, progress, and responsibility in learning. *60. When necessary, use constructive criticism. *61. Effectively praise and reward learning. 62. Use formative evaluation procedures to measure and communicate learner progress and mastery. 63. Whenever possible, use performance evaluation procedures to help the learner realize how to operationalize in daily living what has been learned. 64. Acknowledge and affirm the learners' responsibility and any significant actions or characteristics that contributed to the successful completion of the learning task.
Reinforcement (Ending Activities)	To provide extrinsic reinforcers for learning activities that because of their structure or nature could not induce learner participation or achievement without positive reinforcement. To help learners to be aware of the positive changes their learning behavior has produced. To affirm and to continue learner motivation for significant units of learning.	*65. Use incentives to encourage adult participation in learning activities that are initially unattractive. *66. Consider the use of extrinsic reinforcers for routine, well-learned activities, complex skill building, and drill-and-practice activities. *67. When learning has natural consequences, help learners to be aware of them as well as their impact. 68. Encourage or provide a reinforcing event for positive closure at the end of significant units of learning.

*Can also apply to other time phases.

quence or when there is an established curricular design, the best method for motivation planning is to "superimpose" the six basic questions for motivation planning that follow on the indicated format of instruction for the learning objective. In this manner, you are asking each of these questions to see if your planned instructional activities provide positive answers to each of them. This will allow you to predetermine where the mandatory instructional activities positively respond to these questions and where they do not. For those basic questions that are not positively or adequately answered, you may consider developing learning activities based on the questions' related strategies found in Table 4. (Each of the basic questions for motivation planning emphasizes a major motivation factor, such as attitude, need, or stimulation. Table 4 presents the strategies related to each of these factors.) The main criterion for successful motivation planning, no matter what the instructional plan may be, is that *each time phase (beginning, during, and ending) of the sequence of instruction for the particular learning objective includes significant positive motivational influence on the learners.*

The six basic questions for motivation planning are as follows:

1. What can I do to establish a positive learner *attitude* for this learning sequence? (emphasis on beginning activities)
2. How do I best meet the *needs* of my learners through this learning sequence? (emphasis on beginning activities)
3. What about this learning sequence will continuously *stimulate* my learners? (emphasis on main activities)
4. How is the *affective experience* and *emotional climate* for this learning sequence positive for learners? (emphasis on main activities)
5. How does this learning sequence increase or affirm learner feelings of *competence?* (emphasis on ending activities)
6. What is the *reinforcement* that this learning sequence provides for my learners? (emphasis on ending activities)

It is possible that an instructor may believe that planning for both major motivational factors for each time phase is not always warranted. For example, "I will provide consistent feedback (competence). This should suffice for ending activities. Therefore, I need not concern myself about reinforcement." This is certainly a logical judgment and the criteria for successful motivation planning as stated in the previous paragraph have still been met. The only further comment about such decision making is that it should be based on consideration of the logical flow and efficiency of the instructional process and not based on apprehension that there might be too much positive motivational influence in a particular plan. In general, the goal of the instructor in motivation planning is to make positive motivational influence a continuous stream from the beginning to the end of the learning sequence. When it comes to motivation, it is best for instructors to err, if they must, on the side of generosity.

The reader may be wondering about the specificity of calibration for each time phase. When does the beginning phase end and the during phase begin, or when does the during phase end and the ending phase begin? There is no precise way of determining this because of the great variance in subject matter, learning situations, and particular learning objectives. The best that can be said is that this has to be an individual judgment on the part of the instructor based on the structure of the subject matter, the learning objective, the time available, and the particular learners and learning situation that are involved. In this respect, motivation planning is analogous to writing an essay. We know that the body of the composition (during phase) will usually be longer than either its beginning or ending parts, but to say that any essay for any topic should have only so many sentences for each part would be ridiculous. In motivation planning, the length of any time phase can range from a few minutes to a few days, depending on the factors already mentioned. For example, the beginning phase for a particular learning objective with a group of highly motivated, self-directed adult learners may be very short. However, for a group of unmotivated, insecure adult learners, the beginning phase for the same objective may have to be quite a bit longer to establish positive attitudes and to assess educational needs.

When there is greater instructor and/or learner control over the design of instructional planning, there is another way to

approach motivation planning. This approach places learner motivation as a more influential factor in the instructional process.
Since there is evidence that learner motivation is consistently
positively related to educational achievement, this is a logical
choice (Uguroglu and Walberg, 1979). The instructor will still have
to respect the parameters of the learning objective, inherent structure of the material to be learned, and time available but can focus
instructional planning with motivation as a larger consideration.
An analogous way to look at this process is that all four of these
factors are pieces to a puzzle. They must all fit with one another,
but motivation is a bigger piece of the puzzle. The biggest piece
remains the learning objective, unless it is completely determined
by the needs of the learners. In this case, motivation and the
learning objective would share equivalent status. Under other
circumstances, the learning objective is still the first priority because without it, the motivation of the learners has no direction.
However, once the objective is chosen, the instructor can review the
motivational purposes found in the "Purpose" column of Table 4
to select motivational strategies to guide the choice of learning
activities that fit the structural and time parameters of the learning
objective. In this manner, motivational strategies are not added on
or blended in but become the "source" for structurally congruent
learning processes and activities that respect the time available.

With the *source* approach to motivation planning, the
instructor keeps in mind the learning objective, learners, and
learning situation while he reviews the motivational purposes
(found in Table 4 under "Purposes"), checking off those purposes
that seem particularly important to a successful and motivating
achievement of the learning objective. The designated purposes
guide the instructor to related motivational strategies that are then
selected to develop appropriate learning activities that respect the
structural and time parameters of the learning objective's content.

There may be more than one objective for a motivational
plan because many units of learning contain several objectives that
are structurally related by content or skill. When a motivational
plan is well conceived, it is difficult to tell whether it has been
developed from a *superimposed* or a *source* approach. Both resemble an instructional plan but contain an alignment of motivational

purposes and motivational strategies in a time framework. The examples of motivation plans that follow will begin with simple and short units of learning and move toward longer and more complex units of learning.

Example 1. An instructor is conducting a ninety-minute class session in a college extension course entitled "The Modern American Novel." The topic for the evening is Ernest Hemingway and his novel *For Whom the Bell Tolls.* The learners have been requested to complete the reading of this novel prior to this course session.

Type and number of learners: Fifteen adults ranging in age from twenty-five to fifty-nine. Most of them have had at least a few extension courses previous to this class.

Learning objective: The learners will demonstrate their comprehension of the novel through participation in discussion, a short written critique, and creation of an alternative ending for the novel.

Example 1 contains at least one motivational purpose for each of the six major motivation factors. In this example, seven motivational strategies are used out of a possible sixty-eight. It is conceivable that more or fewer strategies could be used because the example is only illustrative. The particular learning activities and instructor behaviors are what the instructor would do to operationalize the motivational strategies. The next example follows a similar format for learning a technical skill.

Example 2. A staff developer is conducting a seven-hour training session with a small group of instructor trainees on how to use an overhead projector.

Type and number of trainees: Six adults ranging in age from twenty-four to thirty-one. All of them are college graduates.

Learning objectives: By the end of training all the instructor trainees will be able to (1) label the components of an overhead projector, (2) adjust an overhead projector, (3) design and make transparencies, and (4) successfully use an overhead projector to give a fifteen-minute lecture.

Example 2 contains at least one motivational purpose for every major motivation factor except reinforcement. Because performance evaluation procedures and feedback provide a motivationally

Motivation Plan for Example 1.

	Motivational Purpose	Motivational Strategy	Learning Activity or Instructor Behavior
	(Attitudes)		
B E G I N	To build a positive attitude toward the subject and learning situation.	8. Make the first experience with the subject as positive as possible.	1. Begin with an interesting and provocative story about Hemingway the person (over twenty books written about him).
	(Needs)		
N I N G	To satisfy and respect adult safety needs within the content and process of the instructional situation.	28. Introduce the unfamiliar through the familiar.	1. Start a discussion by asking learners to share any situations they read about in the novel which are similar to their own personal experiences.
	(Stimulation)		
D U R I N G	To maintain learner attention.	36. Provide frequent response opportunities to all learners on an equitable basis.	1. Select learners on a random basis to respond during discussion.
	To develop learner involvement.	49. Selectively use application, analysis, synthesis, and evaluation questions and tasks to stimulate learner involvement.	2. Use evaluation questions during discussion such as What part of the novel did you find most enjoyable? Most boring? Most unrealistic? And so forth.

D U R I N G	(Affect) To encourage and integrate learner emotions within the learning process.	53. Selectively emphasize and deal with the human perspective of what is being learned, with application to the personal daily lives of the adult learners whenever possible.	1. Ask learners which character in the novel they most identified with and the emotions that character elicited within them.
E N D I N G	(Competence) To increase learner awareness of progress, mastery, and responsibility in learning in a manner that enhances the learner's confidence, self-determination, and intrinsic motivation.	59. Provide consistent feedback to learners regarding their mastery, progress, and responsibility in learning.	1. Request learners to write a short critique of the novel as they might for a literary magazine. After this task is completed, pass out copies of the actual reviews the novel received in 1940 from the *Book Review Digest*. Ask learners to compare and discuss.
	(Reinforcement) To help learners to be aware of the positive changes their learning behavior has produced.	67. When learning has natural consequences, help learners to be aware of them as well as their impact.	1. Conclude by asking learners to create another ending to the novel. Share and discuss these alternative endings to reveal learner thinking and insights.

Note: The numbers of the motivational strategies correspond to those used in Table 4.

Motivation Plan for Example 2.

	Motivational Purpose	Motivational Strategy	Learning Activity or Instructor Behavior
B E G I N N I N G	(Attitudes) To establish learner expectancy for success. (Needs) To satisfy and respect adult safety needs within the content and process of the instructional situation.	15. Make the learning goal as clear as possible. 16. Make the criteria of evaluation as clear as possible. 17. Use models similar to the learners to demonstrate expected learning. 26. Reduce or remove components of the learning environment that lead to failure or fear.	1. After explaining the value and purpose of the overhead projector, pass out a performance criteria checklist to each trainee for use of this machine and show a fifteen-minute videotape in which a former trainee demonstrates exemplary utilization of the overhead projector. Explain the criteria during the showing of the tape. 1. Explain to trainees that they will have a chance to practice making transparencies and using the overhead projector and that you will be available to them as a consultant during these times.
D U R I N G	(Stimulation) To maintain learner attention. To develop learner involvement.	38. Provide variety in personal presentation style, methods of instruction, and learning materials. 50. Make learner reaction and active participation an essential part of the learning process.	1. Pass out a diagram of the projector among trainees. Have them label it as you point out its components and explain their function with an actual model of the projector. 2. A. Give each trainee an opportunity to adjust a "problem" projector, asking them to label each part they manipulate to solve the problem. B. After passing out the instructions for making write-on and burn-on transparencies to each trainee

(Affect)

DURING

To maintain an optimal emotional climate within the learning group.

58. Use cooperative goal structures to develop and maximize cohesiveness in the learning group.

and demonstrating how to make each type; allow trainees to practice making their own under your supervision.

1. Divide the six trainees into two triads. With assistance from the peers in their triad, each trainee is to develop a fifteen-minute presentation or any topic accompanied by appropriate use of the overhead projector as a visual aid. Each triad will receive one projector for practicing. The trainees are encouraged to use the performance criteria checklist passed out at the beginning of the training session to give feedback and guidance to members of their triad.

(Competence)

ENDING

To increase learner awareness of progress, mastery, and responsibility in learning in a manner that enhances the learner's confidence, self-determination, and intrinsic motivation.

63. Whenever possible, use performance evaluation procedures to help the learner realize how to operationalize in daily living what has been learned.
59. Provide consistent feedback to learners regarding their mastery, progress, and responsibility in learning.

1. Each trainee is videotaped and evaluated while making a fifteen-minute presentation using an overhead projector as a visual aid. Each person is evaluated by the entire group of trainees as well as the staff developer with the performance criteria checklist as the evaluation standard. Any trainee receiving less than an 80 percent average score on the checklist will be requested to make another fifteen-minute videotaped presentation for evaluation by the staff developer.

Note: The numbers of the motivational strategies correspond to those used in Table 4.

sound ending to this learning sequence, there is little apparent need for application of this factor. Example 2 also illustrates the fact that a learning activity can operationalize more than one motivational strategy, as is the case with the activity corresponding to attitudes. It is possible as well that more than one learning activity can be representative of a single motivational strategy. This is exemplified by the second strategy for stimulation, which has two learning activities assigned to it. Instructors need not concern themselves that *every* instructional behavior or learning activity in a learning sequence have a motivational strategy corresponding to it. This kind of minute detail could become obstructive to motivation planning, as it has become with learning objectives when too specific a breakdown becomes more confusing than enlightening for instructional planning (Gronlund, 1978). In general, motivation planning should be thorough enough that each time phase of the instructional sequence for the particular learning objective(s) includes significant positive motivational influence on the learners throughout the entire sequence. As long as this criterion is met, the instructor will have a road map of motivationally effective learning activities to follow and to create a positive overall motivational dynamic for the learners.

Example 3. A community educator is conducting a one-day stress management workshop for a local mental health agency.

Type and number of participants: Eighteen adults from various backgrounds (white- and blue-collar workers as well as homemakers) ranging in age from twenty-three to fifty-five.

Learning objectives: By the end of the workshop all participants will have (1) identified sources of stress in their personal lives, (2) identified their own unique stress responses, (3) experienced several relaxation techniques appropriate for stress reduction, and (4) made a personal plan to prevent and reduce inappropriate stress.

In Example 3 there are two learning activities, one corresponding to stimulation and the flow experience and one corresponding to reinforcement and natural consequences, which have a content that is highly competence-oriented as well. This relationship is emphasized to point out the fact that frequently in motivation planning, a learning activity corresponding to one major motivation factor will overlap with another major motivation factor. Thus, a learning activity can contain a number of characteristics that different motivational theories would explain as having a positive influence on learning. Currently, there is no way to measure or explain the dynamic interaction of all these differently postulated causes of learning behavior within a single learning activity. However, it seems safe to generalize that such activities are relatively strong sources of motivational influence because they have multiple positive effects. For purposes of planning, instructors should consider the primary motivational effect desired by activities that have multiple motivational influences and use this as the guideline for their placement in the motivation plan. The only exception to this would be an activity employing powerful extrinsic reinforcers that might undermine intrinsic motivation (see Chapter Eight for a discussion of the appropriate use of extrinsic reinforcers).

Example 4. An instructor is conducting a two-day in-service unit on personality styles for a group of salespersons from a large company.

Type and number of adults: Twenty experienced members of the company's sales department. All of them are college-educated and range in age from twenty-eight to fifty-six.

Learning objectives: By the end of the in-service training, all salespersons will be able to (1) identify the characteristics of four personality styles, (2) identify the personality styles of their clients, and (3) use their understanding of personality styles to plan a successful meeting with prospective clients.

Example 4 concludes the examples of motivation planning for this book. Each example has been considered as a learning sequence that is a complete unit with beginning, during, and ending time phases so that all aspects of the Time Continuum Model of Motivation could be illustrated for planning. Any complete learning situation can occur in minutes, hours, days, or weeks. The time and qualitative differences between a short presentation and a long-term course are immense. However, even in the latter instance, there will be separate units that can be planned. No matter what the length of a particular learning unit, motivation planning is necessary to sustain continual learner effort and involvement.

Motivation Plan for Example 3.

	Motivational Purpose	Motivational Strategy	Learning Activity or Instructor Behavior
B E G I N N I N G	(Attitudes) To create a positive attitude toward the instructor.	5. Allow for introductions. 1. Share something of value with your adult learners.	1. Introduce yourself and provide a short exercise for participants to introduce themselves to other members of the learning group. 2. To introduce the topic of stress, share a powerful anecdote about stress in your own life and the means you have found to cope with it and prevent it.
	(Needs) To relate instruction to important adult physiological needs.	23. When relevant, select content, examples, and projects that relate to the physiological needs of the learners.	1. Distribute handout, *Sources of Stress.* Have participants select and prioritize the specific sources of stress most prevalent in their personal lives. Explain how the workshop will help them to cope with and prevent the detrimental effects of these sources.
D U R I N G	(Stimulation) To develop learner involvement.	50. Make learner reaction and active participation an essential part of the learning process.	1. Distribute checklist with stress symptoms, and physiological and psychological changes due to stress. After participants have had a chance to analyze their particular symptomatic reactions to stress, give them red and black pencils and drawing paper. Participants are then requested to draw a self-body picture (front and back view) in black and then to color in red the areas of physiological stress as they are manifested in their bodies. These drawings (without identification) are posted around the room for general examination and discussion.

D U R I N G	(Affect) To maintain an optimal emotional climate within the learning group.	58. Use cooperative goal structures to develop and maximize cohesiveness in the learning group.	1. After discussing constructive coping and showing a film on cognitive change methods, distribute a handout that outlines and summarizes these methods. Then divide the group into triads to conduct the following exercise: Each person takes a turn in the triad to describe a current stressful situation in his or her life. The other two members act as consultants, using the constructive coping and cognitive change methods to suggest possible solutions to the stressful situation until each person has had a turn. Visit each group as an observer and general consultant.
	(Stimulation) To develop learner involvement.	52. Create opportunities and conditions for the flow experience.	1. After discussing, demonstrating, and practicing the deep breathing exercises and the passive progressive relaxation technique, pass out the guidelines for each of these skills. Have participants pick partners and choose the skill they most want to learn well. Then have them practice the skill under their own self-direction with their partners actings as feedback monitors until they acquire mastery. Reverse roles.
E N D I N G	(Reinforcement) To help learners to be aware of the positive changes their learning behavior has produced.	67. When learning has natural consequences, help learners to be aware of them as well as their impact.	1. After distributing a handout and showing a slide series that explains how to develop a personal stress reduction program, have each participant create one of their own. Monitor and provide individual feedback during this process.
	To affirm and to continue learner motivation for significant units of learning.	68. Encourage or provide a reinforcing event for positive closure at the end of significant units of learning.	2. To end the workshop, have the learners gather in a circle to participate in an activity in which each individual publicly acknowledges what he or she believes was one of the most important things personally gained from the workshop.

Note: The numbers of the motivational strategies correspond to those used in Table 4.

Motivation Plan for Example 4.

Motivational Purpose	Motivational Strategy	Learning Activity or Instructor Behavior
(Attitudes)		
To create a positive attitude toward the instructor.	5. Allow for introductions.	1. Introduce yourself and provide a short exercise for participants to introduce themselves to other members of the learning group.
(Needs)		
To satisfy and respect adult safety needs within the content and process of the instructional situation.	27. Create a learning environment that is organized and orderly.	1. Give a detailed overview of the course and distribute the participants' handbook.
B E G I N I N G — To ensure that instruction is responsive to learner needs.	22. Use needs assessment techniques to discover and emphasize the normative needs of learners in the learning process.	2. Have participants complete the personality profile sheets in the handbook for two current clients, one with whom they have a highly successful relationship and one with whom they have a highly problematic relationship. Ask them to examine the differences between these two personality styles and indicate how the course will help them with the problematic relationship.
(Stimulation)		
D U R I N G — To develop learner involvement.	49. Selectively use application, analysis, synthesis, and evaluation questions and tasks to stimulate learner involvement. 50. Make learner reaction and active participation an essential part of the learning process.	1. After showing the videotape illustrating the four personality styles and having participants read the descriptive materials in their handbook that cover these as well, have them analyze the characteristics of the two clients they have previously described to place them in two of the four possible categories. 2. After showing another videotape that illustrates the four personality styles but does not identify them, have participants fill out the identification sheets in their handbooks and provide the reasons for the selections they have made. Review and discuss.

(Affect) To encourage and integrate learner emotions within the learning process.	57. When appropriate, help learners to directly experience cognitive concepts on a physical and emotional level.	1. A. With volunteers from the learning group acting as salespersons, role play a prospective client for each of the four personality styles while the rest of the learning group observes. After each simulation, ask those observing to identify the salient characteristics that typify you as a particular personality style. B. Divide the participants into groups of five. Each member receives a script that exemplifies the personality style that that person finds most problematic as a client and role plays this style for the rest of the group with one other member acting as a salesperson. After each person has a turn, members of the group discuss the salient characteristics and their personal reactions to the process. After this exercise has been completed, move to a general discussion with the entire learning group.
(Stimulation) To develop learner involvement.	51. Introduce minor challenges during instruction.	1. Using only an audiotape which simulates each of the four personality styles, challenge the participants to list the salient characteristics and to make the correct identifications. Any participant who incorrectly identifies a personality style is requested to review the related descriptive materials for that personality style in the handbook.
(Affect) To encourage and integrate learner emotions within the learning process.	53. Selectively emphasize and deal with the human perspective of what is being learned, with application to the personal daily lives of the adult learners whenever possible.	1. Ask participants to fill out the personality style worksheets in their handbooks to identify and categorize two of their most important clients.

Motivation Plan for Example 4, Cont'd.

	Motivational Purpose	Motivational Strategy	Learning Activity or Instructor Behavior
D U R I N G	(Stimulation) To build learner interest.	42. When possible, clearly state or demonstrate the advantages that will result from the learning activity.	1. Have participants read materials in their handbooks and view videotapes that demonstrate the most advantageous sales strategies that can be used with each of the four personality styles.
	(Competence) To increase learner awareness of progress, mastery, achievement, and responsibility in learning in a manner that enhances the learner's confidence, self-determination, and intrinsic motivation.	59. Provide consistent feedback to learners regarding their mastery, progress, and responsibility in learning.	1. Give participants guided practice in planning sales strategies based on the personality styles of their two important clients. After this process is completed, have participants divide into groups of five with each participant sharing one sales strategy plan with the group and receiving feedback from its members.
E N D I N G	(Reinforcement) To help learners to be aware of the positive changes their learning behavior has produced.	67. When learning has natural consequences, help learners to be aware of them as well as their impact.	1. As a summary exercise, ask participants to develop an extensive plan for a sales meeting with the client they earlier identified as most problematic for them. The plan is to be based on the personality style of this client and is to include strategies for atmosphere, use of time, gaining acceptance, problem solving, presenting product benefits, and decision making.
	To affirm and to continue learner motivation for significant units of learning.	68. Encourage or provide a reinforcing event for positive closure at the end of significant units of learning.	2. As a culminating activity, have participants post their summary exercises on newsprint around the rooms for general sharing. Afterwards conduct a general discussion where volunteers from the group indicate new sales strategies that were developed for problematic clients as a result of the two-day program. Conclude with appropriate acknowledgments and appreciations.

Note: The numbers of the motivational strategies correspond to those used in Table 4.

The goal of planning with the Time Continuum Model of Motivation is not to confine the instructor to some form of perfect time regimentation but to encourage the use of a structure in which certain motivation strategies have more value and impact when applied with a sense of timing.

The examples given are illustrations. It is quite possible that better and more creative means could be found to approach learner motivation for each of the particular learning objectives. These examples show what might be possible and what is structurally necessary for motivation planning. They are not offered as precise models to follow, but rather as samples that clarify and suggest. It is important to note that there is a practice effect to motivation planning. The more often it is done, the more familiar the Time Continuum Model of Motivation and its related strategies become. This significantly lessens the time required for planning and makes the process more fluid. Also, most instructors develop a shorthand of phraseology for the various purposes, strategies, and learning activities to increase their efficiency in planning.

In review, here are the basic steps for each of the two types of motivation planning. First, the *Superimposed Method:*

1. Clarify instructional objective(s) for the particular learners and learning situation.
2. Estimate amount of time available for instruction.
3. Consider the inherent structure of the material, skill, or knowledge to be learned.
4. Examine the established curricular or instructional design to be followed for the learning unit.
5. Superimpose six basic questions for motivation planning found on page 258 on the indicated format of instruction to see where the mandatory instructional activities positively respond to these questions and where they do not.
6. For any of the six questions that remain inadequately answered, select appropriate motivational strategies from Table 4 and develop related learning activities or instructor behaviors.
7. Final criterion: The sequence of instruction for the particular learning objective(s) includes significant positive motivational

influence on the learners in each time phase (beginning, during, and ending).

Now, the *Source Method:*

1. Clarify instructional objective(s) for the particular learners and learning situation.
2. Estimate amount of time *desirable* for instruction.
3. Consider the inherent structure of the material, skill, or knowledge to be learned.
4. Review the motivational purposes found in Table 4 to select motivational strategies to guide the choice and development of learning activities that fit the structural and time parameters of the learning objective(s).
5. Conduct motivation planning for each time phase.
6. Final criterion: The sequence of instruction for the particular learning objective(s) includes significant positive motivational influence on the learners in each time phase (beginning, during, and ending).

    If each of these steps is properly followed, the adult's perspective while learning is encouraged to be as follows:

1. I have a positive attitude toward my instructor and what I am about to learn, with a reasonable expectancy for successful achievement.
2. I know this learning will lead to the fulfillment of important personal or professional needs.
3. I am stimulated by this learning experience.
4. My emotions are involved while learning and I can contribute as a member of a group to which I feel a mutual sense of affection and respect.
5. I realize I am becoming more competent and I know I am responsible for the success I am having.
6. The way this learning experience is ending helps me to value and want to use what I have learned.

    The above six statements represent what we as instructors want our adult learners to be saying to themselves as they proceed through the instructional process. If learners can make these statements or feel the impact of what they imply, these adults will usually be motivated to learn and to continue learning. This does not mean that adults bear no responsibility for their own motivation during the learning process. It does mean that we as instructors have exercised our professional knowledge and skills to make the instructional experience one that complements and enhances the motivational assets that any learner brings to the learning situation. Learner motivation is a dynamic entity that grows or diminishes itself as it engages and is influenced by the instructional process. In this reciprocal relationship, our responsibility as instructors is to make sure we have used our professional abilities to provide a maximally positive motivational influence to support and nourish the motivational qualities that our learners bring with them to the learning experience. It is wise for us to remember that motivation tends to be affectively oriented and, like any emotion, the quality of its expression is interdependent with the contact it has in its environment. Having made the environment for that contact as positive as possible, we can then reasonably expect people to behave as what they are—responsible adult learners progressing toward excellent achievement.

Other Motivational Models for Instructional Planning

Until quite recently, motivation as a prescriptive and specific aspect of instructional design has received relatively little attention (Reigeluth, 1983). However, there are two comprehensive models of instruction and learning on the horizon that show a great deal of promise. The first is the Interpretive Process Model of Motivated Learning in Classrooms (Corno and Mandinach, 1983). This model views self-regulated learning as the highest form of cognitive engagement, seeing it as critical to the onset and maintenance of learner motivation. Self-regulated learning includes metacognitive and cognitive processes that are referred to as acquisition processes and transformation processes. The researchers indicate that these processes can be acquired by people through training; a number of approaches for training in self-regulated learning skills are recommended. However, most of their efforts, thus far, have been toward what can be done to enhance the personal skills of younger students with little attention to the adult learner or to the instructional side of the process. Nevertheless, if such skills can be acquired and people can learn ways to enhance their own motivation for learning, such training has tremendous potential for the entire field of learning. In support of this general approach, there already exists some research that indicates that learners receiving motivational skills training prior to entering a technical course were more motivated and achieved higher performance scores than a similar group that did not receive this training (McCombs, 1982).

The second comprehensive model of instruction and learning is Keller's (1983) Model of Motivation, Performance, and Instructional Influence. His theoretical framework incorporates cognitive and environmental variables in relation to effort, performance, and consequences. This paradigm also distinguishes among three types of influence of instructional design. These are motivational design, learning design, and reinforcement-contingency design. According to Keller, any instructional event, whether it is a teacher in a classroom or a module on a microcomputer, will have these three influences and the task of the instructional scientist is to understand and control them. His Motivation-Design Model presumes that there are four basic categories of motivational conditions that the instructional designer must understand and respond to in order to produce instruction that is interesting, meaningful and appropriately challenging. These basic categories are interest, relevance, expectancy, and satisfaction. It is important to note that as Keller defines and exemplifies these basic categories, they, albeit indirectly, theoretically include as a totality each of the six major motivation factors of the Time Continuum Model of Motivation. Keller also includes several motivational strategies for each of his basic categories. In my opinion, this is an optimistic and fortunate parallel because both Keller's model and the Time Continuum Model of Motivation are attempting to achieve a similar goal: the synthesis of many lines of research concerned with motivation in order to integrate numerous instructional strategies into the instructional process for the purpose of enhancing learner motivation. Although each of these models uses a different means to categorize motivational strategies and emphasizes a different approach to the planning process as well as different particular strategies to employ, they are both serious attempts to specifically and pragmatically make instruction more appealing.

In conclusion, at this time there appear to be two directions in the development of theory and research to make learning a more motivating experience. The first are those approaches that help learners to acquire and implement specific internally generated strategies for taking control and processing learning, regardless of the external instructional condition (Corno and Mandinach, 1983). The second are those approaches that deal with external instructional strategies that enhance learner motivation (Keller, 1983; and Wlodkowski, 1981). At this time it does not appear that one approach is superior but that both are needed for promoting optimal learner motivation (McCombs and McDaniel, 1983). Learners, adult or otherwise, will be the main beneficiaries of any further synthesis that can be created between these two fields of endeavor.

Evaluating Learner Motivation

You have done your motivation planning and have constructed a comprehensive motivating instructional sequence from the beginning to the end of the learning unit. You are carrying it out. Now, how do you know if and when your learners are motivated? Of all the questions in this book, this is the most difficult one to answer. In fact, based on the present state of knowledge in the field of motivation, it is currently impossible to accurately respond to this query. We just do not have an adequate theory of motivation to develop precise measures of motivation, particularly academic motivation (Keller, 1983). The presently available direct measures of motivation tend not to be highly correlated with performance or with each other (Keller, Kelly, and Dodge, 1978). Until a better theory of motivation develops, it will be difficult to develop better measures of motivation. The primary problem is that motivation as a concept is difficult to operationalize. The choices people make in life and the degree of effort they will exert relative to those choices are influenced by a myriad of personal and environmental variables. Also, motivation is tremendously unstable. People not only vary in their commitment to the choices they have made but also to the associated degree of effort they will expend on behalf of those choices. This is as true in learning as it is in work, play, or interpersonal relationships. To a large extent, all civilized societies have developed oaths and contracts in respect for and fear of the instability of personal motivation.

Psychology continues to make progress and a number of general motivational concepts have been developed along with instruments to measure them. A helpful review of the measures of several of these concepts that are better known, such as achievement motivation and locus of control, in an academic context is available to instructors (Keller, Kelly, and Dodge, 1978). This review also includes several measures of general academic motivation as well. As stated, these measures are all quite imperfect, but for an instructor with a specific purpose who wishes to have a more standardized means to evaluate learner motivation, these instruments may provide some assistance.

Although we cannot precisely evaluate the motivation of adult learners, there are several approaches we can use to estimate and increase our awareness of the presence and quality of motivation among them as they are learning. But first, a cautionary note: Frequently, tests and other indicators of *learning accomplishment* are used by instructors to evaluate learner motivation or as evidence of learner motivation. We think intuitively, "If they are motivated, they will learn." However, learning achievement or accomplishment is strongly influenced by ability and opportunity (instructional design, materials, time available, and so forth) as well as motivation. At best, learner achievement is an indirect indicator of motivation, and unless ability and opportunity have been carefully separated for measurement purposes, it can be a misleading indicator. Other possible means to evaluate learner motivation are instructor-constructed, self-report instruments, such as questionnaires, rating scales, and checklists that elicit the learners' assessment of their own behavior, beliefs, or preferences. These can be very helpful as estimating and feedback devices. However, they have several disadvantages. One is that learners may bias their responses for reasons that range from social desirability to prejudice, and another is that learners are not always that aware of their motives or how to explain them.

Probably the best moment-to-moment method for instructor evaluation of learner motivation is through personal observation. This is, indeed, an imperfect method. Our biases and mood can not only contaminate how we interpret what we perceive but also what we actually choose to perceive. Also, we can never be totally sure that what we see is actually a real indicator of motivation. For example, it is possible that what we see as signs of learners' intensity might be nothing more than their obvious reactions to physical or mental discomfort. Yet, as we instruct, we can only trust our judgment and our professionalism. Also, effort is a direct indicator of motivation (Keller, 1983). It refers to whether the individual is engaged in actions aimed at accomplishing the learning task. We know that adults are motivated by the vigor or persistence of their behavior. Effort is the bottom line when it comes to motivation, and it is seeing learners carry out activities to increase their learning that tells us most persuasively that they want to learn. It has been stated earlier, that if we take the adult learner's perspective of motivation and keep *success* as a constant expectancy, there are at least three important levels: *volition, volition + value,* and *volition + value + enjoyment.* Ideally, in terms of motivation, adults want to be successful in learning activities that they willingly pursue, that fulfill important needs and motives, and that offer some pleasure in the actual process of learning. Observing their effort tells us something about each of these levels. When they begin learning activities without resistance or delay, the volition level would appear to be present. When they continue learning and persevere, especially in the face of obstacles and difficulties, the value level would appear to be present. The quality of their task engagement will tell us something about the enjoyment level. If their outward behavior falls someplace within the range from relaxed and alert to excited and involved (see Chapter Six), it would appear that they are enjoying learning to some extent. Keenly using our observational skills to evaluate these examples of effort on a regular basis in the instructional setting can help us to adjust and to adapt motivational strategies to further enhance learner motivation. Motivation planning may sometimes need such spontaneous refinement, and using the observed quality of learner effort can provide the feedback to guide this process. Also, as stated earlier, it is my firm opinion that each instructor must develop a minimum standard for the quality of effort exemplified within a learning group (see Chapter Six). This can be the percentage of people who willingly begin a learning task, the percentage of people who persevere to overcome a learning obstacle, and/or the percentage of people who appear relaxed and alert while learning. Possession of such standards concretizes effort feedback and encourages us as instructors to be more aware and responsive to continuing instruction that enhances adult motivation to learn.

10

Encouraging Motivation
for Continuing Adult Learning

>   Ideally, the task of educators is to develop the taste for
>   good learning—to develop gourmet learners who are
>   able to tailor and utilize the resources in the learning
>   society to their own needs.   —*K. Patricia Cross*

If we as instructors have been skillful and helpful enough to enhance the motivation of adult learners for successful achievement, there is at least one more pressing question. Will they continue to be motivated once the learning experience has ended? Continuing motivation is potentially as much of an educational outcome as the attainment of any learning objective. In terms of importance, it may be equal to or even greater than the acquisition of a particular skill or concept. In an increasingly complex society where continuous education is a reality, to foster the continued willingness of people to learn may be of greater consequence than to ensure the fact that they have learned some specific thing at a certain point in time

(Maehr, 1976). Cross (1981) emphatically states that the single most important goal for educators at all levels and in all agencies is the development of lifelong learners who possess the basic skills for learning plus the motivation to pursue a variety of learning interests throughout their lives.

Continuing motivation is a complex concept. Maehr (1976) defined it, with qualifications, as an individual's disposition to return to an instructional task at a different time in a different context without external pressures to do so, and when other alternative pursuits are available. This definition would include spontaneously working on science experiments outside of school when no assignment has been given, as well as the inclination of adults to engage in continuing education. However, continuing motivation sometimes has broader implications for practitioners and educators. Each of the following two questions focuses on a qualitatively different aspect of continuing motivation that may be of real concern to adult instructors and those who employ them as well as society in general.

1. How can this learning experience help adults want to learn more about what they have learned?
2. How can this learning experience help adults be more motivated to learn in general?

There is no doubt that business and industry, as well as trainers of basic skills in any area, are vitally interested in continuing motivation as it relates to the first question. Continuing motivation in respect to the second question currently gains the uneasy attention of society and government. We know as a people we cannot afford to develop citizens who do not want to learn. And then there are the adult learners themselves. Who would want to take a course realizing that as a result of it, you would not want to learn more about what you learned and your interest in learning would diminish?

No one has yet developed a guaranteed method for establishing continuing motivation for learning. However, there are a few promising theories and related research studies. Probably the most comprehensive approach offered to help adults want to learn more about what they have learned and to be more motivated to learn in general is cognitive evaluation theory and its related concepts of intrinsic motivation and self-determination (Deci and Ryan, 1985). The reasons for this selection are that this theory corresponds to and fundamentally supports the basic assumptions of andragogy (see Table 5); has developed a body of research that is empirically based, well conceived, and expanding; and is broad enough to include instructional, personality, and developmental dynamics.

Increasing Intrinsic Motivation for Learning

The properties of continuing motivation that deal with desiring to learn more about what has been learned and being more motivated to learn in general can be subsumed under the concept of *intrinsically motivated action*. Intrinsically motivated action is that which occurs for its own sake, action for which the only rewards are the spontaneous affects and cognitions that accompany it. Intrinsically motivated behaviors require no external supports or reinforcements for their sustenance (Deci and Ryan, 1985). Intrinsically motivated learning is learning that meets people's needs to be competent and self-determining (Ryan, Connell, and Deci, forthcoming). This is the type of learning that has the best chance to grow and to enhance the learners' positive motivation for learning in general. As will be discussed, the factors that allow it to flourish enable learners to become more self-confident and self-directed for learning under a variety of circumstances.

The situational (instructional) influence that affects the development of intrinsic motivation for learning is the relative degree of informational versus controlling factors in the learner's environment that allows or limits the learner's self-determination. This aspect of intrinsic motivation has been discussed in Chapter Eight and the reader is advised to review this material. What remains that is essential to elaborate upon are the three specific factors that have been isolated that enhance intrinsic motivation under informational conditions. These are choice, positive feedback, and optimum challenge.

Choice means learners have had some opportunity to initiate and/or direct their own learning. This can range from personal

Table 5. A Comparison of the Assumptions of Andragogy and Cognitive Evaluation Theory.

Subject	Andragogy	Cognitive Evaluation Theory
Concept of the learner	It is a normal aspect of the process of maturation for a person to move from dependency toward increasing self-directedness, but at different rates for different people and in different dimensions of life. Teachers have a responsibility to encourage and nurture this movement. Adults have a deep psychological need to be generally self-directing, although they may be dependent in particular temporary situations.	Human beings have an intrinsic need for self-determination and competence. They develop away from simple responsiveness, toward integrated values; away from heteronomy and toward autonomy with respect to those behaviors not originally intrinsically motivated. Through the process of internalization they attempt to bring into harmony with themselves those regulations that are necessary in their social world. Those conditions (educational and social) that promote intrinsically motivated behavior and also promote the intrinsically motivated process of internalization will be the antecedents of a strong autonomy orientation in human beings.
Role of learners' experience	As people grow and develop, they accumulate an increasing reservoir of experience that becomes an increasingly rich resource for learning—for themselves and for others. Furthermore, people attach more meaning to learnings they gain from experience than those they acquire passively. Accordingly, the primary techniques in education are experiential techniques—laboratory experiments, discussions, problem-solving cases, simulation exercises, field experience, and the like.	People will propel themselves to greater achievement out of their interests and desires for mastery. Environments and approaches that allow this are *active education* and its learning, active learning. People will be active in their learning if the situation allows and supports it.

Readiness to learn	People become ready to learn something when they experience a need to learn it in order to cope more satisfying with real-life tasks and problems. The educator has a responsibility to create conditions and provide tools and procedures for helping learners discover their "needs to know," and learning programs should be organized around life-application categories and sequenced according to the learners' readiness to learn.	People are innately motivated to be effective in dealing with their environment and to master new situations. People need to be competent and self-determining, and those needs are the basis for active learning. People are capable of doing much of the initiating and directing of their own learning rather than being programmed by external forces.
Orientation to learning	Learners see education as a process of developing increased competence to achieve their full potential in life. They want to be able to apply whatever knowledge and skill they gain today to living more effectively tomorrow. Accordingly, learning experiences should be organized around competency-development categories. People are performance-centered in their orientation to learning.	People, when given the freedom to do so, explore new areas and exercise their capacities. They want education to help them to learn what they are competent to do. They want to stretch their skills and seek optimally challenging learning activities to do so. Expanding their competencies contributes to their self-esteem and intrinsic motivation to learn.

Sources: Knowles, 1980, pp. 43–44; Deci and Ryan, 1985; Ryan, Connell, and Deci, forthcoming.

selection of a particular topic of study to personal determination of the level of difficulty of a series of problems one is attempting to solve. The main criterion is that learners believe that they are to a greater than lesser extent self-determining the process of learning. They know that they are the primary locus of causality for their learning. Anything that undermines this belief will undermine their intrinsic motivation. It can be safely said that the majority of researchers who have studied continuing motivation, intrinsic motivation, and self-motivation, as these concepts relate to learning, have emphasized the necessity for helping learners to see themselves as the cause of their own learning behavior in order to develop motivation that does not depend on external control (Thomas, 1980).

Positive feedback has been extensively discussed in Chapter Eight as well. What needs to be accentuated here is that positive feedback must be in the context of perceived autonomy by the learners for it to enhance intrinsic motivation (Ryan, Connell, and Deci, forthcoming). Informing people that they are doing well at a learning task will not increase their intrinsic motivation if they do not feel autonomous in their activity.

Optimally challenging learners means allowing them to pursue learning tasks that are *moderately* difficult to achieve. Such challenges engage their capacities and elicit intrinsic involvement. Challenges that are too easy fail to employ their abilities and result in boredom and disinterest, while those that are too difficult are stressful and anxiety provoking (Csikszentmihalyi, 1975). Learners tend to avoid both and when required to perform such tasks, their intrinsic motivation tends to decrease. An optimally challenging learning task means learners will have to exercise a reasonable amount of effort to achieve it. Often we think that activities that demand *major* effort and are successfully achieved dramatically build adult confidence and pride. This is sometimes true. However, for day-to-day learning, this is a very unrealistic proposition and one that is to be avoided.

To summarize, according to cognitive evaluation theory and research, the learning situations that develop intrinsic motivation are ones that provide positive feedback to people who are engaged in an optimally challenging, self-determined activity (Ryan, Con-

nell, and Deci, forthcoming). The Time Continuum Model of
Motivation has been theoretically organized based on cognitive
evaluation theory and its related strategies have been developed to
be congruent with the specific factors of choice, positive feedback,
and optimum challenge. However, no matter what approach to
motivation planning is used, if an instructor is concerned about
developing intrinsic motivation, these three factors and their related
implications are to be heeded.

At this time, the other approaches to developing continuing
motivation seem to be in an even more initially developmental state.
The Interpretive Process Model of Motivated Learning in Classrooms, discussed in the previous chapter, is particularly promising
(Corno and Mandinach, 1983). Successfully training learners in
cognitive skills that can be used to process and deal with learning
under a variety of instructional conditions as well as to manage
their own motivation would be of inestimable value to society as a
whole. Self-efficacy theory is making progress in this direction as
well (Schunk, 1984). It is possible that someday we will not ask
whether learners are motivated, but whether they have the motivational skills to be motivated.

At this time, the following ideas have not been empirically
proven. But on a theoretical and intuitive level they are informative.
Both the intrinsic motivation and cognitive skill approaches to
continuing motivation tell us that all things being equal, learners
who know they personally cause and determine their own learning
are more likely to be more motivated for any type of learning than
those who do not know this. Also, the more learners experience
intrinsically motivated learning, the more they will want to learn
in general. For example, in an analogous sense, the more you enjoy
reading, the more you will want to read in general. This is where
Cross's (1981) idea of gourmet learners comes in. Gourmet learners
are people who are intrinsically motivated to learn and confidently
realize they can determine their own learning in a variety of
subjects. It is unlikely that they develop spontaneously. Rather, they
probably come about through involvement in a significant number
of intrinsically motivated learning experiences and/or a familial
environment that was supportive of intrinsic motivation for learning. They have two very important personal and societal advan-

tages. They are lifelong learners and they know what good instruction is. As adults, they can assert themselves and request it, and teach their children to do likewise. Learner ignorance maintains ineffective instruction. The more often adults have experienced intrinsically motivating instruction, the less likely they will tolerate inferior methods. By instructing in a manner that supports intrinsic motivation, we not only stand a chance to develop lifelong learners but also to contribute to the positive evolution of our own discipline.

Increasing Intrinsic Motivation for Instruction

It is probably only fair that what works so well for the learner works just as well for the instructor. To experience our jobs as intrinsically satisfying, we need the benefits of optimal challenge, positive feedback, and choice as much as our learners do. The wisdom of this parallel is that if we remain in touch with how much the existence of these three factors means in our own professional lives, we are that much more likely to ensure their existence for our learners. Accordingly, to create circumstances as we instruct that empower this set of factors to become a reality for ourselves gives us the awareness and confidence that we can do likewise for the adults who learn with us.

For ourselves, the cornerstone of optimal challenge is a belief, a faith if you will, that we can get better. This may mean professional growth, personal improvement, skillful competence, or, perhaps, greater self-determination. But as long as we genuinely believe that this is possible, we can maintain a reflective attitude and constant sense of inquiry regarding how to make it happen. Professionals from any walk of life who know they are capable of further development scan their world for the opportunity and means to do so. In the work place, challenges are more often found than given. This confidence in our capacity for professional progress also gives us something much more emotionally powerful than selective perception—commitment. Knowing that we can advance our competence means we will find challenges to enlist our capacities and skills. A challenge nourishes commitment because it offers the chance for growth and renewal. It gives something back to the person who accepts it. It is difficult to commit ourselves to routine work because our skills become repetitive and stagnant. Under such circumstances, a feeling of resignation is much more likely to occur. If we can strengthen ourselves with the belief that we can get better as instructors, the next step is to find those goals within the instructional process that we value and wish to achieve. These could be more expertise, increased learning, refined evaluation, motivating instruction, or simply a better relationship with a particular learner. There are so many possibilities because instruction has no ceiling. The perfect lesson has yet to be found and the path is clearly before us—set a goal, make it moderately difficult, and seek to achieve it.

Challenges naturally bring about the issue of choice because without an adult feeling a sense of ownership or acceptance, a difficult task reduces itself to an oppressive assignment. In this instance, if you carried out the task successfully, you might feel like a good, obedient worker, but you would have some difficulty truly convincing yourself you were a real professional. As a belief in one's capacity for increased competence relates to finding challenges, a belief in one's responsibility for instruction relates to finding a sense of professionalism. My greatest skepticism about instruction today, especially as it exists in business and industry, is that it seems to be governed by a "cult of efficiency" (Sykes, 1983). There is ever-increasing, technical control over the processes and outcomes of instruction. Scientistic technologies abound in the development of curriculum materials and the creation of instructional management systems. A few have even been advertised as "instructor-proof." There is no doubt that science has a tremendous amount to offer for the improvement of instruction. This criticism is certainly not directed at self-instructional or individualized programs of learning. The issue lies with how science is applied and the effect it has on instructors who work with groups of learners. In such other professions as medicine and engineering, scientific advances tend to increase the skills of the practitioners, to enhance their status, and to provide a foundation for the exercise of professional judgment.

However, science as applied to group instruction seems to be moving in the direction of replacing instructor judgment with rules and systems that control and reduce individual discretion. This is potentially alienating and reduces the responsibility as well as the status of instructors. Therefore, our role in the development and utilization of such technology is crucial. We are well advised to ensure that scientific contributions allow for the judgment and decision making that are necessary for a process in which uncertainty and uniqueness are ever present. The motivation of our learners and the quality of their learning experience requires flexibility. Our own sense of responsibility and its relationship to intrinsically satisfying work means that room for our professional judgment and the exercise of that discretion has to be a part of any instructional system. In the final analysis, there is little doubt that, if the system controls us, it controls the learners as well.

The role of positive feedback is immensely important for the development of intrinsic motivation in the instructor during the instructional process. Positive feedback is our "daily bread." On a moment-to-moment basis, it informs us about how successful our instructional efforts are and nurtures us as well. Seeing learners alert, involved, taking notes, smiling, raising questions, volunteering, enthusiastically participating, and, occasionally even laughing at our jokes makes us feel good and tells us we are getting our material across to them. These signals are really more motivational indicators than they are actual evidence of learning. Yet they tell us we are on the right track and learning can be expected. Jackson (1968) has found that these signs are what outstanding teachers have used to judge the effectiveness of their instruction. That such motivational indicators are benevolent to the instructor as well is a remarkable unity of communication—what is motivationally excellent for the learner is excellent for us, too. And this is the entire point. What has been written in this book is not based on some altruistic notion that learning should be appealing or enjoyable. It is the representation of experience and evidence that effective instruction is motivationally sound instruction, a process that enables optimal achievement and provides an inherently rewarding experience for *both* the learner and the instructor.

Many people have written that instruction is a science. Some have argued it is an art. Others have said it is a craft or an intuitive skill. I am not completely sure. But this I know. When it is motivating, when there is a flow of learning and communication between instructor and learner, it is much more than all have written or said it was. It is a dimension. Not something one practices or performs, but something one enters and lives.

References

Alberto, P. A., and Troutman, A. C. *Applied Behavioral Analysis for Teachers*. Columbus, Ohio: Merrill, 1982.

Allen, E. K. "A Study of the Relationship Between Teacher Enthusiasm and Selected Student Variables in Area Vocational-Technical Schools." Unpublished doctoral dissertation, Department of Vocational Education, Temple University, 1980.

Ames, R. E., and Ames, C. (Eds.). *Research on Motivation in Education: Student Motivation*. Vol. 1. New York: Academic Press, 1984.

Apter, M. J. *The Experience of Motivation*. New York: Academic Press, 1982.

Baldwin, A. L. *Theories of Child Development*. New York: Wiley, 1967.

Bandura, A. "Self-Efficacy Mechanism in Human Agency." *American Psychologist*, 1982, *37* (2), 122–147.

Berlyne, D. E. *Conflict, Arousal, and Curiosity*. New York: McGraw-Hill, 1960.

293

Bigge, M. L. *Learning Theories for Teachers.* (4th ed.) New York: Harper & Row, 1982.

Blanchard, K., and Johnson, S. *The One-Minute Manager.* New York: Morrow, 1982.

Bloom, B. S. *All Our Children Learning.* New York: McGraw-Hill, 1981.

Bloom, B.S., and others (Eds.). *Taxonomy of Educational Objectives.* Handbook I: *Cognitive Domain.* New York: McKay, 1956.

Brophy, J. "Teacher Praise: A Functional Analysis." *Review of Educational Research,* 1981, *51* (1), 5–32.

Brophy, J. "Conceptualizing Student Motivation." *Educational Psychologist,* 1983, *18* (3), 200–215.

Brown, G. I. *Human Teaching for Human Learning.* New York: Viking Press, 1971.

Brundage, D. H., and MacKeracher, D. *Adult Learning Principles and Their Application to Program Planning.* Toronto: Ministry of Education, Ontario, 1980.

Bruner, J. S. *Toward a Theory of Instruction.* New York: Norton, 1968.

Bry, A. *Visualization.* New York: Barnes & Noble, 1979.

Carp, A., Peterson, R., and Roelfs, P. "Adult Learning Interests and Experiences." In K. P. Cross, J. R. Valley, and Associates, *Planning Non-Traditional Programs: An Analysis of the Issues for Postsecondary Education.* San Francisco: Jossey-Bass, 1974.

Cary, A. *The Poetical Works of Alice and Phoebe Cary.* Boston: Houghton Mifflin, 1882.

Castillo, G. A. *Left-Handed Teaching.* New York: Praeger, 1974.

Cattell, R. B. "Theory of Fluid and Crystallized Intelligence: A Critical Experiment." *Journal of Educational Psychology,* 1963, *54* (1), 1–22.

Charny, J. "Psychosomatic Manifestations of Rapport in Psychotherapy." *Psychosomatic Medicine,* 1966, *28* (4), 305–315.

Colangelo, N., Foxley, C. H., and Dustin, D. *Multicultural Nonsexist Education.* Dubuque, Iowa: Kendall/Hunt, 1979.

Collins, M. L. "The Effects of Training for Enthusiasm on the Enthusiasm Displayed by Preservice Elementary Teachers." Unpublished doctoral dissertation, Division of Teacher Education, Syracuse University, 1976.

Combs, A. W. "Some Basic Concepts in Perceptual Psychology." Paper presented at the American Personnel and Guidance Convention, Minneapolis, Minn., April 1965.

Combs, A. W., and Taylor, C. "The Effect of the Perception of Mild Degrees of Threat on Performance." *Journal of Abnormal and Social Psychology*, 1952, *47*, 420–424.

Condry, J., and Chambers, J. "Intrinsic Motivation and the Process of Learning." In M. R. Lepper and D. Greene (Eds.), *The Hidden Costs of Reward*. Hillsdale, N.J.: Erlbaum, 1978.

Cooley, C. H. *Human Nature and the Social Order*. New York: Free Press, 1956.

Corno, L., and Mandinach, E. B. "The Role of Cognitive Engagement in Classroom Learning and Motivation." *Educational Psychologist*, 1983, *18* (2), 88–108.

Cross, K. P. "Adult Learners: Characteristics, Needs, and Interests." In R. E. Peterson and Associates, *Lifelong Learning in America: An Overview of Current Practices, Available Resources, and Future Prospects*. San Francisco: Jossey-Bass, 1979.

Cross, K. P. *Adults as Learners: Increasing Participation and Facilitating Learning*. San Francisco: Jossey-Bass, 1981.

Cruickshank, D. R., and others. *Teaching Is Tough*. Englewood Cliffs, N.J.: Prentice-Hall, 1980.

Czikszentmihalyi, M. *Beyond Boredom and Anxiety: The Experience of Play in Work and Games*. San Francisco: Jossey-Bass, 1975.

Csikszentmihalyi, M. "Intrinsic Rewards and Emergent Motivation." In M. R. Lepper and D. Greene (Eds.), *The Hidden Costs of Reward*. Hillsdale, N.J.: Erlbaum, 1978.

Darkenwald, G. G., and Larson, G. A. (Eds.). *New Directions for Continuing Education: Reaching Hard-to-Reach Adults*, no. 8. San Francisco: Jossey-Bass, 1980.

Davies, D. R., Shackleton, V. J., and Parasuraman, R. "Monotony and Boredom." In R. Hockey (Ed.), *Stress and Fatigue in Human Performance*. New York: Wiley, 1983.

Day, H. I. (Ed.). *Advances in Intrinsic Motivation and Aesthetics*. New York: Plenum Press, 1981.

deCharms, R. *Personal Causation: The Internal Affective Determinants of Behavior*. New York: Academic Press, 1968.

Deci, E. L. *The Psychology of Self-Determination.* Lexington, Mass.: Heath, 1980.

Deci, E. L., and Ryan, R. M. "The Dynamics of Self-Determination in Personality and Development." Paper presented at the International Conference on Anxiety and Self-Related Cognitions, Berlin, July 1983. To appear in R. Schwarzer (Ed.), *Self-Related Cognitions in Anxiety and Motivation.* Hillsdale, N.J.: Erlbaum, 1985.

Deutsch, M. "Cooperation and Trust: Some Theoretical Notes." In M. R. Jones (Ed.), *Nebraska Symposium on Motivation.* Lincoln: University of Nebraska Press, 1962.

Dewey, J. *How We Think.* (Rev. ed.) Lexington, Mass.: Heath, 1933.

Ellis, A. *Reason and Emotion in Psychotherapy.* New York: Lyle Stuart, 1962.

Ellis, A., and Greiger, R. (Eds.). *Handbook of Rational-Emotive Therapy.* New York: Springer, 1977.

Elstein, A. S., Shulman, L. S., and Sprafka, S. A. *Medical Problem Solving: An Analysis of Clinical Reasoning.* Cambridge, Mass.: Harvard University Press, 1978.

Epstein, J. (Ed.). *Masters: Portraits of Great Teachers.* New York: Basic Books, 1981.

Flavell, J. "Cognitive Changes in Adulthood." In P. B. Baltes and L. R. Goulet (Eds.), *Life-Span Developmental Psychology.* New York: Academic Press, 1970.

Frederiksen, N. "The Real Test Bias: Influences of Testing on Teaching and Learning." *American Psychologist,* 1984, *39* (3), 193–202.

Freud, S. "Letter to C. G. Jung, December 6, 1966." In E. Jones, *Sigmund Freud: Life and Work.* Vol. 2. London: Hogarth Press, 1955.

Fuhrmann, B. S., and Grasha, A. F. *A Practical Handbook for College Teachers.* Boston: Little, Brown, 1983.

Gage, N. L. "The Generality of Dimensions of Teaching." In P. L. Peterson and H. J. Walberg (Eds.), *Research on Teaching: Concepts, Findings, and Implications.* Berkeley, Calif.: McCutchan, 1979.

Gage, N. L., and Berliner, D. C. *Educational Psychology.* (3rd ed.) Boston: Houghton Mifflin, 1984.

Gephart, W. J. (Ed.). "Teacher Enthusiasm." *Practical Applications of Research,* 1981, *3* (4), 1-4.

Gephart, W. J., Strother, D. B., and Duckett, W. R. (Eds.). "Instructional Clarity." *Practical Applications of Research,* 1981, *3* (3), 1-4.

Gilbert, T. F. *Human Competence: Engineering Worthy Performance.* New York: McGraw-Hill, 1978.

Glaser, R., and Cooley, W. "Instrumentation for Teaching and Instructional Management." In R. Travers (Ed.), *Second Handbook of Research on Teaching.* Chicago: Rand McNally, 1973.

Good, T. L. "Classroom Research: A Decade of Progress." *Educational Psychologist,* 1983, *18* (3), 127-144.

Goodman, J. "Humor, Creativity, and Magic: Tools for Teaching and Living." Unpublished manuscript. Sagamore Institute, Saratoga Springs, N.Y., 1981.

Grabowski, S. *Training Teachers of Adults: Models and Innovative Programs.* Syracuse, N.Y.: National Association for Public Continuing and Adult Education and Educational Resources Information Center Clearinghouse in Career Education, 1976. (ED 131 184)

Gronlund, N. E. *Stating Objectives for Classroom Instruction.* New York: Macmillan, 1978.

Haan, N., and Day, D. "A Longitudinal Study of Change and Sameness in Personality Development: Adolescence to Later Adulthood." *International Journal of Aging and Human Development,* 1974, *5* (1), 11-39.

Halpin, A. W. *Theory and Research in Administration.* New York: Macmillan, 1966.

Harper, D. O., and Stewart, J. H. *RUN: Computer Education.* Monterey, Calif.: Brooks/Cole, 1983.

Hill, W. F. *Principles of Learning: A Handbook of Applications.* Sherman Oaks, Calif.: Alfred Publishing, 1981.

Hockey, R. (Ed.). *Stress and Fatigue in Human Performance.* New York: Wiley, 1983.

Hockey, R., and Hamilton, P. "The Cognitive Patterning of Stress States." In R. Hockey (Ed.), *Stress and Fatigue in Human Performance.* New York: Wiley, 1983.

Hofmeister,, A. *Microcomputer Applications in the Classroom.* New York: Holt, Rinehart and Winston, 1984.

Holding, D. "Fatigue." In R. Hockey (Ed.), *Stress and Fatigue in Human Performance.* New York: Wiley, 1983.

Hollander, E. P. *Principles and Methods of Social Psychology.* New York: Oxford University Press, 1976.

Hoover, K. H. *College Teaching Today.* Boston: Allyn & Bacon, 1980.

Hunt, J. McV. *Intelligence and Experience.* New York: Ronald Press, 1961.

Hurt, H. T., Scott, M. D., and McCroskey, J. C. *Communication in the Classroom.* Reading, Mass.: Addison-Wesley, 1978.

Jackson, P. W. *Life in Classrooms.* New York: Holt, Rinehart and Winston, 1968.

Johnson, D. W. "Attitude Modification Methods." In F. H. Kanfer and A. P. Goldstein (Eds.), *Helping People Change.* Elmsford, N.Y.: Pergamon Press, 1980.

Johnson, D. W., and Johnson, F. P. *Joining Together: Group Theory and Group Skills.* (2nd ed.) Englewood Cliffs, N.J.: Prentice-Hall, 1982.

Johnson, D. W., Johnson, R. T., and Maruyama, G. "Interdependence and Interpersonal Attraction among Heterogeneous and Homogeneous Individuals: A Theoretical Formulation and a Meta-Analysis of the Research." *Review of Educational Research,* 1983, *53* (1), 5-54.

Johnson, D. W., and others. "Effects of Cooperative, Competitive, and Individualistic Goal Structures on Achievement: A Meta-Analysis." *Psychological Bulletin,* 1981, *89* (1), 47-62.

Jones, E. E., and Gerard, H. B. *Foundations of Social Psychology.* New York, Wiley, 1967.

Jourard, S. *The Transparent Self.* New York: Van Nostrand, 1964.

Karoly, P. "Operant Methods." In F. H. Kanfer and A. P. Goldstein (Eds.), *Helping People Change.* (2nd ed.) Elmsford, N.Y.: Pergamon Press, 1980.

Kazdin, A. E., and Bootzen, R. R. "The Token Economy: An Evaluative Review." *Journal of Applied Behavior Analysis,* 1972, *5,* 343-372.

Keller, J. M. "Motivational Design of Instruction." In C. M. Reigeluth (Ed.), *Instructional-Design Theories and Models: An*

Overview of Their Current Status. Hillsdale, N.J.: Erlbaum, 1989.

Keller, J. M., Kelly, E. A., and Dodge, B. *Motivation in School: A Practitioner's Guide to Concepts and Measures.* Syracuse, N.Y.: Syracuse University and Educational Resources Information Center Clearinghouse for Information Resources, 1978. (ED 169 953)

Kennedy, J. J., and others. "Additional Investigations into the Nature of Teacher Clarity." *Journal of Educational Research,* 1978, *72* (1), 3-10.

Kerman, S. "Teacher Expectation and Student Achievement." *Phi Delta Kappan,* 1979, *60,* 716-718.

Kidd, J. R. *How Adults Learn.* New York: Association Press, 1973.

Knowles, M. S. *The Adult Learner: A Neglected Species.* (2nd ed.) Houston: Gulf, 1978.

Knowles, M. S. *The Modern Practice of Adult Education: From Pedagogy to Andragogy.* (Rev.) Chicago: Follett, 1980.

Knox, A. B. *Adult Development and Learning: A Handbook on Individual Growth and Competence in the Adult Years.* San Francisco: Jossey-Bass, 1977.

Korman, A. H., Greenhaus, J. H., and Badin, I. J. "Personnel Attitudes and Motivation." *Annual Review of Psychology,* 1977, *28,* 175-176.

Kruglanski, A. W., Stein, C., and Riter, A. "Contingencies of Exogenous Reward and Task Performance: On the 'Minimax' Principle in Instrumental Behavior." *Journal of Applied Social Psychology,* 1977, *7,* 141-148.

Lepper, M. R. "Extrinsic Reward and Intrinsic Motivation: Implications for the Classroom." In J. M. Levine and M. C. Wang (Eds.), *Teacher and Student Perceptions: Implications for Learning.* Hillsdale, N.J.: Erlbaum, 1983.

Lepper, M. R., and Greene, D. (Eds.). *The Hidden Costs of Reward.* Hillsdale, N.J.: Erlbaum, 1978.

Levin, T., and Long, R. *Effective Instruction.* Alexandria, Va.: Association for Supervision and Curriculum Development, 1981.

Levy, J. "Research Synthesis on Right and Left Hemispheres: We Think with Both Sides of the Brain." *Educational Leadership,* 1983, *40* (4), 66-71.

Lewin, K. *A Dynamic Theory of Personality.* New York: McGraw-Hill, 1935.

Lindeman, E. C. *The Meaning of Adult Education.* Montreal: Harvest House, 1961.

Luft, J. *Group Processes: An Introduction to Group Dynamics.* (3rd ed.) Palo Alto, Calif.: Mayfield, 1984.

McClelland, D. C. *Power: The Inner Experience.* New York: Irvington, 1975.

McCombs, B. L. "Learner Satisfaction and Motivation: Capitalizing on Strategies for Positive Self-Control." *Performance and Instruction,* 1982, *21* (4), 3–6.

McCombs, B. L., and McDaniel, M. A. "Individualizing Through Treatment Matching: A Necessary but Not Sufficient Approach." *Educational Communication and Technology Journal,* 1983, *31* (4), 213–225.

McGraw, K. O. "The Detrimental Effects of Reward on Performance: A Literature Review and a Prediction Model." In M. R. Lepper and D. Greene (Eds.), *The Hidden Costs of Reward.* Hillsdale, N.J.: Erlbaum, 1978.

McLagan, P. A. *Helping Others Learn: Designing Programs for Adults.* Reading, Mass.: Addison-Wesley, 1978.

McLagan, P. A. *Models for Excellence.* Washington, D.C.: American Society for Training and Development, 1983.

Madsen, K. B. *Modern Theories of Motivation.* New York: Halstead Press, 1974.

Maehr, M. L. "Continuing Motivation: An Analysis of a Seldom Considered Educational Outcome." *Review of Education Research,* 1976, *46* (3), 443–462.

Mager, R. F. *Developing Attitude Toward Learning.* Belmont, Calif.: Fearon, 1968.

Maslow, A. H. *Motivation and Personality.* (2nd ed.) New York: Harper & Row, 1970.

Messick, S. "Personality Consistencies in Cognition and Creativity." In S. Messick and Associates, *Individuality in Learning: Implications of Cognitive Styles and Creativity for Human Development.* San Francisco: Jossey-Bass, 1976.

Moenster, P. A. "Learning and Memory in Relation to Age." *Journal of Gerontology,* 1972, *27,* 361–363.

Monette, M. L. "The Concept of Educational Need: An Analysis of Selected Literature." *Adult Education,* 1977, *27* (2), 116–127.

Moore, D. E. "Assessing the Needs of Adults for Continuing Education: A Model." In F. C. Pennington (Ed.), *New Directions for Continuing Education: Assessing Educational Needs of Adults,* no. 7. San Francisco: Jossey-Bass, 1980.

Morgan, M. "Reward-Induced Decrements and Increments in Intrinsic Motivation." *Review of Educational Research,* 1984, *54* (1), 5–30.

Naisbitt, J. *Megatrends.* New York: Warner, 1982.

Nietzsche, F. W. *The Antichrist.* New York: Knopf, 1920.

Otto, H. A. *Group Methods to Actualize Human Potential: A Handbook.* (4th ed.) Beverly Hills, Calif.: Holistic Press, 1975.

Penland, P. *Individual Self-Planned Learning in America.* Washington, D.C.: Office of Education, U.S. Department of Health, Education and Welfare, 1977.

Penland, P. "Self-Initiated Learning." *Adult Education,* 1979, *29* (3), 170–179.

Pennington, F. C. (Ed.). *New Directions for Continuing Education: Assessing Educational Needs of Adults,* no. 7. San Francisco: Jossey-Bass, 1980.

Peters, T. J., and Waterman, R. H., Jr. *In Search of Excellence: Lessons from America's Best-Run Companies.* New York: Harper & Row, 1982.

Petri, H. L. *Motivation: Theory and Research.* Belmont, Calif.: Wadsworth, 1981.

Pittman, T. S., Boggiano, A. K., and Ruble, D. N. "Intrinsic and Extrinsic Motivational Orientations: Limiting Conditions on the Undermining and Enhancing Effects of Reward on Intrinsic Motivation." In J. M. Levine and M. C. Wang (Eds.), *Teacher and Student Perceptions: Implications for Learning.* Hillsdale, N.J.: Erlbaum, 1983.

Reigeluth, C. M. (Ed.). *Instructional-Design Theories and Models: An Overview of Their Current Status.* Hillsdale, N.J.: Erlbaum, 1983.

Robinson, R. D. *Helping Adults Learn and Change.* Milwaukee, Wis.: Omnibook, 1979.

Rogers, C. R. *Freedom to Learn.* Columbus, Ohio: Merrill, 1969.

Rosenshine, B., and Furst, N. "Research on Teacher Performance

Criteria." In B. O. Smith (Ed.), *Research in Teacher Education: A Symposium.* Englewood Cliffs, N.J.: Prentice-Hall, 1971.

Rosser, R. A., and Nicholson, G. I. *Educational Psychology: Principles in Practice.* Boston: Little, Brown, 1984.

Ryan, R. M. "Control and Information in the Intrapersonal Sphere: An Extension of Cognitive Evaluation Theory." *Journal of Personality and Social Psychology,* 1982, *43* (3), 450–461.

Ryan, R. M., Connell, J. P., and Deci, E. L. "A Motivational Analysis of Self-Determination in Education." To appear in C. Ames and R. E. Ames (Eds.), *Research on Motivation in Education: The Classroom Milieu.* New York: Academic Press, forthcoming.

Ryan, R. M., Mims, V., and Koestner, R. "Relation of Reward Contingency and Interpersonal Context to Intrinsic Motivation: A Review and Test Using Cognitive Evaluation Theory." *Journal of Personality and Social Psychology,* 1983, *45* (4), 736–750.

Saint-Exupéry, A. de. *The Little Prince.* (K. Woods, Trans.) New York: Harcourt Brace Jovanovich, 1943.

Sanders, D. P. "Educational Inquiry as Developmental Research." *Educational Researcher,* 1981, *10,* 8–13.

Sarason, I. G. (Ed.). *Test Anxiety: Theory, Research and Application.* Hillsdale, N.J.: Erlbaum, 1980.

Schmuck, R. A., and Schmuck, P. A. *Group Processes in the Classroom.* (4th ed.) Dubuque, Iowa: Brown, 1983.

Schunk, D. H. "Self-Efficacy Perspective on Achievement Behavior." *Educational Psychologist,* 1984, *19* (1), 48–58.

Scott, J. P. "A Time to Learn." *Psychology Today,* 1969, *2* (10), 46–48, 66–67.

Scriven, M. "The Methodology of Evaluation." In R. Stake (Ed.), *Perspectives of Curriculum Evaluation.* Chicago: Rand McNally, 1967.

Seligman, M. *Helplessness.* San Francisco: W. H. Freeman, 1975.

Shavelson, R. J., Hubner, J. J., and Stanton, G. C. "Self-Concept: Validation of Construct Interpretations." *Review of Educational Research,* 1976, *46,* 407–442.

Sheehy, G. *Passages: Predictable Crises of Adult Life.* New York: Dutton, 1976.

Sheikh, A. A. (Ed.). *Imagery: Current Theory, Research, and Application.* New York: Wiley, 1983.

Shipman, V., and Shipman, F. "Cognitive Styles: Some Conceptual, Methodological, and Applied Issues." In E. W. Gordon (Ed.), *Human Diversity and Pedagogy*. Westport, Conn.: Mediax, 1983.

Shostak, R. "Lesson Presentation Skills." In J. M. Cooper (Ed.), *Classroom Teaching Skills: A Handbook*. Lexington, Mass.: Heath, 1977.

Sigel, I. E., Brodzinsky, D. M., and Golinkoff, R. M. (Eds.). *New Directions in Piagetian Theory and Practice*. Hillsdale, N.J.: Erlbaum, 1981.

Simon, S. B., Howe, L. W., and Kirschenbaum, H. *Values Clarification*. New York: Hart, 1972.

Singer, J. L., and Pope, K. S. (Eds.). *The Power of Human Imagination*. New York: Plenum, 1978.

Skinner, B. F. *Verbal Behavior*. New York: Appleton-Century-Crofts, 1957.

Skinner, B. F. *The Technology of Teaching*. New York: Appleton-Century-Crofts, 1968.

Smith, B. J., and Delahaye, B. L. *How to Be an Effective Trainer*. New York: Wiley, 1983.

Smith, R. M. *Learning How to Learn*. Chicago: Follett, 1982.

Smith, R. P. "Boredom: A Review." *Human Factors*, 1981, *23* (3), 329–340.

Spence, J. T. (Ed.). *Achievement and Achievement Motives*. San Francisco: W. H. Freeman, 1983.

Spence, J. T., and Helmreich, R. L. "Achievement-Related Motives and Behaviors." In J. T. Spence (Ed.), *Achievement and Achievement Motives*. San Francisco: W. H. Freeman, 1983.

Surber, J. R., and Anderson, R. C. "Delay-Retention Effect in Natural Classroom Settings." *Journal of Educational Psychology*, 1975, *67*, 170–173.

Sykes, G. "Contradictions, Ironies, and Promises Unfulfilled: A Contemporary Account of the Status of Teaching." *Phi Delta Kappan*, 1983, *65* (2), 87–93.

Thomas, J. W. "Agency and Achievement: Self-Management and Self-Regard." *Review of Educational Research*, 1980, *50* (2), 213–240.

Tomkins, S. "Affect as the Primary Motivational System." In M. B.

Arnold (Ed.), *Feelings and Emotions.* New York: Academic Press, 1970.

Tough, A. *The Adult's Learning Projects.* (2nd ed.) Austin, Tex.: Learning Concepts, 1979.

Travers, R. M. W. (Ed.). *Second Handbook of Research on Teaching.* Chicago: Rand McNally, 1973.

Tucker, D. M. "Lateral Brain Function, Emotion, and Conceptualization." *Psychological Bulletin,* 1981, *89* (1), 19–46.

Uguroglu, M., and Walberg, H. J. "Motivation and Achievement: A Quantitative Synthesis." *American Educational Research Journal,* 1979, *16,* 375–389.

Ungar, F. (Ed.). *Goethe's World View.* New York: Ungar, 1963.

Vaill, P. B. "The Purposing of High-Performing Systems." *Organizational Dynamics,* 1982, Autumn, 23–29.

Valenti, J. *Speak Up with Confidence.* New York: Morrow, 1982.

Van Houten, R. *Learning Through Feedback.* New York: Human Sciences Press, 1980.

Vargas, J. S. *Behavioral Psychology for Teachers.* New York: Harper & Row, 1977.

Walberg, H. J., and Uguroglu, M. "Motivation and Educational Productivity: Theories, Results, and Implications." In L. J. Fyans, Jr. (Ed.), *Achievement Motivation: Recent Trends in Theory and Research.* New York: Plenum, 1980.

Wang, M. C., and Lindvall, C. M. "Individual Differences and School Learning Environments." In E. W. Gordon (Ed.), *Review of Research in Education.* Vol. 11. Washington, D.C.: American Educational Research Association, 1984.

Watson, J. S., and Ramey, C. G. "Reactions to Response-Contingent Stimulation in Early Infancy." *Merrill Palmer Quarterly,* 1972, *18,* 219–228.

Watzlawick, P. (Ed.). *The Interactional View.* New York: Norton, 1977.

Weiner, B. *Human Motivation.* New York: Holt, Rinehart and Winston, 1980a.

Weiner, B. "The Role of Affect in Rational (Attributional) Approaches to Human Motivation." *Educational Researcher,* 1980b, *9* (7), 4–11.

Weiner, B. "Principles for a Theory of Student Motivation and

Their Application Within an Attributional Framework." In R. E. Ames and C. Ames (Eds.), *Research on Motivation in Education: Student Motivation.* Vol. 1. New York: Academic Press, 1984.

Weinstein, M., and Goodman, J. *Playfair.* San Luis Obispo, Calif.: Impact Publishers, 1980.

Whaba, M. A., and Bridwell, L. G. "Maslow Reconsidered: A Review of Research on the Need Hierarchy Theory." *Organizational Behavior and Human Performance,* 1976, *15,* 212–240.

White, R. W. "Motivation Reconsidered: The Concept of Competence." *Psychological Review,* 1959, *66,* 297–333.

Wittrock, M. C. "Learning as a Generative Process." *Educational Psychologist,* 1974, *11,* 87–95.

Wittrock, M. C. "The Cognitive Movement in Instruction." *Educational Psychologist,* 1978, *13,* 15–29.

Wittrock, M. C., and Lumsdaine, A. A. "Instructional Psychology." *Annual Review of Psychology,* 1977, *28,* 417–459.

Wlodkowski, R. J. "Making Sense Out of Motivation: A Systematic Model to Consolidate Motivational Constructs Across Theories." *Educational Psychologist,* 1981, *16* (2), 101–110.

Wlodkowski, R. J. *What Research Says to the Teacher: Motivation.* (Rev. ed.) Washington, D.C.: National Education Association, 1982.

Wlodkowski, R. J. *Motivation and Teaching: A Practical Guide.* Washington, D.C.: National Education Association, 1984.

Woolfolk, A. E., and McCune-Nicolich, L. *Educational Psychology for Teachers.* (2nd ed.) Englewood Cliffs, N.J.: Prentice-Hall, 1984.

Zajonc, R. B. "On the Primacy of Affect." *American Psychologist,* 1984, *39* (2), 117–123.

Zinker, J. *Creative Process in Gestalt Therapy.* New York: Brunner/Mazel, 1977.

Index